The
BEST
BUSINESS
SCHOOLS'
ADMISSIONS SECRETS

UPDATED EDITION

A Former Harvard Business School
Admissions Board Member Reveals
the Insider Keys to Getting In

CHIOMA ISIADINSO, M.Ed.

 sourcebooks

Grateful acknowledgment is made for permission to reprint the following copyrighted material:
Byrne, John A. "MBA Class of 2015: Harvard vs. Wharton." Table: *A Tale of Two Business Schools—Harvard vs. Wharton*. Poets & Quants. July 19, 2013. Accessed April 29, 2014. www.poetsandquants.com/2013/07/19/class-of-2015-hbs-vs-wharton. Permission granted.

This publication is designed to provide accurate and authoritative information in regard to the subject matter covered. It is sold with the understanding that the publisher is not engaged in rendering legal, accounting, or other professional service. If legal advice or other expert assistance is required, the services of a competent professional person should be sought.—*From a Declaration of Principles Jointly Adopted by a Committee of the American Bar Association and a Committee of Publishers and Associations*

Published by Sourcebooks, Inc.
P.O. Box 4410, Naperville, Illinois 60567-4410
(630) 961-3900
Fax: (630) 961-2168
www.sourcebooks.com

Library of Congress Cataloging-in-Publication Data

Isiadinso, Chioma.
   The best business schools' admissions secrets : a former Harvard Business School Admissions Board member reveals the insider keys to getting in / Chioma Isiadinso, M.Ed.—Second edition.
      pages cm
   Includes bibliographical references and index.
1. Business schools—Admission. 2. Master of business administration degree. 3. Business education. I. Title.
   HF1111.I85 2014
   650.071'1—dc23

                                    2014018560

               Printed and bound in the United States of America.
                      POD 10 9 8 7 6 5 4 3 2

*To Ari and Aku. You are a **blessing** and a constant joy in my life.*

CONTENTS

FOREWORD

I FIRST MET CHIOMA ISIADINSO in 2005 when I was the CEO of one of the largest banks in Nigeria. Chioma had recently finished her time as an admissions assistant director at Harvard Business School (HBS) and was recruiting in Nigeria on its behalf. She had invited me to participate on an HBS alumni panel for a prospective students' event. I was halfway through a decade-long period as CEO of the bank, an experience I never imagined I would have when I was starting my MBA at Harvard Business School in 1980.

With degrees from Oxford and Cambridge in the UK, I thought that an MBA would position me for a top placement at a state-owned firm upon my return. Over the next thirty years, I ended up acquiring and running a large bank and investing in and leading a major mobile technology operator in Nigeria. I have had the opportunity to lead and manage people in two different industries at companies that were at different stages of growth. I can directly attribute my success in these ventures to the training and confidence I acquired during my MBA at Harvard Business School.

When I was applying to the MBA program at HBS, I knew what I was looking for in an MBA program. I wanted a program that would provide me with a comprehensive overview of various aspects of running businesses, including areas such as finance, management, marketing, and governance. I wanted a program that would prepare me to lead an organization in the future rather than just be a specialist in any one functional area. I wanted a program that would equip me with the skills to pursue opportunities across various industries rather than being a prisoner to one particular sector. As Chioma would say, I was looking for a school whose brand was connected with developing leaders.

Applying to top MBA programs these days is much more difficult compared to when I applied in 1980. Given my education and personal background at the time, standing out in the MBA applicant pool was not as difficult as it is today. I did not have to spend a lot of time developing and communicating my personal brand. I was able to stand out from the crowd much more easily because there were so few in the crowd that had a similar brand. Today, if I were to apply to a top MBA program, I would have a hard time standing out from the crowd. That is why this book is so important to business school applicants of today and tomorrow.

The book is divided into three parts. Part One encompasses the first five chapters of the book, which provide you with a big picture overview of the MBA admissions process and teach you how to develop your personal brand and how to pick MBA programs whose brands are a natural fit for your brand. Part Two covers the next four chapters, which dive into the details of the actual MBA application and teach you how to weave your personal brand throughout your entire application. Part Three includes the final five chapters, which give you advice on how to choose which business school admittance you should accept, how to overcome potential challenges that may put your application at a disadvantage, and how to fund the MBA program you decide to attend.

As a former HBS admissions officer, when it comes to advising you on how to successfully apply to top business school programs, no one is better qualified to do so than Chioma. She wrote the book on it in 2008—*The Best Business Schools' Admissions Secrets*. In this updated version of her bestselling book, she has packed it chock-full of valuable insights and advice that she has gained from years of expertise in the MBA admissions process.

This book is like an MBA application blueprint—Chioma teaches you how to successfully develop your personal brand and then leverage your brand throughout the MBA application process. When Chioma asked me to write this foreword, I was more than happy to do so. I remember what it was like for me to apply to business school in 1980 and recognize how helpful this book would have been for me at that time. As the competition increases each year to win a coveted spot in one of the top business school programs around the world, I can envision how so many applicants will benefit from developing the personal brand advice and strategies that Chioma provides in this updated version of her book.

Hakeem Belo-Osagie
HBS MBA '80
Chairman, Etisalat Nigeria

PREFACE TO THE SECOND EDITION

W HY WRITE A SECOND edition? Well, the simple answer is that a lot has changed in the six years since I first wrote *The Best Business Schools' Admissions Secrets*. Countries such as Greece have gone bankrupt. Lehman and Bear Stearns, financial powerhouses, are no longer in existence. The world's population has grown to more than seven billion. We've witnessed some firsts; the United States of America elected its first African American president, and South Africa became the first African country to host the World Cup in 2010.

Major changes have also taken place in the world of business school admissions. International Master of Business Administration (MBA) programs are developing a stronger reputation across the globe, giving the U.S. MBA programs some serious competition. International MBA programs offered by Instituto de Estudios Superiores de la Empresa (IESE) and Instituto de Empresa (IE) in Spain, Institute for Management Development (IMD) in Switzerland, and Hong Kong University of Science and Technology (HKUST) have moved ahead of many top U.S. MBA programs like New York University's Stern Business School, Northwestern University's Kellogg MBA program, and Duke University's Fuqua School of Business in the 2014 *Financial Times* rankings. All of this has happened in a span of only ten years. Business school applicants should always keep a critical eye on the international landscape, because it is constantly evolving. Do your research—schools that have been historically considered to have "go-to programs" in the past may no longer be a good fit. Schools that have previously been overlooked may be coming into the forefront. In this new edition, I focus more on international programs and international students to provide a balanced perspective for applicants regardless of where they are applying from.

In light of the changes to many top MBA programs, this book will better prepare readers to apply and secure admission in this new admissions climate. One of the main differences is that a majority of MBA programs have changed their applications. In the sixteen years that I have been in the admissions industry, I have never seen such a level of change sweeping across multiple MBA programs as I've witnessed this year. Harvard Business School's decision to reduce its essay requirement to only one and to make writing the essay optional ushered in a sea of similar changes across many business schools. While the fundamental essay-writing principles remain the same, I feel that it is important to address these changes at schools like Harvard Business School, as well as the new essays that have cropped up across different business schools around the globe.

There is no highly rated MBA program that has not embraced social media such as Twitter and Facebook. What's new, however, is how schools are adopting technology in the actual application process. Many schools now rely on Skype interviews instead of phone interviews to ensure that the person they are interviewing is actually the person who applied to the program. Skype also is allowing schools greater leeway in assessing responses, as well as the body language and unspoken data that can be gathered through the video format. Schools like the University of Toronto's Rotman School of Business, Yale School of Management, and Northwestern University's Kellogg School of Management have taken digital technology to even greater depths by requiring applicants to respond in real time to targeted questions on camera. I cover tips on how applicants can prepare for this new format as well as the Skype interview in Chapter Eight: The Interview.

While we are still on the subject of technology, it's worth noting some interesting changes happening in the online space as well. Not too long ago, there were no rankings for online MBA programs. Today, there are several: *U.S.News & World Report*, *Financial Times*, and *Bloomberg Businessweek*. Schools like the University of Virginia's Darden Business School and Wharton MBA have forayed into Massive Open Online Courses (MOOCs) to bring business education to thousands of people without geographic boundaries. MBA programs are also embracing technology as they offer hybrid classes to combine in-class and online education. This trend is driving some of the growth in online MBA programs and will remain an interesting trend to watch in the future. With its growing popularity, the online MBA is beginning to lose some of the stigma associated with it, and we'll likely continue to see online MBA programs become more popular.

Since the first edition of my book, many MBA programs have begun accepting the Graduate Record Examinations (GRE). Look to Chapter Five: Understanding the Admissions Criteria to learn more about the GRE and find key information to consider when deciding to apply with this test. The Graduate Management Admission Test (GMAT) has undergone some changes as well. Chapter five also covers new information on integrated reasoning and how schools utilize the GMAT compared to the GRE in their evaluation processes.

I'm excited that you have chosen to use the second edition of my book as a resource throughout your business school application process. I've heard applicants from around the globe share how the first book has helped them to successfully gain admission to their dream MBA programs. I hope you will find this second edition equally informative and instructive. I welcome your feedback and look forward to hearing from many of you. You can email me directly at chioma@expartus. com. I wish all of you continued success with your life and your MBA admissions application.

ACKNOWLEDGMENTS

THERE WERE COUNTLESS INDIVIDUALS who were instrumental in making this book a reality.

I'd like to thank my husband, Obinna, for your entrepreneurial spirit that has somehow rubbed off on me. Your ability to envision possibilities and your unwavering support have enabled me to write this book.

I happen to believe in fate and faith, and I have to thank Rita Rosenkranz, my agent, for believing in me and taking a step of faith with me on this journey. I extend a heartfelt thanks to Fern Reiss, who provided me with the opportunity to meet my wonderful agent. I would like to also thank the publishing team at Sourcebooks for their professionalism and commitment to this book. A special thanks to Suzy Bainbridge and Lindsay Newton for your support in editing the second edition of the book.

I am grateful to the many talented clients I have had the fortune to work with through my consulting practice, EXPARTUS. Your stories continue to inspire me and I am thrilled for your successes. I want to also thank all the business school alumni and students who volunteered to share their essays for this book. Thank you for opening up your lives and essays. Your stories will help many future applicants glean insights on how to tell their stories in a compelling way. Many thanks to everyone who participated in interviews for this book: Fred Chima, Selena and Khary Cuffe, Fernando D'Alessio, Recy Dunn, Associate Dean Sean Ferguson, Ivan Kerbel, Bukky Olowude, Jevelyn Bonner-Reed, Chris Ryan, Dennis Tseng, Rachel Zlotoff, and the Veritas Prep team, especially Brian Galvin and Scott Shrum.

I would also like to thank Michael and Bonnie Carter, Nadja Fidelia, and Dr. Gloria Hill, for your mentorship. This book talks about the importance of having brand champions, and you have been a major blessing! Mariela Dabbah, thanks for believing in the vision of this book from the very beginning. To Mr. Hakeem Belo-Osagie, your support of my book has been priceless and it means a lot to me to have you behind it. Catherine Bickersteth, Ladun Omojokun, and Abiola Anyakwo, you have been true friends. Thank you for all your support throughout the writing of this second edition of the book.

I would be remiss not to thank the amazing individuals I have had the fortune to work with both at Harvard and at Carnegie Mellon. Particularly, Kirsten Moss, Eileen Chang, Patty Dowden, Dee Leopold, (Prof) James Cash, Brenda Peyser, Mark Wessel, Ty Walton, Barbara Brewton, Elizabeth Casale, Carol Young, (Prof) Janusz Szczypula, and Provost Mark Kamlet. My amazing team at EXPARTUS, thank you for being a joy to work with.

A special thanks to all my family and friends for their patience and support. Dr. Maria Obiechina, you are an amazing role model. I am blessed to have you as my mom, and you continue to motivate me to do the best I can. I'm thankful to my late dad, Professor Emmanuel Obiechina, who encouraged me to become a writer in the first place. I know you are busy with your red ink pen in heaven! I will be forever thankful to my beloved mother-in-law, Mrs. Rose Isiadinso, for her calm spirit and encouragement as I juggle entrepreneurship and motherhood. I am grateful for the opportunity to live my passion of helping people access the best education possible. For this, I am blessed and thankful to God.

INTRODUCTION

I HAD BEEN IN THE admissions business for three years (Carnegie Mellon) when I moved to Cambridge to take on an assistant director role at Harvard Business School. From the open houses to information sessions to the countless phone calls that barraged the admissions offices every day, one thing was clear: applicants to business school were stressed out about their applications. Business schools, sensitive to the stress that surrounds the application, have made strides to create more admissions transparency and provide applicants with more opportunity to "connect" with the admissions board. But it is safe to say that, with rejection numbers still in the 80 to 90 percent range, applicants recognize that they are up against significant odds to earn an admission spot at their top MBA program.

After a few years of declining application numbers due to the poor economy, business schools are beginning to experience an increase in their application volume. According to the Graduate Management Admission Council (GMAC) 2013 Application Survey, 52 percent of full-time two-year MBA programs and 53 percent of full-time one-year MBA programs reported an increase in their application numbers. Poets & Quants, an MBA admissions forum, confirms this trend by revealing that all top ten U.S. MBA programs—with the exception of Wharton—saw an increase in their number of applications.

It is this sheer competition that drives applicant sentiment to a frenzied pitch. In this high-stakes world, many intelligent individuals discard common sense for myths and hearsay.

COMMON ADMISSIONS MYTHS
YOU SHOULD WATCH OUT FOR

The folklore surrounding admissions to elite business schools is legendary and endless. Some of it includes bets that applying in particular rounds can guarantee a favorable admission outcome; other stories focus on the belief that recommendations from alumni are a shoo-in (as opposed to recommenders who do not have a brand-name degree); others center on jumping on bandwagons that applicants believe are popular.

The social enterprise bandwagon is one such example. While on the admissions board at Harvard Business School, I saw my fair share of the social enterprise tack-on stories that were simply an attempt on the part of the applicants to say, "Look, I have my quota of socially conscious contributions." This is demonstrated in the example of an applicant who has worked in a for-profit career for his entire professional life but then states in his application that his greatest passion in life is to work in the nonprofit sector. Without prior evidence of genuine social sector interest, no one on the admissions board will buy his story. In fact, the admissions board will see such a statement as a gimmick and will discount his application.

Two additional career bandwagons that have become quite popular recently include social investing and renewable energy. The temptation to claim an interest in a career path simply because you've heard that schools like individuals from those backgrounds should be curtailed. Have these two career paths become more popular in terms of MBA career options? Yes. But that doesn't mean candidates need to fake an interest in these areas to get admitted. If you don't have a genuine interest in these emerging careers, then saying you do will only confirm to the admissions board that you are not authentic. Ultimately, this will cast doubts upon you and your candidacy.

Of course, one can't talk about the misconceptions of business school admissions without encountering the issue of legacy. Unlike undergraduate admissions, where children of alumni get a slight bump, legacy does not have much bearing in the admissions process at the top MBA programs. It is important for candidates to know ahead of time that having parents who are alumni of Stanford, or any top school for that matter, will not get them admitted.

One of the most popular myths surrounding MBA admissions is the perception that there is a certain profile or formula that leads to a coveted offer. I often hear candidates lament the fact that they don't come from blue-chip firms like Google, Microsoft, Goldman Sachs, TPG, McKinsey, and Schlumberger. Others focus on the fact that they attended South Dakota State University and worry that they can't compete with the Ivy-educated applicants who saturate the admissions pool. This perspective could not be further from the truth. The reality is that there isn't a hidden formula that guarantees acceptance to a top business school. Certainly, you will find a good number of Ivy-educated candidates from name-brand firms in the applicant pool. But you will also find a sizeable number of non-Ivy-educated candidates from firms that do not fall in the "usual-suspect" category. The diverse backgrounds of admitted students show that there isn't a cookie-cutter profile to the selection process.

But the process of selecting who gets admitted and who doesn't is a combination of science (the numbers) and art (the branding). The MBA boards evaluate candidates on limited information (a few pages in an application and a thirty- to forty-five-minute conversation) to decide which candidates are a fit and have the most compelling stories. This is why it is very common to see two applicants with nearly identical backgrounds (as far as raw numbers, educational history, and work experience) apply to the same business school, but one receives a rejection letter while the other is admitted.

The difference in outcome is usually a result of how each candidate markets himself or herself. We have all heard of the 750 GMAT, 3.7 GPA, Ivy-educated Wall Street superstar analyst who received interview invitations from Harvard, Stanford, Wharton, and Columbia, only to be rejected by all four schools. Clearly this candidate had the numbers, but having the numbers isn't enough to guarantee admission. It's how you position the data and what that information reveals about you that can make or break the application outcome. Successful applicants present a profile that is differentiated from others with similar backgrounds. It is this differentiation that tips the scale on who gets a congratulatory phone call and who doesn't.

These differentiated candidates often have one thing in common: they were memorable. I pondered what these candidates had that gave them an edge in the application process. It wasn't until after I left the Harvard Business School admissions board and launched my consultancy firm, EXPARTUS, that it dawned on me that successful business school applicants had figured out what many consumer goods companies know too well: the importance of selling one's value proposition to the customer. The 20 percent of applicants who are admitted to top business schools understand that the application process is a marketing exercise. These successful candidates have a strong sense of their personal brand (what sets them apart from their competition) and are effective in communicating their uniqueness to admissions boards.

YOUR ADMISSIONS PROCESS AND THE IMPORTANCE OF PERSONAL BRANDING

I focus *The Best Business Schools' Admissions Secrets* on personal branding as it relates to the admissions process. After many years in the admissions business, I am convinced that the greatest mistake that business school applicants make is that their applications lack a compelling brand. Most applicants pay way too much attention to trying to "game" the system and figure out what admissions boards want to hear, instead of taking a step back to assess their own stories and to present them in an authentic, powerful way.

Developing one's personal brand requires significant introspection, something that is a make-or-break factor in the application process. Being extremely smart with an 800 GMAT, perfect GRE score, and near-perfect GPA isn't enough to guarantee admission to your dream business school. The applicant pool is teeming with candidates with exceptional academic backgrounds. Being brainy can be a necessary but insufficient prerequisite in the application process. Conversely, there are enough instances of successful candidates with academic data that are below the school's admissions range. An interesting and compelling brand can help candidates land admission to their dream schools, even when their academic numbers are not exceptional. Nonetheless, this is not an excuse to ignore the academic components of the application.

The Best Business Schools' Admissions Secrets will examine how applicants can use branding techniques to achieve admissions success. I will begin by discussing why you would even consider an MBA in the first place. I will also discuss the three main admissions criteria that you will be evaluated on (academic ability, leadership track record, and uniqueness) and will provide specific insights on how to address each of them. I will provide anecdotes to convey the nuanced differences that lead to successful brand positioning. I will also devote a chapter to each of the application components (essays, résumé, recommendations, and interviews). Wherever applicable, I will present a case study to illustrate how you can navigate the application process.

The Best Business Schools' Admissions Secrets will also examine the common admissions mistakes candidates make as well as offer practical tips so you can avoid making the same application errors. I'll examine admission outcomes and how to effectively manage each of them.

I often hear applicants raise the issue of financing the MBA, so I have also devoted a chapter to discussing financing resources and how to go about planning to fund the business education. I have also interviewed students and alumni of top business schools, as well as a GMAT test provider and former admissions board member, to present additional insights to help you navigate the challenging admissions terrain.

The idea of individuals as personal brands is a relatively new way of thinking made popular by personal brand guru Tom Peters. Peters describes personal branding as:

> ...your promise to the marketplace and the world. Since everyone makes a promise to the world, one does not have a choice of having or not having a personal brand. Everyone has one. The real question is whether someone's personal brand is powerful enough to be meaningful to the person and the marketplace.

(Source: www.tompeters.com)

The question applicants have to answer during their application to business school is whether their personal brand is strong enough to be meaningful to the admissions board reviewing their application. Robin Fisher Roffer, author of *Make a Name for Yourself*, describes the power of personal branding when she says, "Branding makes you an active partner in fulfilling your destiny in business and life." Adopting the personal branding advice throughout this book will not only help you stand out in the competitive pool but will also empower you to become better at being your authentic self.

HOW TO USE THIS BOOK TO APPLY SUCCESSFULLY

I have written *The Best Business Schools' Admissions Secrets* not only to help candidates gain admission to top business schools but also to help them develop a clearer sense of who they are and what matters to them—their brand. It has been personally rewarding for me to hear from numerous applicants that the first edition of this book helped them to gain greater clarity about their brand and that they are using the personal brand tools they learned to make career decisions while they are in business school. I hope this updated edition will do the same for you.

Books that have been the most meaningful to me often have every other page marked up, highlighted, or overrun with a lot of notes. I encourage you to write down your thoughts as you read this book. It should be a good reference even after you have read it once, and you should go back and revisit sections that are relevant when you begin working on your application.

While I don't expect that this book will answer every single question you have about the application process, I anticipate that it will answer the majority of the burning ones. I have written this book for anyone who is seriously considering an MBA and wants to maximize his or her chance of gaining admission to a top business school. When I wrote this book six years ago, I had focused primarily on top business schools in the United States. In this edition, I expand my examples to include top MBA programs in Europe and Asia to provide a more balanced representation of business education worldwide. This book will give you an inside perspective of how top MBA admissions boards think and how they evaluate candidates.

The Best Business Schools' Admissions Secrets is also designed to empower you to reach for your dreams and to begin to take the necessary steps to live a passion-filled life. It is more than simply getting into the school of your dreams. It is about finding fulfillment in your life, tapping into what matters most to you, and charting a plan to achieve those things that bring you meaning.

I believe that every individual has a God-given set of talents and passion, and when you pursue your dream, you have no choice but to succeed. I ultimately believe that if you spend most of your time doing what you truly enjoy, you will become brilliant at it and will achieve success in other areas of your life. Getting into your dream MBA program is one of the steps along the journey of living a passionate and purpose-driven life. I wish you great success along the way.

CHAPTER ONE

Deciding on the MBA

W ANTING AN MBA IS a good thing. It suggests that you are ambitious and willing to push yourself to achieve a goal. But before starting on your application, you should examine what an MBA means to you. Be clear on your motivations and goals before embarking on the extremely challenging and expensive application process.

All top business schools will expect you to address why you want an MBA, whether they ask in an interview or earlier within the application process. How the schools pose the question can differ, but fundamentally, they each want to understand your career goal and whether an MBA is necessary to help you achieve it. Equally important to the MBA admissions board is understanding whether your MBA aspiration reflects your true passion or is simply a way for you to get your ticket punched. The issue of fit is also very important to business school admissions boards. They want to ensure that their program is right for you and that you are right for their program.

The justification for an MBA will vary from one applicant to the next. The important thing is to remain true to who you are when presenting your rationale for pursuing an MBA. In this chapter, I will examine the four most popular reasons applicants cite for wanting to attend business school and how admissions boards view these reasons. I will also review the benefits of obtaining an MBA and the different variables that candidates use in selecting a business program.

THE COST OF YOUR MBA

Applying to business school will cost you a fair amount of money. The average application fee is $200, and given the acceptance rate of 10 to 20 percent, most applicants apply to four or more schools. In addition to application fees, applicants have to pay for standardized tests. Registration for the Graduate Record Examinations (GRE) is $185. It is $250 for the Graduate Management Admission Test (GMAT). With average test-prep programs charging about $1,100 to $1,500 (not including one-on-one tutoring), you should expect to shell out at least $2,000 just to apply to business schools. If you decide to hire an admissions consultant to guide you along the way, this figure can increase significantly. The MBA itself is a very expensive investment, with costs north of $180,000 for two-year programs and more than $80,000 for one-year programs. And I haven't even touched on the opportunity cost of leaving a lucrative job and forfeiting a salary and bonus for one to two years. If you include the lost income, the MBA price tag can easily be more than $250,000–$350,000. So before you take the application plunge, make sure the MBA is necessary to achieve your career goals.

The good news is that although the MBA costs a considerable amount of money, the payoff can be substantial, with many graduates from top programs earning twice what they used to earn prior to receiving an MBA. But the payoff isn't only monetary. Many MBA graduates receive other perks, such as greater career exposure, contacts, skills, and so on. Before delving deeper into the benefits of the MBA, which I will further examine in this chapter, let's take a look at two major admissions traps that applicants fall into: jumping on MBA bandwagons and applying because they are unemployed.

THE RIGHT REASONS FOR GETTING YOUR MBA

The MBA admissions board will be checking to make sure you are not simply getting on the MBA bandwagon because all of your friends are applying to business school. The MBA board also wants to ensure that you are not applying simply because your firm has a structure where employees complete a two- or three-year analyst program and then have to leave. Analysts and consultants in investment banking and strategy consulting face this issue the most. It is understood that a majority of analysts and consultants will "move on" after two to three years and a significant number will end up pursuing their MBA degree. But this expectation of going for your MBA is not a strong enough reason to convince the MBA admissions board that you are serious about the degree. Candidates in these categories need to make a clear pitch for what their specific MBA goals are and how the particular program is best positioned to help them achieve their future success.

Be wary of trying to game the system. Someone once asked me whether I thought she should join a private equity (PE) shop after working two years in consulting in order to get PE experience. My answer to her was to focus on her long-term goals. If her passion is to start or lead a PE company, then making the leap now is fine. On the other hand, if joining a PE shop is simply to get a stamp, then it isn't the right path to take. More recently, the opposite has been the case; some schools have admitted fewer PE applicants than in the past, leading some to question whether they should change careers away from private equity before applying to business school. Instead of trying to read the tea leaves of each school to decipher what they will do each year, you are better off zeroing in on what you truly care about and making a passionate case for why you will be a great addition to that school.

MBA admissions boards can also see through the ploy of leaving a consulting or engineering job to join a nonprofit organization right before applying to business school specifically to get a social enterprise stamp of approval. On the other hand, if social philanthropy is a genuine interest, then make sure you connect the dots to other evidence in your professional and personal life to show that social enterprise isn't just a passing fancy.

Quite frankly, there is no set profile or work experience that guarantees admission to a top business school. So, at best, simply jumping on trendy bandwagons will signal to the MBA admissions board that you are not authentic about your career goals. Because each candidate's story varies, it is important to embrace your unique circumstances and articulate how the MBA fits with your goal and how it will transform your career.

PURSUING AN MBA DESPITE A PINK SLIP

Another potential red-flag reason applicants give for applying to business school is that they lost their job and have nothing better to do. Obviously this situation is likely to yield an unfavorable outcome. Many casualties of the dot-com disaster contributed to the unprecedented application volumes seen at many leading business schools in 2001. Not surprisingly, many of the applicants did not gain admission to business school.

The 2007–2008 economic meltdown has led to job cutbacks across different industries, with financial services taking the greatest hit. The worldwide economic recovery is still ongoing. Some of those who received pink slips may still be struggling to rebuild their careers. One silver lining that has emerged in admissions recently is that MBA programs have become more accommodating of "hiccups" in candidates' CVs and résumés. It is also important to acknowledge that there are some variations in terms of the work options that applicants pursue within the United States versus outside of the United States. For example, while living in the United Kingdom for a few years, I noticed that more professionals there took on contract work that lasted for shorter periods compared to the United States, where there is more of a culture to secure employment in roles that are longer-term in duration. I expect that U.S. MBA programs are becoming more attuned to this cultural variation and will take into consideration the applicant's context.

Should you find yourself in the unfortunate situation of being unemployed, avoid saying that you are pursuing the MBA as a way to get back into the job market. I know, it sounds obvious, but I have come across this rationale enough times to know that the obvious isn't always "obvious." Even if you don't explicitly state this reason for why you want an MBA, if you receive a pink slip and do not find alternative employment, the MBA admissions board will still likely conclude that you are seeking the degree because you do not have anything better to do.

However, unemployed candidates are not necessarily doomed to rejection. I have worked with several unemployed candidates through my consultancy, EXPARTUS, and despite receiving pink slips, each was able to gain admission to elite business schools. If you are unemployed, the important thing you should keep in mind is to use the time wisely to reassess your plans and to engage in activities that reinforce your brand. Using the time to learn a new language, to develop real skills that you truly care about, or to engage in activities that affect people's lives through focused and committed volunteerism can be justifiable reasons for how you have spent your time.

For instance, if you were a varsity squash player and have always been interested in community involvement now that you are not working an eighty-hour workweek, you can join a volunteer organization like StreetSquash to lend your skills to empower and impact the lives of inner-city kids through athletics. Better yet, if you are trying to make a switch, for example, from finance to marketing, you can lead marketing initiatives in a nonprofit enterprise, helping it grow its donor base and secure more funding. The brief marketing experience you gain can provide insightful material for your essays and reinforce your justification for the career change. This is what one of my former clients did, enabling him to secure admission to a top business school despite the challenge of not being currently employed when he applied.

While schools have softened their response to employment gaps on résumés and CVs, the pressure is still on the applicant to explain the circumstances surrounding the job loss and what you have done since. And it goes without saying that the shorter the unemployment gap, the easier it is to explain.

TOP FOUR MOST POPULAR REASONS FOR PURSUING AN MBA

Striving for an MBA solely for the sake of jumping on the MBA bandwagon will only hurt your chances of admission. The same goes for applying simply because you have lost your job. So what are the common rationales that are acceptable for desiring an MBA? In this section, I will review the four most common reasons that drive MBA applicants' decisions to apply to business school, as well as how the MBA admissions board feels about each of them.

Responses to why you want an MBA often fall into four categories: financial reward, intellectual challenge, personal development, and professional advancement. Let's examine each and discuss how admissions boards view them.

Financial Reward

There is no doubt that the return on investment of an MBA (especially for top MBA programs) is very high. A glance at career brochures or websites of leading MBA programs reveals that after graduating from business school, the average starting salary for the newly minted MBA is about

$100K. According to the GMAC 2013 Alumni Perspectives Survey, the financial payoff of the MBA is high, with graduates of both two-year and one-year MBA programs reporting earning a median salary of $100,000. And these data points do not include the bonuses that can often be in the tens of thousands of dollars, depending on the industry. You don't have to be a math whiz to recognize that the MBA offers significant financial reward that pays for itself. If this is your main reason for pursuing an MBA, that's fine—but I recommend keeping it to yourself. The MBA admissions board already recognizes that financial reward is one of the key reasons people choose to study for an MBA. Stating this reason as your main driver for an MBA means not taking advantage of your opportunity to share a deeper reason like personal or professional fulfillment, reasons that can show more depth of character and insight as far as the admissions board is concerned. We will get to those shortly.

Intellectual Challenge

For many candidates, the draw of the MBA is the intellectual stimulation and challenge that they will experience in the classroom. Without a doubt, the MBA builds skills and equips students with new insights to business issues. The joy of learning new material and concepts makes the MBA attractive to candidates who welcome the intellectual and invigorating conversations inside and outside the classroom. Stretching yourself intellectually is a fine rationale for why you want an MBA. Schools are attracted to intellectually curious students who enjoy learning and discovery. However, this rationale can raise flags for the MBA admissions board if you have multiple graduate degrees but no work experience; candidates with this background can be seen as "degree collectors" or "perpetual students." Your comfort level operating in the real world may be called into question. So regardless of what your background is, it is important to balance your quest for knowledge with practical experience. Mention the importance of growth and development on an intellectual level, but also express how you anticipate using your new knowledge toward achieving your life goals.

Personal Development

The personal development justification for the MBA is often tied to professional benefits as well. The draw for many people who choose to pursue the MBA is the personal confidence and credentials that an MBA gives them. As an MBA alumna phrased it, "My MBA gave me the courage to think bigger, step farther, and pursue my lifelong dream." The one thing that most MBAs have in common is an ambitious spirit and a desire to achieve something significant—the teacher who wants to create charter schools across the nation, the cellist who plans to transform her national music conservatory in Bulgaria, or the business analyst who wants to run an emerging market hedge fund. What all these individuals have in common is a desire to have greater impact beyond where they are in their lives. The confidence that an MBA provides allows many individuals to achieve significant goals, and this remains a major driver for many who seek a graduate business education. One can't talk about the personal development impact of the MBA without addressing the incredible social network that surrounds the MBA experience. Through lifelong friendships and diverse networks, many MBAs are able to achieve their goals. It is no surprise that personal development is a popular rationale given by many applicants for why they want an MBA. This rationale makes complete sense to admissions boards.

Professional Advancement

The majority of applicants indicate that they are seeking an MBA for the career development benefits. More specifically, they say that they want the MBA to increase their understanding of the business world. This is a popular and compelling reason to give for why you want an MBA.

For some candidates, an MBA is a necessary next step to jump-start a stalled career. For others, they have been bypassed on promotions because they lack the degree. And then there are those applicants who are ready for a significant management role but who lack some fundamental skills that would be necessary to succeed in the new position. Entrepreneurs also find the MBA environment to be a great value in building their skill set and helping them refine their business model, reposition their product, and learn more successful ways to scale an already successful enterprise. A case in point is seen in the story of Victoria Ransom, a New Zealander from a small farming town of sixty-five people who ended up starting a social media marketing company. She sold her company, Wildfire, to Google for $350 million. Wildfire wasn't her first foray into business. In fact, she had been an entrepreneur since her early twenties.

However, the skills she learned from Harvard Business School helped her launch Wildfire while she was a student there.

And of course, there are the career changers—I can't talk about the professional development benefit of the MBA without discussing career changers. Many MBA candidates can be characterized as such. In fact, more than 70 percent of MBA students change their industry, function, or location after attending business school. If you are a career changer, you probably see the MBA as a bridge to enable you to transition into a new industry or function. And indeed, that is one of the major benefits of the MBA.

However, it is not enough to say you plan to use the MBA to change your job. You must be able to show that you have made a significant impact in your current career. It is also important that you present strong evidence based on your brand that you have what it takes to make a career switch. Regardless of whether you will change careers or remain in your current industry, it is acceptable to use professional development as your justification for why you seek an MBA.

I will discuss career changers and branding in greater detail in the chapter on building and selling your brand.

THE VALUE OF THE MBA

The MBA is an expensive investment. Ask anyone applying to business school, and you are likely to hear that they believe that the return on their investment can be significant. The numbers from graduates of top business schools support this: 86 percent of women and 89 percent of men surveyed in a Catalyst study reported that they were very satisfied with their MBA career after attending business school.

Often, the value of the MBA can be characterized as falling within one of these ten benefits:

1. Management skills
2. Strategic skills
3. Analytical and quantitative skills
4. Technical skills
5. Soft skills (leadership, communication, negotiation, agility in thinking on your feet, team management, etc.)
6. Increased knowledge

7. Significant salary bump
8. Access to new careers
9. Incubating and starting a business
10. Expanded network

The Graduate Management Admission Council (GMAC) 2013 Alumni Perspectives Survey reveals that 95 percent of the alumni polled indicated that the benefit of their MBA was good to outstanding. According to this study, the top three drivers for the value of the MBA were:

• Taking on challenging and interesting work
• Gaining managerial knowledge and technical skills
• Starting a business

(Source: GMAC Alumni Perspectives Survey, 2013)

So if you have decided that the MBA is for you, and you are clear on why you want to pursue this degree and what it will offer you in the long term, let's examine the specific influences that shape which MBA program you choose.

DIFFERENT TYPES OF MBA PROGRAMS

MBA programs have evolved over the years and many offer different options. The most prevalent MBA options are as follows: full-time two-year MBA, full-time one-year MBA, part-time MBA, executive MBA, and online MBA. Although this book focuses on full-time one- and two-year MBA programs, I will discuss some other options to give you a sense of what each program offers and the type of student for whom it is a good fit. MBA programs tend to have strict transfer policies, so do not count on being able to switch from a part-time MBA program to a full-time MBA program at a top business school. To avoid disappointment, you should do your research early to ascertain the program that is the best fit before enrolling in business school.

Two-Year MBA Program

The two-year MBA program is extremely popular in the United States, although the one-year program is beginning to gather steam. The full-time MBA program is ideal for career changers for two reasons: (1) it offers greater opportunity to step back and reflect on their experiences and goals; and (2) it provides them with greater flexibility to take many classes in the new career they are pursuing. This option also offers students the opportunity to pursue an internship the summer after their first year to assess whether the new career interest is a good fit.

The curricula of two-year MBA programs provides students with the opportunity to gain a broad exposure to the different business areas as well as a chance to develop a specialization. MBA programs vary in how much curriculum flexibility they offer to students. Chicago Graduate School of Business (GSB) is one of the most flexible, allowing students the greatest freedom to opt out of classes and to design their own schedules. Since the first edition of *The Best Business Schools' Admissions Secrets*, several schools have undergone significant curriculum changes. Wharton, for example, now offers greater flexibility for the core classes based on students' backgrounds. It allows students to take elective classes in their first year, something that usually happens in the second year at most other two-year business schools. It also allows course customization, which enables students to tailor their courses to relate to their long-term goals. Wharton has also placed greater emphasis on communication (both written and verbal) as well as on experience-based learning through its global modular courses, in which students work in small groups in different countries to tackle a real-world business challenge.

But Wharton isn't alone in revamping its curriculum. Several other schools that have changed their MBA curricula include UC–Berkeley's Haas School of Business and Columbia Graduate School of Business. Some, like ESADE Business School in Spain, are planning future curriculum changes. Harvard Business School has embarked on a multi-year curriculum change. The heralding of a new dean, Nitin Nohria, at HBS, has brought some changes as well. In a three-year curriculum review, HBS has introduced a new required course, Field Immersion Experience for Leadership Development (FIELD), which will take students to different emerging markets, where they are given the chance to translate what they have learned into action. But the curriculum change at Harvard doesn't stop there. The school is also planning to introduce more opportunities for students to put their learning into practice while experiencing greater course integration.

Applicants who pursue the full-time two-year MBA program find that it is the most expensive MBA option, given the price tag and the lack of income for two years. Some firms offer sponsorship for their star employees to pursue a full-time MBA program. Find out what your company's policy is for sponsorship by speaking with your manager and by talking to individuals you know who have gone to business school and returned to the firm. The expectation is usually that you will return to your firm if you receive financial support from your firm. For some individuals, this golden handcuff may be too high a price to pay, and they may pass on the employee sponsorship if they already know that they would prefer to work at a different firm or in a different industry.

If you are a career changer who plans to work in strategy consulting or in investment banking, then you should definitely pursue a full-time two-year MBA program. The availability of a summer internship will provide you with entrée into banking or consulting, which will make you more marketable to the banks and consulting companies.

One-Year MBA Program

The one-year MBA program is more popular outside of the United States. A majority of the European MBA programs, including INSEAD in France, Cambridge Judge, Oxford Saïd, IMD, IE, and ESADE, are all one-year programs. A few European exceptions include the London Business School, which can be done in as little as fifteen months and up to twenty-one months, and IESE in Spain, which is completed in two years.

Students in two-year MBA programs often complain that the time went by too quickly, so you can imagine the pace at which everything is done in the one-year program. For this reason, there has been the assumption that you can't pursue a career change in a one-year MBA program. However, students who thrive in this intense and accelerated environment are those who can juggle a lot of things at the same time and maintain a laserlike focus on what they want to get out of their MBA. Therefore, while there isn't the traditional summer internship opportunity in the one-year MBA program, these organized and focused students can still pursue a successful career change within this compressed time frame. Cambridge Judge Business School, for instance, reports that about 50 percent of their graduates are career changers. This very high number should be reassuring to business school candidates that they too can pursue a successful career change in a one-year MBA program.

Some of the other students who are drawn to the one-year MBA program are those who are already in their career of choice but are looking to strengthen specific business skills. Also, entrepreneurs who plan to return to a family business or to start one of their own will find the one-year MBA option attractive as well.

Part-Time MBA Program

The part-time MBA program is a popular choice for individuals who want to remain in their job while developing their business skills. Many firms are supportive of employees who wish to pursue a part-time business degree because they are able to retain them. Some even offer the option to sponsor the applicant with some stipulation on the number of years the employee must remain at the firm. Each firm varies in terms of their policy on sponsorship eligibility. You may even have to take the GMAT and score at a certain level for your employer to sponsor your application. It is important to find out if your firm offers tuition reimbursement and the terms associated with it.

The part-time MBA option is not ideally suited for career changers for different reasons. The most prominent is the inability to "test out" a new career during the summer internship. Nonetheless, there are still examples of graduates of part-time MBA programs who have successfully transitioned to a new career.

An attractive feature of the part-time MBA program lies in the fact that students get to immediately put into practice what they are learning. The flexible schedule through evening and weekend classes makes this option appealing to many professionals who want the business education without having to forfeit their jobs.

Executive MBA Program

Of all the MBA program types, the executive MBA varies the most (a combination of weekends, evenings, onsite engagements where students congregate on campus, and online study). Many top institutions offer an executive MBA program, while others offer certifications and other short-term executive education training. An example of the latter is Harvard Business School's executive programs that last for a few days to several weeks and focus on developing the managerial skills of business leaders across the private, public, and nonprofit sectors.

Executive MBAs often provide exceptional employees with sponsorship. Even if your firm does not have a formal sponsorship policy, it is worth speaking to your manager to explore whether your firm would be able to sponsor you. Besides the financial sponsorship, it is also important to get your firm's support, because most executive MBA programs require students to leave their jobs to be on campus for periods of time.

Deciding whether an executive MBA (EMBA) is the right option for you will depend on where you are in your career and why you want the MBA. If you are at a relatively early stage in your career, the EMBA is not typically a good fit, since it is designed for individuals who are further along in their career and have substantive professional responsibilities and management experience. It is no surprise, then, that the majority of students in executive MBA programs are over thirty and have a decade of professional experience. The EMBA is also ideal if you are looking for credentials, deeper industry knowledge, and expanded skill sets as opposed to making a major career change.

Online MBA Programs

While online programs carried a very negative stigma a few years ago, today such programs are becoming more acceptable, and their popularity is growing. Even business leaders like Jack Welch are getting into the online MBA market. Welch has partnered with Strayer University to create the Jack Welch Management Institute to provide an online executive MBA program. While online MBAs aren't the focus of this book, they warrant some discussion. Some applicants find online MBA programs attractive for a variety of reasons, including lower cost, flexibility (you can fit the program into your life), continuity with employment, career advancement, and immediate skill growth that is applicable to your job.

But buyers beware. There are a great number of fly-by-night online programs that are scams and don't deliver on the education they purport to provide. Applicants targeting an online MBA program should do careful research to identify programs that are actually accredited and have a track record of delivering what they promise.

One practical thing applicants to online MBA programs can do is to take a free online course first to test whether this option suits their needs. Start by checking out companies like EdX, a collaboration between Massachusetts Institute of Technology and Harvard University, that provides massive open online courses for free.

SELECTING THE RIGHT MBA PROGRAM

Having discussed the different variations of the MBA program, I would like to more closely examine the variables that applicants consider when selecting a program. Here are the top ones that influence applicants' selection decisions.

Length of the Program

As I discussed earlier, a number of variables affect your decision of whether to pursue a full-time two-year, full-time one-year, part-time, or executive MBA program. Is time a factor for you? Are you trying to complete the MBA in as short a time as possible? Is the high cost of an MBA prohibitive? Are you already in the industry you want to be in? Can you bypass the summer internship? If you answered yes to these questions, it may be worth exploring MBA programs that are less than two years. Some of the top business schools in the United States have one-year or accelerated MBA programs. Chicago, Kellogg, and Columbia are just a few examples that come to mind. The MBA programs outside of the United States are also good options if time is a major factor for you or if you are seeking an international career. INSEAD, IE, Judge, Saïd, and IMD are popular programs in Europe that offer a full-time MBA program in less than two years.

Geographic Location

Is geography of critical importance to you? Some candidates cannot imagine themselves in an urban environment; hence schools like London Business School, Haas, Chicago, Columbia, and HBS will not make sense for them. There are applicants for whom the small-town community at schools like Darden, Tuck, and the Johnson School at Cornell University is ideal. Individuals seeking international exposure must take the geographic location into account. Candidates planning to pursue a career in Europe may want to consider programs like IMD (Switzerland), INSEAD (France), Bocconi (Italy), and London Business

School (UK). Geography can also impact career opportunities for MBA graduates. For instance, if you don't speak Chinese and you attend a Chinese MBA program, it will be tougher for you to secure employment in China without polishing your Mandarin skills. It is always in your best interest to find out the career opportunities available in the region you are targeting and the visa policies that you will have to adhere to. Be aware that regions that are still struggling economically will tend to have fewer available jobs, so think carefully about the geography of the MBA program before you apply.

Size of the Program

The size of the class can also play a significant role in where an applicant chooses to apply. The small program size of IMD, Haas, Tuck, Yale School of Management, HKUST, and Stanford Graduate School of Business could be a major draw for some applicants and a turnoff for others. So decide whether you are someone who will thrive in a large environment or a smaller, more intimate one. Having clarity on the ideal environment for you will save you the hassle of going through business school unhappy with where you are.

Teaching Method

We can't discuss variables affecting school selection without addressing the teaching methodology of the programs. Darden, IESE, and HBS may be appealing to some applicants for their emphasis on the case-study method, whereas this idea can be terrifying for other applicants. Also, some candidates believe you cannot teach finance effectively through the case method and would be loath to attend a program that is primarily case-focused.

Flexibility of the Program

MBA programs differ in the range of flexibility they offer their students. MBA programs like Chicago GSB are among the top programs with significant curriculum flexibility. This level of curriculum option is ideal for candidates who are seeking a program where they can exempt out of classes they have taken before in order to create space to take new materials. Stanford GSB's revised curriculum a few years ago added greater flexibility for its students to customize their MBA experience.

Many other MBA programs have seen the value of providing flexibility in their curricula and have made changes accordingly.

International Business Exposure

Some applicants are attracted to international business. So although these students may opt for an American MBA, it is important to them to attend a program that offers the opportunity to either study abroad or tackle an international project that allows them to live abroad.

The Ross MBA at Michigan, Johnson MBA at Cornell, Wharton, and Kellogg are some of the programs that offer significant international experience and exposure. At Ross, for instance, you can take a semester exchange at one of the finest MBA programs in Europe, Australia, or Asia. Stanford GSB, since overhauling its curriculum, can be added to the list of MBA programs with a strong international exposure. Stanford addresses its goals to "globalize the experience" of their students by stating:

> The School will continue to globalize its cases and course materials, and a global experience will be required of each student during his or her two years at the School. This can be fulfilled by a study trip, an international internship, an overseas service-learning trip, or a student exchange, such as the School's new program with Tsinghua University's School of Economics and Management in China.
>
> *(Source: Stanford GSB website)*

But few MBA programs can boast of their international reach and brand as much as INSEAD, which has campuses in three countries: France, Singapore, and United Arab Emirates. There, students are able to take classes at one of the campuses as well as have the opportunity to study abroad in various MBA programs around the world.

Brand of the Program

Last but not the least is the overall brand of the MBA program. There is a certain feel and culture that permeates each MBA program. By visiting the programs and attending classes, you will be in a better position to ascertain whether a program is right for you. Each MBA program also has areas that it is brilliant at and is known for. I encourage all applicants to take the time to thoroughly research each program to ensure that they select the ones that fit their brand and goals. We address the topic of MBA programs as brands in the next chapter.

By now, I anticipate that you have a clearer sense of whether the MBA is worth it for you. You also have a practical sense of admissions traps to avoid when making the decision to apply. Furthermore, you should be aware that whatever rationale you give to the admissions board for why you wish to pursue an MBA will be scrutinized. Assess your own circumstances carefully before deciding on your particular reason(s) for an MBA. But equally important is selecting the right type of MBA program given different variables that are important to you. I have covered the main variables that influence MBA program selection, and I hope this information has helped you to decide whether a two-year, one-year, part-time, or executive MBA program is ideal for you. Taking the time to assess what you need from an MBA program and knowing yourself well will help you make the appropriate decision in the long run. A $180,000 misstep is too costly a mistake to make, and I'm glad you are investing in the research and assessment early in the process.

CHAPTER TWO

Personal Branding and the
MBA Application Process

S O WHAT EXACTLY DOES personal branding have to do with the admissions process? Everything! Applicants with strong and compelling brands distinguish themselves from the pack and capture the attention of admissions boards. But applicants are not the only ones who have to think of themselves as brands. MBA programs are also brands, and the MBA admissions board is charged with identifying the best candidates who are a fit with the brand of their program.

In my sixteen years in the admissions industry and from my experience running my admissions consultancy, EXPARTUS, I have come to recognize that there is a special chemistry that admitted candidates bring to the table: a strong and clear sense of who they are, what matters most to them, and where they are heading in the future. What comes to mind when an admissions board member thinks about the candidate he or she just read about? What unique characteristics emerge that set that candidate apart from all the other individuals within the same category? It is the candidate's salient attributes and unique perspective and experience that set him or her apart in the application pool. Making sure that your unique brand stands out is critical to achieving admissions success.

A brand is what differentiates a product (or person, in the case of MBA applicants) from the pack. Jeff Bezos, founder of Amazon, puts it this way: "Your brand is what people say about you when you are not in the room." Simply stated, your brand precedes you. Let's look at a few strong brand examples. Who do you think of when you hear the phrase "motivational talk-show maven"? If you guessed Oprah, you're right. While she has ended her iconic show, her reputation as the most powerful talk-show host remains intact. How about "international rock star activist"? One might think of Bono, of the rock group U2. Okay, you might be thinking, "Bono and Oprah have one thing in common; they are famous people with tons of money." The point is taken. However, not all famous people have brands or a strong characterization that accompanies their names.

Make no mistake about it—business school application is an exercise in marketing; it requires you to be able to sell the value you will offer to an MBA program. Successfully marketing your story to an admissions board requires a clear understanding of your personal brand.

WHAT EXACTLY IS A BRAND?

As personal branding guru Peter Montoya, in his 2002 book *The Personal Branding Phenomenon*, explains, "Strong brands instantly communicate simple, clear feelings or ideas to us about a product, company, or person." What attributes come to mind when you think about a product, person, or company? Do you have a positive or negative reaction? Or worse, are you indifferent, which can suggest the absence of a brand?

What feeling or idea does your brand communicate to the MBA admissions board? What image does the admissions board have of you after reading your application? Does it match the message that you set out to convey? Understanding the elements of successful brands will help you begin to think of yourself as a brand as you present your story to the admissions board.

I will discuss four fundamental brand rules that help MBA applicants differentiate themselves. I will also use case examples of individuals and companies that apply these branding principles to illustrate how you can do the same to make your application stand out.

THE FUNDAMENTAL RULES OF PERSONAL BRANDING

- Rule #1: Be focused.
- Rule #2: Be an expert.
- Rule #3: Be a leader.
- Rule #4: Excel and deliver results.

Rule #1: Be Focused

Let's look at the case of two companies and the effect the rule of focus has had on them.

Branded companies know a secret: branding requires focus. Racing fans across the world hold Lamborghini cars in great esteem. Automobili Lamborghini S.p.A is a company that stays true to its brand of producing exotic, high-powered racing cars. Started in 1963 by Ferruccio Lamborghini, the company has focused on its brand as a company that produces luxury sports cars, and it owns that brand in the market along with its archrival, Ferrari. This focus has enabled the company to generate a lot of money, over €469 million in 2012. While many car manufacturing companies have struggled financially, Lamborghini has managed to achieve revenue increases for the past four years. Now, let's look at General Motors (GM). If I asked you to tell me what type of car GM specializes in, you may be hard pressed to come up with a quick phrase that captures its essence. If you said "sporty, all-terrain, average all-American car" you would be right—this statement describes the Corvette, Hummer (H2), and Saturn, all GM cars (although the latter two are no longer manufactured). But one of GM's biggest problems is that it doesn't own a message in the consumer's mind. By diversifying so much and offering products that appeal to the widest customer base, the brand of the company has been diluted in the process. It is no wonder GM filed for chapter 11 bankruptcy on June 1, 2009. It took a U.S. government bailout in excess of $19 billion to give GM a new lease on life. This bailout came with strings attached, including forcing GM to simplify its product offering from eight car types to four (Chevrolet, Buick, Cadillac, and GMC). Companies that try to be all things to all people are very quick to lose the attention of the consumer, and GM has learned this tough lesson.

The rule of focus applies to applicants to business school in a similar way. You should identify one or two things that you are brilliant at and focus on using them to create value at your firm. By focusing on these core elements, you will be able to build a reputation and develop a track record that establishes your brand. Avoid spreading yourself too thin, because it only creates confusion about what you stand for. Applicants who try to be different things at the same time (innovator, change manager, operations guru, accounting whiz, and human capital champion) run the risk of creating confusion about their brand and ultimately raise red flags for the admissions board. Pick the few themes that are core to your value, skills, and goals, and build your brand on them. As an MBA applicant, you will increase your chances of success if you can identify key attributes or brand elements that differentiate you from your competition. I go into more detail on brand attributes in the chapter on building and selling your personal brand.

Rule #2: Be an Expert

Microsoft is a company that has leveraged its expertise—software—to become a multibillion-dollar company. With few exceptions, one can't turn on any personal computer worldwide without having to rely on a Microsoft Office product to perform basic functions. Microsoft's expertise developing "easier, faster, smarter" software has enabled it to capture significant market share, which translates to billions of dollars in revenue.

In another example, YouTube, a company started by three young former PayPal employees, has revolutionized the way information is transmitted around the world. Their tagline, "Broadcast Yourself," is at the heart of their brand, providing a vehicle for anyone to get their message out to a global audience. In the space of a few years, they have transformed the way video files are shared. Google's purchase of YouTube for more than $1 billion is evidence of the power a brand can have when it focuses on its expertise and uses it to meet a need in the marketplace.

Applicants to business school must look for ways to create value for their firm, team, or clients. What is a need that is not being met at your firm? Is there a new product that can improve the revenue stream at your company? Do you have knowledge that can help facilitate that? Are you an athlete who has special understanding of the sports product business? For instance, you may be a marketing associate at Nike and can draw from your experiences as an athlete to shape the development of the latest sneakers design that is being introduced in the market. As a minority, you may be able to offer unique insights into how your company should position itself when marketing to minority communities. A Chinese national with experience working on the mainland can help her company navigate its expansion into China given her geopolitical awareness of the region.

Even personal experiences can influence the development of a candidate's expertise. For example, you may develop an interest in pharmaceutical products because of health issues. Your own self-study and research can position you as a resident expert in the area of health-care and pharmaceutical topics at your firm. Your knowledge could become valuable to help your firm expand its knowledge base in health-care/drug industry deals.

International experience can also be an option. European applicants have an edge in language ability compared with their U.S. counterparts. Leveraging strong language ability, many candidates opt for international deals where they are able to use their linguistic expertise when working with clients. This is the case for a Turkish woman who works in mergers and acquisitions in London and—because she speaks fluent German—is able to work on many prominent German deals at her firm. The insights she gleaned working in the United Kingdom and Germany, combined with her awareness of her home country, Turkey, bring meaningful understanding of what is required to work in international settings. Regardless of your specific experience, it is important to figure out where you have unique, value-added expertise, which you should begin to use immediately to differentiate yourself from your peers.

Rule #3: Be a Leader

Branding requires a commitment to step up and stand for what you believe. Taking action and leading is another key to branding. The power of branding goes beyond companies and products and applies to people as well. Two great examples of individuals who demonstrate the rule of leadership in cultivating their brands are Bono and Wangari Maathai.

Bono has been a leader in addressing humanitarian problems and alleviating poverty, disease, and hunger in the poorest areas of the world. His steadfast commitment to social justice has led to his brand as an activist rocker. By raising funds, investing his own resources and money, and bringing to the attention of the world many of the issues plaguing Africa, his brand as an activist was born. Bono clearly represents an example of someone with an authentic brand who is living his passion, creating change, and making an impact on the lives of millions. Today, Bono is viewed as the preeminent rock star leader in advocating for the poor.

Wangari Maathai is another great example of an individual with a powerful brand built upon the rule of leadership. Known as the "Tree Lady," Wangari Maathai had a distinct brand as a fearless conservationist who refused to be cowed by Kenya's former dictatorial government despite death threats and imprisonments. To the majority of the world, she was known as Africa's first female Nobel Peace Prize Laureate. She founded a grassroots environmental organization called the Green Belt Movement, which introduced a vision of empowerment for women and conservation through the planting of trees. Maathai clearly lived her passion of improving the environment until her death in 2011. Pursuing this vision led to an environmental revolution the likes of which had never been seen in Africa. In 2004, she received a Nobel Prize, but before this honor was bestowed on her, she had already established an enduring brand as an eco-activist.

I'm not suggesting that all applicants to business school should become activists tomorrow. Leadership does not always require activism. Rather, it requires commitment and a willingness to take a risk to pursue your passion.

You may be passionate about education and may want to consider taking on leadership roles in a nonprofit educational organization. Denise is an applicant who had the guts to pursue her passion by changing her career before business school. Doing very well in a Wall Street firm, Denise chose to turn down her third-year analyst offer to join a relatively young educational organization. Her two years at this organization enabled her to build credibility as an education advocate and future leader and gave her ample opportunity to tackle significant leadership challenges. Shortly after, she was admitted to a top business school, where she plans to establish a strong network and broaden her skill set before running charter schools.

Many of you may not be interested in changing your career as Denise did. You can still demonstrate leadership in a practical and tangible way within your firm. For instance, parlaying your analytics expertise to overhaul and lead the new training program at your firm may be the exact leadership role that works for your brand. That's exactly what Sunil did while working at his private equity firm. He drew on his achievements in helping train and develop the junior staff at his firm as a way to differentiate himself from other well-qualified MBA candidates and ultimately secured admission to both Stanford and Harvard Business Schools.

Some of you may be like Fred, a pharmaceutical engineer from an emerging market country whose leadership impact is shown through working within the established system in his firm. Fred realized that his firm had much stricter regulations regarding the shelf life of pharmaceutical drugs than his home country did, and because of those policies, perfectly good drugs were going to be thrown away. Fred's impact was to seize the opportunity to partner with his firm to distribute the drugs, which otherwise would have been wasted, to hospitals and clinics in his home country. Or you may be like John, who started a small tutoring program in New York to empower inner-city kids whose grades suffered as a result of the abysmal education they were exposed to in their public schools. What is important is that whatever leadership role you choose to cultivate, pick one that reinforces your brand and make sure you deliver impact with it. Authenticity is critical to the branding process, so focus only on the things that you are truly committed to.

Rule #4: Excel and Deliver Results

Like her or not, Martha Stewart has established a brand as the grande dame of home improvement. She is known for scrutinizing every item or product associated with her brand before putting her seal of approval on it. Some may see this as overkill; the reality, however, is that because she has been this closely involved with her products and has maintained a judicious vigilance in the quality associated with her brand, she has been able to build a multimillion-dollar business.

Although the majority of the applicants to business school have not started multimillion-dollar companies, adopting a Martha Stewart–like scrutiny to the product or service you deliver can pay dividends in the application process. Delivering excellence in everything you do—including the services you provide to clients, the products you develop, or the teams you manage—will ensure that you have a track record that will stand out when you apply to business school.

Although Martha Stewart has been successful in building a strong firm, she also represents a cautionary story of what happens when your personal actions are negative. Because Martha Stewart, the person, is intimately connected to her eponymous company, her conviction for perjury during her insider-trading trial had an enormous impact on her company, with stock prices plummeting. Martha Stewart's example shows how one negative action can unravel years of establishing an excellent reputation. Applicants to business school must be careful not to make a mistake that can derail the reputation they have earned at their jobs. Consistently delivering quality results will solidify your positive reputation/brand among your colleagues, superiors, and clients. After all, it is precisely this track record of excellence that your brand champions will rely on to support your application.

Applicants who show commitment to excellence and high-caliber work have an edge over their competition. Let's look at an example.

John was a second-year analyst and was extremely committed to producing quality work. His work ethic of being the first in and the last to leave the office enabled him to manage his work effectively. His sharp intellect and the high quality of work that he became known to produce made him very popular among managing directors at his firm, many of whom would specifically request that he be staffed on their deals. This reputation soon allowed John to work on many of the high-profile deals at his firm and gave him unusual access to senior leadership beyond what his peers were exposed to. Before long, John became known as a leader among his peers, as many analysts would also seek him out to get his perspective since he had worked on more complicated deals and could provide information on analytics and how to "manage up." You can imagine the type of recommendation an applicant like John would receive.

If your work isn't at the level of individuals like John, it is never too late to begin to establish a reputation of excellence. Make the commitment today to begin operating beyond your job responsibility by looking for ways to fill an existing void at your firm as well as raising the bar in the quality of work you produce.

Individuals who understand the power of personal branding recognize the importance of consistent commitment to excellence and results. Producing a track record of excellence on a regular basis is one clear way to differentiate yourself from your peers who just do a "good job." Doing your job well is not enough. Going beyond what is expected of you and delivering excellent results regularly is one sure way to stand apart from your competition.

Even the physical application to an MBA program needs to demonstrate this brand of excellence. The mistake that some applicants make is to underestimate the importance of each aspect of the application. An unpolished and mistake-ridden résumé can tip the scale to a rejection. That means that every aspect of the application, from standardized test scores to essays, recommendations to transcript, and everything in between, should be of high quality. Never cut corners. It is the fastest way to earn a negative brand reputation.

But applicants to business school are not the only ones for whom branding matters. MBA programs are also seen as brands, and applicants often apply to them based on how they view their brand.

MBA PROGRAMS AS BRANDS

Each business school is distinctive and has a different culture or feel to it. As such, it is critical to understand the brand of each program in order to select the ones that best fit with your personal brand.

MBA candidates are not the only ones who use marketing to differentiate themselves. Even MBA admissions boards are not impervious to marketing. They too do their fair share of marketing to ensure that their programs' brands are adequately communicated to their target applicants. It is no surprise that each year, dozens of members of MBA admissions boards embark on a grueling recruitment schedule across the nation and the world to "market" their unique MBA program and convince diverse and talented prospective candidates to apply. Whether admissions boards are marketing their program through their annual fall open-house events or through other means, including dynamic websites, active social media engagement, glossy brochures, and on-campus events, their pressing goal is to attract the most talented, diverse, and accomplished individuals who are a fit with their program's brand.

Some MBA programs have done a brilliant job defining and marketing their brands. By contrast, there are those whose brands are quite ambiguous to the customer, making it difficult for people to articulate what the program stands for. MBA programs that attempt to be all things to all people without having a key component that they master face the possibility of owning zero percent of the customer's mindshare. (Similarly, MBA candidates who do not have a clearly articulated and compelling brand capture zero market share in the mind of the MBA admissions board.) It is therefore quite usual to see MBA programs and universities as a whole invest a lot of money to conduct a brand study to refine and revamp their brand. This exercise often involves extensive communication with alumni, current students, recruiters, and other stakeholders who are familiar with the program.

Make no mistake about it—business schools are not trying to simply admit a prototype applicant. Take a school like Columbia Graduate School of Business. Although Columbia has a fantastic brand as a finance program—after all, value investing was invented here—it isn't looking to admit all its students from finance backgrounds.

Neither is Kellogg trying to admit an entire class of marketing people. That would be extremely limiting and would defeat the overall purpose of a top business school: students from diverse backgrounds (both professionally and personally) interacting with each other and learning from the different perspectives covered in the classroom. The brand of an MBA program goes beyond the career area it specializes in, although this is important in shaping the brand of the school. Kellogg, for instance, has a strong reputation as a marketing program but is also known for its extremely collaborative culture and emphasis on teamwork. Does that mean you can't find teamwork at Columbia? Of course teamwork is a part of Columbia's culture (and of most top business schools). But Kellogg's emphasis and devotion to the collaborative community will always make it one of the premier team-oriented business schools in America. Tuck is another program that has a similar brand focus on teamwork and collaborative community.

Understanding and deciphering the brand of MBA programs isn't a simple, cut-and-dried process. It requires in-depth research. Applicants need to:

- Speak with products of the business school, in particular, alumni, current students, MBA admissions boards, and faculty
- Visit the schools to get a firsthand experience of the program, its culture, and teaching style, not to mention the people who might someday become classmates

- Talk to people in the industry to understand how the program is perceived and thereby get a better feel for the program's brand

Top MBA programs have a lot in common. They all have high-caliber faculty, smart students, adept admissions boards, dedicated career services, and active alumni. They are similar in their value of diversity. Diversity is defined not simply by gender and ethnicity alone but includes socioeconomic backgrounds, geographic backgrounds, upbringing, career experiences, and unique perspectives. Despite these similarities, however, many top business schools have unique and differentiated brands. Here are a few examples.

Stanford Graduate School of Business

The mission of Stanford Graduate School of Business (GSB) is to "Change Lives. Change Organizations. Change the World." This captures the heart and soul of the school. This is a school where change is welcomed and students are nurtured to maintain a worldview that ultimately asks what impact they have had on the people around them, the organizations where they have worked, and the part of the world where they have lived. Like its biggest competitor, Harvard, Stanford wants people who have done something, left a mark, and have a leadership story to tell. The good news is that the expectation is less about formal positions and more about character. The school wants to know that you are someone who stands for something and who does something, big or small, in each environment you find yourself in. But that is only part of the story of Stanford's brand. The other half of its brand is centered on entrepreneurship.

A recent Poets & Quants survey of the top one hundred business schools with the highest number of successful start-ups (companies that have raised a minimum of $1.6 million) ranked Stanford number two, behind Harvard Business School. The GSB enjoys a strong reputation of honing and developing entrepreneurship. Partly a result of Stanford's proximity to Silicon Valley, the world's entrepreneurial capital, or perhaps the long history of innovation from Stanford alumni and faculty alike, Stanford's brand as the preeminent entrepreneurial MBA program is long established. That said, Stanford GSB is more than an entrepreneurial MBA program. It has many diverse offerings, including the

Center for Global Business and the Economy, as well as a strong culture of social enterprise, as seen in its dedicated Center for Social Innovation, Certificate in Public Management, and sizeable alumni base engaged in socially responsible businesses.

The reality is that if you are looking for an MBA program that will stretch you intellectually as well as creatively to explore new ventures and start your own business, Stanford GSB may be the ideal program for you. A large number of entrepreneurs (or aspiring entrepreneurs) are likely to be attracted to Stanford. Given Stanford GSB's commitment to diversity, you will find students who have not started a business and sold it for millions. However, what these admitted students have in common is an entrepreneurial mind-set, affinity for innovation, out-of-the-box thinking, and disparate experiences where they took a risk to try something new within an old guard company and they changed it for the better. It is for these reasons that Stanford students are often described as eclectic and "free spirits."

With that said, if you are looking to enter a career in general management, you will find Stanford to be a great environment where you can develop general management skills across different business areas.

Columbia Graduate School of Business

Columbia Business School is another great example of an MBA program with a powerful brand. It is known as one of the leading finance business schools in the country. Its location in New York City, the financial capital of the world, the sizeable number of alumni who pursue finance-related careers, and the phenomenal faculty with excellent track records in finance all contribute to Columbia's finance brand. I would be remiss if I stopped here, particularly given Dean Glenn Hubbard's innovative changes. He has introduced online components to the Columbia curriculum as well as greater integration across different business disciplines. Hubbard's vision to equip MBA students to tackle business problems with multiple lenses will help differentiate the school as a place that trains multidisciplinary business leaders.

Columbia GSB is a school that values diversity and will continue to attract students in other areas in which they are looking to establish their brand. Columbia's January program also offers the added advantage of attracting entrepreneurs who work for family businesses or for themselves and is a natural brand extension of the school.

Although Columbia can likely succeed in attracting more entrepreneurs into its program and creating an overall stronger perception in the marketplace of being a place of entrepreneurship and innovation, it is unlikely that Columbia will fundamentally shift to become an entrepreneur-only program at the expense of its brand as one of the leading finance MBA programs in the nation.

Kellogg School of Management

Another example of a school with a strong brand is Northwestern University's Kellogg Graduate School of Management. It is rare that you hear someone talk about a marketing MBA program in the United States without Kellogg being at the center of the conversation. Even the name, Kellogg, is tied to the multibillion-dollar consumer products company. Although Kellogg has a dominant brand as a marketing MBA program, it offers much more than marketing to its "customers." In fact, Kellogg offers an extremely flexible curriculum that allows students to specialize in a variety of functional business areas, with finance and strategy as the first and second most popular areas of study, respectively. Kellogg also has owned the brand of being a highly team-oriented and collaborative environment for a long time. However, over time, the school's hold on these two brand qualities has weakened as more MBA programs have introduced strong marketing disciplines as well as greater team collaboration in their programs.

The challenge for Kellogg's new dean, Susan Blount, is to reposition Kellogg in the marketplace in a way that is relevant, authentic, and believable. She has hired a chief marketing and engagement officer, Tim Simonds, and for several months has engaged faculty, alumni, students, and external customers to better define Kellogg's new brand.

Dean Blount's rebranding plans have resulted in a new focus for Kellogg, one that invites us to see Kellogg through a different lens: "Think bravely: We believe that business can be bravely led, passionately collaborative, and world changing." It is still early for Kellogg's new brand to fully take hold, and only time will tell whether the school will emerge with a successful brand that customers will buy into.

Ross Business School (Michigan)

Putting one's arms around the Ross brand is somewhat challenging because it is an MBA program that isn't necessarily known for one particular area. It is accurate to describe Ross as a well-rounded MBA program. However, I think the better way to categorize the Ross brand, beyond being well-rounded, is that it is action-oriented and has a culture of constant improvement. I think these two elements have enabled Ross to get top rankings in recent years. Even its motto of "Leading in Thought and Action" speaks to the brand of the program: it offers extensive opportunities to infuse the business education with real-life experience. The Multidisciplinary Action Project (MAP), a required first-year course offered in the second half of the second semester, gives Ross students an opportunity to test many of the first-semester business ideas and theories in a real-life environment. The Ross School was several years ahead of many business schools that are just now beginning to introduce structured, hands-on practical experiences into their programs. At Ross, the students work on a consulting engagement to resolve a business challenge a real company faces. So candidates looking for a well-rounded program and hands-on experience for their MBA will be attracted to Ross Business School.

Harvard Business School

One can't talk about an MBA program that builds its brand fundamentally on leadership without thinking of Harvard Business School (HBS). Does that mean that HBS is the only place where leaders can be found? Of course not! One can find a ton of leaders across the nation's top MBA programs. In fact, all of the top schools highlight leadership as a core aspect of their programs. However, Harvard's mission of "developing leaders who care about the well-being of society" strikes at the heart of what the program stands for.

Leadership permeates the HBS experience and is not only about formal roles (student leadership in organizations or career titles) but includes situational leadership where candidates seize opportunities to make a difference regardless of their role. The structure of the curriculum, the teaching methodology (case-based learning), and the projects outside of the classroom are all designed to challenge students to refine, rethink, confirm, and establish their perception of leadership and transform their own unique way of leading.

Even Harvard Business School recognizes the importance of brand building and marketing. HBS hired Brian Kenny as its first chief marketing officer in 2008 with a focus to help the school articulate its brand message to alumni, students, applicants, and other external stakeholders. In an interview with Mashable, Kenny asserts that "if we allow others to tell our story for us, then we're doing ourselves a disservice... my job is to help tell that story." What story exactly is Kenny referring to? He is talking about the perception of HBS as an über-competitive place filled with blue bloods and arrogant students. The other view that people have of the HBS brand is that it *isn't* the leader in innovation and entrepreneurship. MIT Sloan and Stanford GSB often own this brand in the minds of applicants. Yet interestingly enough, there is strong evidence (including the fact that HBS has the highest number of entrepreneurial faculty) to confirm that Harvard is a dominant force in entrepreneurship. The school is committed to showing the public that it is collaborative, diverse, and entrepreneurial. This interest can often filter through in the admission decisions of the school, and applicants who demonstrate some of these brand qualities will naturally be attractive to Harvard Business School.

INSEAD

INSEAD, the Business School for the World, is the best-known global business school and owns that brand in the marketplace. It attracts the most international minds around the world. The school's massive size compared to its European competitors (with the exception of London Business School), as well as the wealth of its resources across multiple MBA disciplines, allow it to own the claim that it is truly one of the best MBA programs, if not *the* best program outside the United States.

The fact that the school has campuses in Singapore, Abu Dhabi, and France confirms its claim that it has a world reach that is unrivaled. Most business schools are forced to simply partner with other programs in different parts of the world, while INSEAD stands in a league of its own as an MBA program with three locations training the best business minds for varied careers around the world.

But INSEAD's brand doesn't end here. It is a program that cultivates entrepreneurship. In fact, more than 70 percent of our clients who have gone to INSEAD over the years have eventually started their own businesses around the world. This is a school that knows what it is and is continuing to chart a course that will allow it to remain ahead of the pack in the years to come. It's not a school for everyone, but if you are looking for a very international MBA program or you wish to start your own business either straight out of school or in the future, INSEAD remains a school you should take a close look at.

The previous examples are a snapshot of some of the MBA programs that proactively manage their brands. Of course, there are other solid MBA programs not covered, and I encourage each applicant to use the research steps described earlier in this chapter to further investigate the programs they are interested in.

Now, let's focus on the MBA admissions board to get a better understanding of who they are and how they operate in the convoluted application process.

THE MBA ADMISSIONS BOARD

The MBA admissions board's role can be likened to that of a portfolio manager. Their job is to pick the right stock that will yield the greatest level of return to the program. Just as portfolio managers assemble diverse stocks, MBA admissions boards admit applicants with backgrounds and experiences that are unique and that will enrich the overall community. Applicants who have strong brands that are a fit with the MBA program will have a higher chance of being selected. Ultimately, the expectation is that these admitted students will graduate to become brand extensions of the program and will continue to strengthen their alma mater's brand.

Understanding the MBA admissions board should at the very least make them more approachable and increase your comfort level when interacting with them. Also, understanding where they are coming from and precisely what their role is will give you a clearer perspective of how to present your application as a whole.

First and foremost, the MBA admissions board members are human and compassionate. They are single and married, mothers and fathers, young and old. They are passionate about their jobs. They are not in it for the money and often consider their roles true labors of love. Some of them are alumni of the MBA program; many of them have an MBA or a graduate degree (although not all do). Some programs also include students as members of the admissions board. Chicago GSB, the Johnson School at Cornell University, and Wharton are a few examples of MBA programs where second-year students serve on the admissions board.

Typically, these students would do the first read and assess the candidate; then the application is evaluated a second time by an assistant or associate director of admissions before a final outcome is determined. (Admissions policy variations may exist from school to school and can change from one year to the next.)

Each year, these talented and dedicated board members embark on a grueling recruiting schedule (from August to November) after receiving marching orders to identify smart, talented candidates with excellent leadership potential and track records. They're forced to admit only a limited number of applicants, which is further complicated by an application pool that is full of talented individuals who have achieved significant levels of success in different environments. Because there is no formula to weed out weak applicants, the MBA admissions board invests in carefully evaluating each candidate. Admitting a diverse class made up of different perspectives (for example, industry, country of origin, talents, gender, ethnicity, and personal and professional experiences) while maintaining a balance presents a significant challenge.

Typically, each application is evaluated by at least two board members. If both board members' votes are in agreement, then the application often moves forward in the process. Of course, sometimes the two board members are in disagreement. In such situations, the application may be evaluated by a third board member. Another option may be to bring the application to the admissions committee, where the merits of the candidate will be discussed and a decision rendered. These meetings can be quite spirited as board members argue passionately about the candidate in question. Ultimately, at some business schools, the MBA admissions director has the final say in the fate of a candidate if there is dissension among the board members. At other business schools, such as Yale, the decisions are made primarily in a committee setting, and the decision is based on the admissions board members' reaching a consensus.

The admissions season is long and strenuous. The MBA admissions board works extremely long hours during the busy season, which lasts from the end of August to the end of May. Each week, board members pick up bins filled with applications that need to be evaluated and returned within a small time window. Many board members work very late into the night, and it is easy for many essays to blur into the next when they lack originality. MBA admissions board members love to read applications where they can really see who the candidate is and the rationale driving the choices that person made, both personally and professionally. (This is why applicants should pay attention to the PGII factor—passion, guts, impact, and insight—which I will further discuss in the chapter on essay fundamentals.)

Board members are not spared during holidays either. November is the heart of the application season for round one, and applications are often reviewed even during holidays like Thanksgiving. Most people take vacations to spend time with their family during the holidays. Given a compressed admissions season where decisions have to be made by a certain deadline, board members do not usually take time off during special holidays. So board members have to carve out time during their holidays to review applications. You want to write interesting and captivating essays that are worth reading, especially if someone is giving up family time to evaluate your candidacy.

Successful applications are usually the ones that have a clear and strong brand message. After reading a well-branded application, the typical response from the MBA admissions board should be something like, "This is the visionary engineer who solves business problems creatively" or "I just read the application of a smart, unconventional banker who consistently focuses on developing junior talent." They can't come to these conclusions if the stories you have recounted in your applications are generic and lack focus.

I've often heard applicants say, "I'm not good at marketing and promoting myself." And my answer is, "Start practicing!" If you are not comfortable selling yourself to the MBA admissions board, you will likely leave out compelling aspects of your story in your application.

Although I am a big promoter of self-marketing and branding, I don't endorse false marketing. Not only is it unethical, it will likely come back to haunt you. This book does not promote falsifying your story or presenting a brand that does not authentically reflect your personal and professional life.

The reason I am so bullish about developing your personal brand is so that you have a realistic and up-to-date awareness of who you are and what you have done in your life. Your grades and GMAT or GRE score are not going to be enough to communicate why you should be admitted to a particular MBA program. Writing essays that convey your brand's distinction will help your application stand out to the MBA admissions board. It will also enable the board member who evaluates your application to become an advocate on your behalf. The clearer and more impressive your brand is, the more likely he or she will be able to argue for your application when your candidacy is discussed in an admissions committee meeting.

Ultimately, your goal is to turn the admissions board member reading your file into a brand champion. The board member has to "buy" your story in order to "sell" it to colleagues or the admissions committee. And just as with traditional marketing, only products with powerful and compelling brands stand out. MBA applicants must have distinctive brands that capture the mindshare of the MBA admissions board. At the end of the day, your job is to get the board to say, "Wow! I'd love to meet this person."

Finally, applicants have to be careful in deciding how much contact, including face time, they need with the admissions board. MBA programs vary drastically in their preference for face time with candidates. Tuck, for example, has one of the most liberal policies and encourages candidates to visit Hanover and interact with the admissions board. Other programs may find it to be a nuisance if a candidate asks to meet with board members during a (non-interview) visit. Similarly, sending lengthy emails and making multiple phone calls to the admissions board can annoy the board members. It is important to follow instructions regarding sending additional materials to the MBA admissions board after the deadline. Some MBA programs (for example, Wharton and HBS) explicitly request that applicants not send additional materials, even if they are wait-listed. On the other hand, programs like Chicago Booth MBA and Kellogg School of Management have been open to receiving additional information if it reflects a new update that isn't covered in the existing application. Typically, most programs are open to a short and polite thank-you card after an interview. However, a two-page letter to the MBA admissions board where you wax eloquent about your achievements is unlikely to have the desired results. I have been approached multiple times by desperate candidates who have not heard back from MBA programs and who, in their panic, plan to have an alumnus of the program contact the school to find out what is holding up the interview invitation. I always advise the distraught candidate to resist having an alumnus call and harass the MBA admissions board. Calling the board will likely backfire and hurt the candidate's chance of admission. Exercising patience is the best strategy. At the very least, candidates should find out what each program's policy is and adhere to it. Remember that the MBA admissions board is short on time and is already burdened with a very challenging workload. Annoying them ensures that they will not become advocates for your candidacy.

As long as the business school admissions process remains competitive, applicants will continue to face significant pressure to communicate why they are unique and worthy of a coveted admission spot. Candidates who recognize the differentiating power of branding will maintain an edge over their competitors.

CHAPTER THREE

Building and Selling Your Brand

A PERSONAL BRAND IS IMPORTANT to helping you live a life that is passion-driven and grounded in your values. By having a clear sense of your personal brand, you can actively engage in the things that matter to you, deliver results that you can be proud of, add value to those around you (both personally and professionally), and live a life that has meaning and impact. Building your brand will help you chart a clear path to achieve your goals and live your passion. Beyond these benefits, however, having a powerful, clear personal brand before you embark on the application process can be extremely effective. Applicants who have a clear sense of their personal brand often emerge successfully from the application process. Let's look at how to build your brand.

One of the first things necessary to develop your personal brand is to identify your passion.

WHAT IS YOUR PASSION?

Are you living your passion both personally and professionally? Is what you do bringing you fulfillment? Is there a major disconnect between how you see yourself and how others see you? Will getting an MBA enable you to achieve your vision for your life? It is important to take the time to address these questions; the answers will help you gauge whether you are living a life driven by passion.

The word "passion" is thrown around in various contexts in our everyday communication. But phrases like "I'm passionate about baseball" or

"My passion is doing the rumba" do not quite capture the essence of what I mean by passion. Passion is not a hobby or simply what you like to do for fun. I have a slightly different perception of passion as it relates to business school applications. I define passion as what gives meaning to our lives.

A conversation I had at my old neighborhood coffee shop best illustrates the elements of a passion-filled life. I had posed this simple question, "What is your passion?" to Kim, a fellow customer indulging in a latte. Her face immediately lit up, and she replied, "Teaching and affecting the lives of my students." Kim has been teaching for several years in New York City elementary schools, and she is successful at what she does. She chose a teaching profession because it fit with her values to help kids succeed. As she described her work with her kids, it was impossible to miss the pure joy and fulfillment in her voice. The excitement that accompanied her description could not be faked. When you are living your passion, your life will reflect the energy and joy that accompanies a passion-filled life.

So, is what you are doing currently true to your passion? Stop for a minute to reflect on this question. The important thing is to assess whether what you do brings meaning to you, whether it reflects your values, skills, and interests. If that's not the case, then it may be time for self-exploration to determine what matters to you and to begin to integrate that into your professional and personal life. A simple way to assess whether you are living a passion-filled life is to ask yourself whether you would do your job if you were not paid for it.

I encourage you to take a few minutes to complete the passion survey to see how aligned your passion is with what you are currently doing.

EXPARTUS PASSION SURVEY

For each question, rate your response from 1 to 3: 1 = not really, 2 = somewhat, 3 = absolutely. After completing each question, tally your scores.

- Are you aware of what your greatest passion is?
- Is your passion connected to your personal brand?
- Are you living your passion outside of your job?
- Are you living your passion in your job?

- Do you enjoy your job?
- Do you have the right skills to live your passion?
- Would you keep working in your industry if you weren't paid for your job?
- Are you still being challenged by the work you do?
- Does what you do have an impact on the lives of others?
- Are you proud of your accomplishments?

Scores that range from 22 to 30 indicate that your job is in sync with your passion. Scores that range from 12 to 21 suggest that some changes are in order; this may not require a career change but more active investment in aligning your passion with your career. Scores of less than 12 call for a major overhaul. Consider a thorough brand audit to assess what matters most to you and begin incorporating it in your life. Be open to a career change.

After completing the passion survey and determining whether your life is aligned with your passion, you can go a step further to assess and develop your personal brand. This process requires that you undergo a personal brand audit to identify your key brand themes and ultimately to distill your story into a personal brand statement. Let's get started first with an audit of your personal brand.

HOW TO BUILD A COMPELLING PERSONAL BRAND

Personal Brand Audit

The first step in building a powerful brand is undergoing a personal brand audit (PBA). The PBA is a candid assessment of who you are. It includes your values, goals, skills, and passion. Included in this assessment is a review of your strengths and weaknesses, your past achievements and failures, your track record, your perception of yourself, and how other people perceive you. After completing this audit, the next step is to distill it down to the core of what matters to you. You could start by picking key values, goals, interests, and achievements. If you can, try to further focus on the most critical value, goal, interest, or significant achievement from your life. It can be challenging to drill down at this level, because as human beings we are complicated and have varied backgrounds, interests, values, and so forth. However, this exercise, as frustrating as it may be in the beginning, forces you to objectively look at what you are dealing with (the good, the bad, and the ugly). Then you have to apply honesty balanced with judgment in piecing together the most compelling aspects of who you are.

A MINI PERSONAL BRAND AUDIT (PBA)

In completing the PBA, be as candid and introspective as you can. It is also extremely important to cite examples when answering each question. The more vivid and specific your examples are, the more effective they will be in enabling you to pull out stories from your background that reflect your brand.

Passion

- I am most passionate about:
- My work inspires me in the following way:
- If I could live my passion, I would:

Values

- What do I value the most about myself?
- What do people value the most about me? (Ask colleagues, friends, family.)
- What three things do I cherish the most in life?
- My values are a fit with my career in the following way:
- My values are misaligned with my career in the following way:

Skills

- My three greatest strengths are:
- My three greatest areas of development are (describe what you are doing to improve them):
- The most significant impact I have had on a person is:
- The most significant impact I have had on a team is:
- The most significant impact I have had on an organization is:

Goals

- My short-term goal is:
- My reason for seeking an MBA now is:
- My long-term goal is:
- Without the MBA, it will be nearly impossible to achieve my long-term goal because:

Brand Themes

In the course of completing your PBA, you will notice some recurrent brand themes. Evaluate these themes to determine whether they reinforce your brand and whether they qualify as major themes (central elements for your story) or minor themes (elements you could add to your story if there is room).

Brand themes are not just your job descriptions or obvious variables of your story. They are consistent and recurrent elements that reflect who you are at the most meaningful level. Brand themes are not typically what you write in your résumé. They are subtler than your job title and job description. Brand themes reflect how you do what you do, the characteristics and values that drive your actions and choices, the distinctive and memorable traits that people see in you.

One can argue that brand themes can be fuzzy and "touchy-feely." A tech guy I know happens to be exceptionally charismatic and very outgoing. He absolutely does not embody the stereotype of a reserved, nerdy tech guy. When applying to business school, had he focused simply on his job role or title, he would have been ineffective in conveying his charismatic brand. By tapping into instances that demonstrate how he operates in a team environment and by sharing personal stories, he was able to convey an accurate brand picture of himself: one that is dynamic and engaging instead of limited by his work role.

Your job titles or roles do not constitute your brand themes. It isn't the title or label but the intrinsic and motivating elements behind what you do and your own identity (values, passions) that make up your brand theme.

Here are a few examples of what a brand theme is *not*:

- Smart investment banker
- Ivy-educated engineer
- Top-ranked consultant
- Hardworking private equity analyst

You will notice that these examples are generic and not differentiating. In other words, if you want to build your application around being a smart banker, you pigeonhole yourself with the other thousand smart bankers in the applicant pool. The same goes for each of the other examples. To stand apart, you need brand themes that are differentiating. So although you are a smart banker, one of your key brand themes could be a connector. A connector is someone who thrives on building bridges and bringing disparate people and teams together to solve problems. They enjoy people, are well connected, and make good use of their social network to create positive impact wherever they are. Connectors do not hoard information or sit on the sidelines when a problem needs to be resolved. They love to jump in and partner with people to bring about results. More than that, they are gifted at working with different types of people and can bring out the best in them. Being a connector is what differentiates you from the pack. Nowhere in your application do you explicitly state "I'm a bridge-connecting banker!" Rather, the stories you choose to recount when addressing the essay questions can convey and reinforce this connector brand, which then leads the admissions board to draw the conclusion based on the evidence. The same can be said for your recommender. The anecdotal accounts that he shares about your connecting ways will lead the admissions board to draw the same conclusion about your brand.

The challenge in sharing your brand with the MBA admissions board is that you need concrete examples from your personal and professional life to substantiate any themes you select. One of the laws of personal branding is focus. So with selecting your brand themes, it is important to pick three to four that are most reflective of who you are and what matters to you. You may be wondering, why three or four? Because the application has a limited space, it is important to focus on the most salient themes in your story. Furthermore, you don't want to come off as scattered by throwing in too many attributes and themes. By selecting a few focused themes, you can then use the application essays to reinforce a consistent message that supports your personal brand. Your recommenders would also need to be aware of the key brand themes you are presenting, so that the examples they use to illustrate your story remain consistent with your branding strategy. Applicants who have a strong online brand presence through blogs, websites, or other social media platforms can also capitalize on this by including this information on their applications. Having a consistent brand online will only reinforce your personal brand message in real life.

At the end of the day, it is less about having the "right" themes and more about tapping into meaningful attributes and elements from your life experiences. Here are just a few examples of brand themes of successful applicants to business school:

SAMPLE BRAND THEMES

Empowerer of women	Engenderer of trust
Articulate communicator	Risk taker
Global citizen	Multicultural citizen
Charismatic leader	Contagious optimist
Connector	Unrelenting value-seeker
Bootstrapper	Bridge builder
Diplomatic rebel	Investor in junior talent
Turnaround expert	Idea guy
Motivational manager	Astute negotiator
Dancer of life	Trailblazer

These themes are by no means exhaustive. Brand themes are endless and should be reflective of the candidates' experiences. The examples offered here are only snapshots of potential brand themes from successful applicants. These applicants were able to successfully brand their way into top business schools, not because they had perfect stories but because they committed to the introspection necessary to identify their personal brand. Articulating what mattered to them and why they had made the different choices that they made (connecting the dots of their lives) allowed the MBA admissions board to differentiate them from their competition.

PERSONAL BRAND THEMES

List the four brand themes/attributes that best describe you. Make sure you cite examples to back them up.

1.

2.

3.

4.

Now that you have identified your brand themes, go over them to see if they accurately represent you. What words come to mind as you read through your responses? Do you notice any surprises? With branding, it is equally important that those around us reach the same conclusions about our brand. Ask two people who know you well (they can be colleagues, family members, or friends) whether the themes you selected are reflective of who you are or if other themes are more relevant to your brand. If there are inconsistencies, then be willing to go deeper to determine whether you need to take steps to better communicate your personal brand.

A major mistake applicants make is that they don't invest in enough introspection to identify their brand themes before embarking on their essays. As a result, many business school application essays are disjointed, boring, and superficial. Let's explore how a candidate can use a brand theme, global citizen, to sell her personal brand. The candidate doesn't even have to mention the brand theme in the actual essay. Rather, she can select stories that depict her as a global citizen.

Let's say she has three essays for her application; she can use one to two different stories to convey her comfort level in international settings. The first could be of a key project she worked on managing an international team spanning two continents; this project shows how her sensitivity to the nuanced cultural differences enabled her to lead effectively. Or she may wish to share a personal story about the study abroad program she did in a remote region of the world and her personal "aha" cultural moment. Finally, she may wish to write about her involvement with a nonprofit group that helps immigrants from different regions of the world adjust to their new lives in America. These examples, plus the fact that she has lived in many countries around the world, speaks multiple languages, and has recommendations that reinforce her global-citizen brand, can paint a strong message about who she is in the MBA admissions board's mind.

With schools like HBS offering applicants only one essay, you may be wondering how you can convey your personal brand on this compressed canvas. It is absolutely doable. The same branding process applies. You have to decide which of your three or so brand themes are the most compelling to share with HBS. The branding law of focus still applies here. You may want to focus on one brand theme, the strongest one that you have, and share multiple stories across the different parts of your life (personal, community, professional), or you could choose to be broad and highlight two or three brand themes with one example or anecdote for each. The trick is for you to be honest with yourself and clear about what the key message is that you want HBS to know about you. The quality of the example and what it reveals about you remains the crux of the issue. If the HBS admissions board member doesn't walk away after reading your essay with a strong sense that you are a leader or that you are an interesting person who brings some unique set of experiences or viewpoints to the program, you have failed in your goal to win over the admissions board.

Once you have identified the themes to your story, it is important to distill them into a summary, the personal brand statement, which speaks to the heart of who you are. Clearly, as human beings, we are a lot more complicated than a one-sentence statement. I'll be the first to acknowledge this. However, given that you have thirty seconds to make a lasting impression and that the application comes down to a few minutes of review before a decision is rendered, I encourage applicants to go through the exercise of summarizing their salient attributes into one sentence: their personal brand statement.

Personal Brand Statement
If you had about twenty-five words to describe yourself, what words would you use? Many people refer to this as your one-minute introduction or

elevator pitch. I refer to it as your personal brand statement (PBS). The PBS is important because it summarizes who you are in a memorable way. To write a focused application that reinforces the core of your brand, it is important to have a clear PBS.

The PBS is made up of three parts:

1.   Who you are (values, passions, etc.)
2.   What you have done (skills, track record, etc.)
3.   Where you plan to end up (vision and goals for your life)

Here are some PBS examples from MBA candidates who have gained admission to top programs:

- Gutsy Asian female with a passion for empowering women who plans to transform family business by infusing fair-trade practices
- Athletic, team-driven leader with passion for investing who plans to leverage international investing experience to build a world-class investment management firm
- Energetic Midwesterner with accelerated cross-functional leadership roles at media company who plans to run an entertainment company focused on educational programs for children
- African American bootstrapper with significant leadership track record who plans to create and run a VC fund to help revitalize inner-city communities

Why is the PBS important? The MBA admissions board reads thousands of pages of applications and has the challenge of distilling a candidate's information into a descriptive summary, the equivalent of a PBS. After wading through countless application pages, the admissions board needs to be able to point to a clear takeaway of what they think is distinctive and memorable about you. When candidates start out with a personal brand statement, it serves as a road map for their application. They are able to ask themselves whether each story (essay) reinforces their personal brand statement. Given the limited space allotment of admissions essays, a personal brand statement allows you to maintain a laserlike focus when selecting topics to write about as you position your story. Also, by having a clear sense of your PBS before you complete the application, you will be able to refer back to it at each step of the application process to determine whether your essays, recommendations, résumé, and even the answers you provide in an interview reinforce your personal brand.

So now that you know how important it is to complete a PBA to understand your brand, you know what brand themes look like, and you have reviewed PBS examples, let's practice. Try summarizing your story in one sentence (your PBS), keeping in mind that although there may be different things that you would like to cover, the law of focus is critical.

YOUR PERSONAL BRAND STATEMENT

_____

_____

_____

_____

After you have developed your PBS, continue to refine it and work on keeping it succinct (about twenty-five words).

Once you have completed this entire branding process, you are now ready to tackle the application. In a couple of chapters, I address the selection criteria used by admissions boards at leading business schools to evaluate candidates. But before I leave this branding chapter, I want to share a few thoughts on career changers.

CAREER CHANGERS

No applicant is more in need of personal branding than career changers. Applicants in this category have to convince the MBA admissions board that they need an MBA and that the new career goal makes sense given their current experience.

Although MBA admissions boards welcome career changers to apply, the expectation is that there should be a strong connection between who you are, what you have done, and what you wish to do in the future. A derivatives trader, for instance, with little to no community service experience helping nonprofit groups who simply says that she wants the MBA so that she can run a nonprofit organization, is going to have an extremely difficult time convincing the MBA admissions board that her goals are authentic. The immediate questions on the mind of the board are how realistic is the goal and does the applicant have elements in her background that reinforce her identified passion of nonprofit management.

Many career services offices have come under fire in the past few years regarding the placement statistics of graduating students. It is not enough to show interest in a new career; applicants today must keep in mind that they will need to find a job in the new career at the end of their program. The bigger the gap between your experience and future role, the tougher it is to convince recruiters to hire you in the new career. Career changers are likely to be rejected if their goals are inconsistent and don't seem achievable. I address the consistency and credibility issues in greater detail in the chapter on essay fundamentals.

The first step career changers should take is to find ways to begin incorporating their passion into their lives. If you find that there is a gap between what you want to do and what you do currently, you may be able to create credibility for your goals by using your extracurricular activities and community service involvement to establish a track record of commitment to the new career. Doing this will create more synergy between your passion and your actions.

Successfully positioning yourself as a career changer requires planning, time, and a good dose of patience. Simply stating that you are an engineer who wishes to make a switch to finance will not cut it. It is a huge career leap. There have been many engineers who have successfully gone into banking post–business school. Your awareness of the difficulty of making this transition and a plan or strategy for how you will do it will help assure the MBA admissions board that you are not setting yourself up for great disappointment when you begin the recruitment process as a student. After all, you will be competing with many former bankers who will have a significant advantage over you. You will need to express why a career in finance matters to you. How will you use the new career to effect change? It will be helpful to identify some of the skills that you will need to be a successful banker and connect them to some of the skills you already have both through work and beyond. Career changers need to be very specific when making a case for a new career. They have to demonstrate specific knowledge about the new career so that it is clear that it isn't simply a passing fancy. In addition, having congruence between your personal life and your professional life is equally important. The following cases illustrate the importance of creating consistency in one's brand.

Case Study: Pre-MBA Career Changers
Ann: Auditor to Real Estate Entrepreneur

Ann had been working as an accountant and auditor for a somewhat obscure company and felt quite dispassionate about her career. She enjoyed numbers and had studied accounting in college, and shortly after became a certified public accountant (CPA). After a few years as an accountant and auditor, she noticed that despite having mastered her responsibilities and having received multiple promotions, she was beginning to plateau in her professional development. More than that, she realized that as she ascended her career ladder, she was becoming more specialized, leaving her less excited about accounting. For the past two years, Ann had been dabbling in buying real estate, but she always considered it a hobby, not her bread and butter. Ann began to question what was missing. Why was she not excited about the prospect of another potential promotion? Why was she more interested in closing the next real estate deal for her sideline "hobby"?

After completing a personal brand audit, Ann realized that her true passion was indeed real estate and that an entrepreneurial track was what was missing in her current role, where there was limited room for innovation. Further reinforcement came through her brand audit as she began to recall early memories of tagging along with her real estate entrepreneur uncle as he made his Saturday rounds to review his development sites.

Delving deeper into what attracted her to real estate, Ann discovered that she enjoyed the research involved in locating the right deal, structuring the financing, negotiating with lawyers and sellers, and managing the overall process. Ann carefully saved enough money and eventually quit her job to focus on real estate full-time.

Because her passion and brand were intrinsically tied to real estate, Ann also became involved in community service organizations to help low-income residents access affordable housing.

Ann has successfully rebranded herself as a real estate entrepreneur in a consistent and credible way. Her passion and goals come from the heart and are clear to anyone who meets her. Her community involvement isn't simply to check off the box on the application but is a result of what matters to her. If she decides to apply to business school in the future, she will have the advantage of applying with a clear and distinctive brand, which will likely lead to a successful application.

Jenny and Scot: Bankers to Nonprofit Managers

Not all career changers will have the luxury of quitting their jobs and starting a business they are passionate about. So what else could a career changer do to strengthen his or her application?

Take Jenny, an investment banker who had decided she wanted a career in nonprofit management. Her challenge was that she did not have community service experience, and her extracurricular activities boiled down to some social events that she planned through her sorority in college. Given her lack of a track record in volunteering for nonprofit organizations or any related activities, Jenny's goal of starting or managing a nonprofit organization most likely would not pass the credibility test in the application. If Jenny applied without developing a track record at a nonprofit group, her brand would be strongly tied to finance, and it would be unlikely she would be offered admission at a top-tier MBA program.

Contrast Jenny with Scot. Scot too was a banker who wanted to run or start a nonprofit organization in the future. He had spent most of his professional career working as an investment banker. However, his extracurricular involvement, both while he was in college and currently in his community, was strongly tied to nonprofit leadership. Scot's track record of having started several socially conscious organizations in college and beyond enabled him to pass the credibility test. Clearly, an MBA admissions board would be more likely to admit Scot over Jenny because his socially responsible interest was strongly tied to his brand and he had solid evidence of having started organizations in this area. In fact, Scot gained admission to Harvard and Stanford!

The lesson here is if you want to change your career and rebrand yourself, it is best to show a track record through work or outside activities. Are there skills that you currently use in your career that are transferable to your new career? Highlight them in your application. Are there opportunities to work part-time or as a volunteer in the new career? A consultant who discovered that her passion was in the restaurant business spent most of her weekends working in a restaurant. She didn't simply fall back on the fact that she worked long hours. She invested the time to gain some exposure to the new career. Some may think this is too extreme, but it made the difference in her acceptance to her top MBA program.

But what about after you gain admission to business school? Career changers still have a tough road ahead of them in transitioning to the new career. The two-year MBA program is ideal for a career changer because there is more time built into the curriculum to allow for hands-on experience in the new career. That's not to say that career change is impossible if you are attending schools like INSEAD or Oxford Saïd Business School. Many of the graduates of one-year MBA programs have also had success changing their careers.

Case Study: Post-MBA Career Changers

Felix: Engineer to Investment Banker

Felix was an engineer for five years and was interested in switching to investment banking. After his first year in business school at a top program, he interned for a financial advisory firm during the summer. This experience enabled him to land a position in a small private equity group in his home country. His ties to his country, coupled with a name-brand institution, gave him an advantage in securing this position. His goal is to build up his private equity experience to develop a track record before making a move into a larger, more established private equity shop.

Valerie: Nonprofit Manager to Marketing Associate

Valerie is another career changer who used the MBA to land a job at a leading firm that is her passion. She had worked in the nonprofit sector prior to attending business school. She knew from the minute she arrived in business school that she wanted to change careers, and she set out to build skills and gain experiences that would make her competitive in the career search. Her goal was to switch into marketing. Instead of targeting the summer for internships, she realized that she needed marketing experience to land a coveted internship. She joined the marketing club, began networking with classmates with marketing backgrounds, and met with marketing professionals visiting the school. During the winter break, instead of going on a leisure trip with friends, she secured an internship with a consumer goods company. At the company, she made sure to network with key individuals in the marketing and business development group. Her focused efforts paid off, as she received a summer internship at the firm. When she graduated from business school, she had multiple offers from the top consumer goods companies.

Applicants who invest in defining and cultivating their personal brand enjoy great success in the MBA application process. And even beyond the application, your self-awareness will help you navigate your career during business school and beyond. There is a certain reassurance that you gain when you know who you are and what makes you tick; personal branding enables you to be anchored and not to chase the fads that come along over the course of your career.

Now that you know how to assess and present your brand, we'll turn to the admissions process.

CHAPTER FOUR

The Full Cycle of Admissions

A CRITICAL MISTAKE THAT MANY applicants make is not fully understanding the importance of the entire admissions cycle. It has three stages: preapplication, application, and postapplication. Each stage is important, and ignoring any one of them can negatively affect your admission outcome.

The business school application requires a fair amount of time and resources. Beginning to plan for the MBA two years before applying to business school allows candidates to address any holes in their stories. Applying shortly before the deadline (while it may work for some candidates) is not optimal, because it does not allow enough time for candidates to build up a track record or to address any potential weaknesses in their stories. Quite frankly, it is never too early to start preparing for the application. While you are still in college is the ideal time to begin planning for business school. Taking quantitative business classes, acing the GMAT or GRE, and ensuring you have a fantastic leadership track record in college are all practical steps you can take to solidify your background before you begin the application to business school.

I'm often asked what happens to the physical application once it is submitted, and I'll answer that question in this chapter. I will also address the process an application goes through after you hit the Submit button, the actual evaluation process, and the follow-up process after the application has been reviewed and a decision is made.

THE PREAPPLICATION PROCESS

The preapplication stage is when you can do your due diligence to determine which MBA program is the best fit for you. During this stage, candidates can research MBA rankings, review program websites and marketing materials, attend open-house events, visit campuses, and refine their brands. What a candidate does during the preapplication period can significantly change his or her odds for admission to an elite business school. Conducting a personal brand assessment now helps you identify and address your weaknesses before they turn into admissions barriers.

Another important component of the preapplication period is standardized test preparation. These tests cover high school mathematics, data interpretation, reading comprehension, critical reasoning, and other skills. When was the last time you were tested on a sentence completion exercise? By taking a test-prep course during this period, you can increase your test performance when you take the exam. If you are not satisfied with your score, you will still have ample time to retake the exam.

In addition, starting early gives you the opportunity to take multiple courses to strengthen your quantitative background (especially if your GPA is low or you do not have a business background). I had a male client who was an engineer and who had attended five universities before finally graduating with a 2.9 GPA. He was able to strengthen his academic background by taking two business classes and earning an A in both of them. Taking the initiative to attend finance and accounting courses and demonstrating that he had the intellectual aptitude and discipline to handle rigorous coursework was exactly what he needed to do to mitigate the low GPA. His GMAT score was, of course, very high as well. He ended up gaining admission to a top MBA program and received several thousand dollars in scholarships.

A caveat to this client's story, however, is that applicants can't assume that taking one or two classes will simply erase years of academic deficit— and there isn't one magic bullet that solves *all* academic weaknesses either. Failure to acknowledge any gap in your academic performance and to do something about it creates a hole in your application that puts you at a disadvantage. But you also need to recognize that even if you do address and improve your academic weaknesses in some way, the MBA admissions board will still factor those weak grades on your report card into their decision.

Lack of leadership is another common reason that applicants are rejected. The preapplication period presents a great opportunity for you to assess where you can improve your leadership track record. Devoting a year or two to address those gaps can make you more competitive in the future when you apply to business school. Early preparation for the application will also allow you to make a candid assessment of your personal brand to determine whether there are gaps and devise a plan to tackle them. We've seen enough candidates come through my consulting company, EXPARTUS, who would have had a stronger profile had they come to us a couple of years prior to applying. This would have allowed them to develop an application plan that would help them pursue their passions, interests, and goals in a strategic way, enabling them to become more competitive as candidates when they apply a few years in the future. For instance, realizing that your community leadership is weak will allow you enough time to take on community leadership roles and develop a track record, which will put your application in a positive light. If you have demonstrated little leadership at work, you can use the preapplication period to beef up your professional leadership (whether it is starting a new initiative at work or taking on leadership responsibility to manage junior team members).

The brand assessment can also be helpful to those who are career changers. With a two-year head start, you can try to make a move into the industry in which you are interested or at least become involved on a volunteer basis in the area that you wish to transition to in the future. For candidates who lack international exposure, this is the perfect time to request an international assignment or to change jobs to gain more global experience.

Let's take a closer look at the specific steps and variables that can guide candidates as they prepare themselves to embark on the application.

Rankings

The popular ranking entities for business schools are *U.S.News & World Report*, *Businessweek*, *Wall Street Journal*, *Financial Times*, *The Economist*, and Poets & Quants. Poets & Quants is the newest among these and was started by John Byrne, the originator of the *Businessweek* ranking system. Byrne created Poets & Quants just a few years ago, and it has grown to become one of the most popular social media communities where applicants go to learn the latest MBA trends and school-specific information from leading MBA programs around the world.

My general opinion of rankings is that they are a good starting point to gain perspective on the brands of programs and how they are viewed by students, alumni, and recruiters. However, I caution applicants about using rankings as the only determinant for their decision to apply to a particular program. The methodologies for ranking business schools vary from one ranking entity to another, and a large amount of the information is subjective. Therefore, it is quite common to have a wide discrepancy between the ranks that are conferred to each MBA program (for instance, a program can be ranked first and tenth by different agencies in the same year). It is also important to remember that just because a program is top-ranked does not mean you will fit in there. You should conduct a thorough investigation to ensure that the program will offer you the right environment to grow and meet your professional and personal objectives.

Open-House Events

Each summer and fall, MBA programs embark on an extensive recruitment schedule that includes on-campus information sessions and open-house events across the globe. These events are designed to introduce prospective candidates to the MBA program through presentations from MBA admissions board members, faculty, current students, and alumni. Invitations are extended to prospective candidates living in the area. Prior to each event, the MBA admissions board sends out an invitation to individuals in their inquiry database. I recommend that you provide your contact information to the admissions office as soon as possible so that you can be invited to open-house events held in your city. These give you access to board members with whom you may not get an opportunity to engage outside of this context. Also, for individuals who do not have access to alumni from their MBA program of interest, open-house events are great opportunities to meet with alumni and to gain perspective about the direct impact and value of the specific MBA program for them.

Marketing Materials

MBA programs are quite savvy with their marketing, often creating glossy brochures and elaborate websites to attract prospective applicants. Relying on the marketing materials of business schools without visiting the schools may only give you a superficial view of the program. For instance, some MBA websites may say they have a global focus, but further investigation can reveal that opportunities to pursue a global education or to study abroad may be severely limited. This is why you can't simply take materials at face value without speaking with alumni and current students and visiting the schools to get a firsthand experience of the program. I can't tell you how many candidates swear that a particular program is ideal for them simply based on the marketing materials they read. I know of a candidate who was admitted to a school in the Midwest that she had set her mind on attending. After realizing it wasn't a good fit, she found herself stuck because it was the only admission offer she had in hand. Because she couldn't remain at her current job, she had to scramble to find an alternative. The result was that she eventually found a job in a far-flung region of the world as she planned her reapplication strategy. The wasted time, money, and angst could have all been avoided had she taken the time to visit the programs she was applying to. You can bet that, the second time around, she will be sure to visit every single school she plans to apply to.

Campus Visits

Although the websites of business schools can be useful tools when getting started in application research, it eventually becomes more important to speak with individuals who are products of the programs to get their firsthand perspective. A campus visit allows you to attend classes, experience the faculty and their teaching styles, and interact with current students to learn about the academic and social culture of the program. I have always said that the application to business school is an exercise in marketing; as you spend more time with the students, faculty, and administrators of a business school, the more familiar you will be with the program's brand. In turn, the more face time you have with your "customer," the MBA admissions board, the more likely you are to convey *your* brand. There is a caveat to this: stalking the admissions board by camping out at the admissions office will only send the wrong message and therefore have the opposite effect you wish to have. Limit your visits to a couple of trips to campus and ensure that you get full exposure to classes, student life, and the admissions board (when available) during your visit.

Webinars and MBA Social Networks

MBA programs have become very savvy about leveraging technology to reach prospective applicants around the world. There is no good business school that doesn't have a social media presence, whether it is a Facebook page or a Twitter feed. MBA programs are also leveraging technology through webinars and podcasts to provide prospective students with more real-time feedback on their school. This isn't just the domain of the admissions office. Professors and deans of many business schools are engaged with applicants through technology. Even Harvard Business School has introduced weekly webinars hosted by the admissions board. It customizes its webinars to appeal to different demographics, such as the LGBTQ community. Other targeted webinars cover specific events for international students, minorities, women, and military candidates. HBS is also customizing its webinars to target regions (e.g., a Latin American webinar) and industries (e.g., consumer goods and marketing). These tailored communication outreaches at HBS and other MBA programs will provide greater opportunity for applicants to engage with the schools directly without having to incur enormous travel costs.

THE APPLICATION PROCESS

Once you have identified the MBA programs in which you are interested, the next step is tackling the application. Applying to business school can be extremely stressful for most candidates. The combination of knowing that you have a 10 to 20 percent acceptance chance and the time-consuming, involved nature of the application process creates anxiety. Stressful as it may be, you should avoid skipping any steps in the application process. For instance, passing up an opportunity to interview at programs for which interviews are an option may communicate to the MBA admissions board that you are not fully committed to their program.

In the following sections, I'll go over some specific questions that often arise concerning the actual application.

When Are MBA Applications Typically Due?

Applications vary from one MBA program to another, and it is important to review each program's application requirements and deadlines to ensure that you fulfill each appropriately. Most leading MBA programs in the United States and abroad have set deadlines that focus on discrete rounds. To further complicate things, you will find that some programs, such as Tuck, have an early-application (priority) deadline that is not binding if you are admitted; on the other hand, Columbia's early-decision deadline and Fuqua's early-action deadline *are* binding, and candidates who are admitted to them are required to withdraw their applications at other schools. If you are unsure whether a school is for you, you should not apply through its binding admissions programs. Contact the schools directly to get the information on its exact deadlines and admissions policies.

MBA programs have strict policies surrounding deadlines, so plan to start the application process early and make sure you know all the deadlines for the schools you are planning to apply to. Most MBA programs have at least three application deadlines, and some have more than six. London Business School, for example, has five deadlines (October, November, January, March, and May) that it refers to as stages. Columbia uses an unconventional system that starts with a binding early-decision deadline in early October, and then admits students on a rolling basis until its regular admissions deadline in April. Application deadlines at some schools begin as early as September. Most MBA programs have their first deadline between the months of September and October. The second application deadlines are usually in January, though some schools squeeze in two admissions deadlines between October and December, as is the case at Tuck. The third application deadline is usually in March, followed by a May deadline. Regardless of which round you intend to apply for, you should give yourself a minimum of four to six months to complete your application. Note that incomplete applications are typically pushed to the next round, and exceptions are rarely granted, even when an incomplete application is the result of an errant recommender.

When Is the Ideal Time to Submit My Application?

International MBA programs tend to have more rounds than their U.S. counterparts. But regardless of whether you are applying to a U.S. or non-U.S. business school, you should plan to apply earlier in the admissions cycle rather than later. In the case of U.S. schools, you should target the first or second round. In the case of non-U.S. schools, you should target the first three rounds. You should apply when you are ready, not because you are trying to "game" the system by targeting a particular round you think may have better odds of acceptance. Many programs explicitly state that applicants should avoid applying in the later rounds because most admissions spots are taken by then. It may also become tougher for international students to secure their visas if they apply late.

There are a few candidates for whom applying later may not have as detrimental an effect: a classic example is the nontraditional candidate with an excellent GMAT score and academic record and a solid track record of leadership. A candidate like this can "round out" the class and, with no academic issues, could be admitted in a late round. Also, someone who is applying from a country that is underrepresented in the applicant pool could get away with a later-round application if they are solid in all three admissions criteria. (I'll go into great detail in the next chapter on the admissions criteria used to evaluate candidates.) The operative word here is "could." You always run the risk of being rejected if there are only a few spots available. I have heard of some MBA programs informing candidates that their application was strong but that its lateness resulted in their being denied admission. Preparing yourself early in the preapplication stage and judiciously executing the application will help you avoid any mishaps.

What Do I Need to Include in My MBA Application?

The MBA application is composed of several items, including the résumé, recommendations, essays, transcripts, GMAT or GRE score, and a completed online application. Each aspect of the application is important and carries significant weight in the decision to admit a candidate. The goal for applicants is to present a strong application across all the evaluation materials. The stronger each element of the application is, the higher the chance of being admitted. I will discuss each of the application components in later chapters.

What Happens Once I Submit My Application?

In the past several years, admissions offices have moved to a paperless application. Moving to an online application model has streamlined the application process and created more efficiency for MBA programs. Operations teams in admissions offices are now able to spend less time entering application data, thus enabling MBA admissions boards to quickly begin the application evaluation. Even the submission of recommendations has become more efficient. Instead of relying on the postal service to deliver a recommender letter on time, you can take the guesswork and stress out of the recommendation process by having letters submitted online. Once you identify who will write your recommendations, you can enter their names and email addresses, giving your recommenders access to the online application. The trick, however, is to make sure that the recommender does not submit the recommendation before you have had a chance to discuss your overall strategy and key brand message. This has happened to a few unsuspecting candidates, so be sure to communicate to your recommenders that you plan to discuss your branding before they submit their recommendations.

Once you have submitted your application and all supplemental materials, your status will change to reflect that your application is complete or under review. The operations staff then prints out a copy of your application and creates a folder for you. Applications are not reviewed or considered complete until all required materials have been received.

Can I Influence When My Application Is Reviewed?

No, you can't. With the exception of schools that have a rolling admissions policy, under which applications are reviewed in the order in which they are received, applications are reviewed in random order, and the timing of the review does not impact who will receive a favorable outcome. At most schools, when your application is reviewed comes down to when your physical application is created and when the MBA admissions board member picks up the application bin that happens to contain your application.

Let me paint a vivid picture for you to illustrate my point. The operations room is the hub of any admissions office. It is here that the applications are printed, folders created, and bins (containers that board members use to lug applications back and forth between their homes and schools) assembled. Let's say your completed application is printed in the beginning of the week and placed in a bin, and it happens to be a week where a higher number of applications are printed and assembled. Even though your application was printed at the beginning of the week, by Friday, when the board members stop in to pick up their bins, yours may be in the back, making it logistically difficult to get to. The board members will grab the bins that are up front and make their way to the back. Candidates whose folders were created later in the week will be in bins that are more accessible. The good news is that every application will receive the necessary evaluation—thorough scrutiny from multiple different board members—that it deserves, regardless of when it is reviewed. So you see, there isn't much a candidate can do to influence when their application is evaluated, and investing energy into figuring out how to do so is a useless exercise. A better use of your time is to create an appealing and interesting application that will capture the mindshare of the admissions board.

Can I Send Additional Materials to the Admissions Office?

Schools vary in their policies with regard to accepting additional materials after the application deadline. It is imperative that you know what the program's policy is so that you are not surprised. A safe assumption is that the MBA program will not accept new materials after the deadline. A few exceptions may exist at some schools for wait-listed candidates, but again, you should check with the MBA program to find out exactly what their policy is and adhere to it.

What Happens if My Application Is Not Complete by the Deadline?

An email is the most common way that candidates are notified of their incomplete status. If your application status doesn't change from pending to complete, it is worth contacting the admissions office. A top reason for an application remaining incomplete is a delay in the recommendations. It is your responsibility to touch base with all your recommenders to ensure that they submit their letters on time. If you are like me, a little on the cautious side, you may want to contact your recommenders at least a couple of weeks before the submission deadline to make sure they have everything they need and that they will meet the deadline.

Contacting admissions offices multiple times to inquire if they received your recommendation letters or any other materials is not the best way to make a positive impression. Be sensitive to the admissions board's overstretched schedule and don't inundate them with calls or emails. You are better off controlling the process by staying in touch with your recommenders and making sure that they fulfill their commitment. Giving them more than three months to write a recommendation for you will help you limit any problems that may crop up.

How Are Applications Reviewed?

MBA programs vary in the specific evaluation processes that they use in assessing candidates. Some schools have a strong committee process (Rotman MBA and Yale are good examples of this), while others (like Harvard Business School) involve a more independent assessment. I am often asked questions regarding how many people evaluate candidates at Harvard, for how long applications are evaluated, and the gender of MBA admissions board members. Those are the wrong questions to focus on, because answers to these questions do little to prepare you for presenting a powerful application, nor do they influence the admission outcome.

Here is what is more useful to know. All applications are reviewed by a member of the admissions board, and they are all given the same consideration. In other words, applications are not sorted based on standardized test scores, with top-scoring candidates being reviewed while those with lower scores are cast aside. Some schools involve students in the admissions process; in these cases, students typically review applications during the first reads, and then they are passed on to a board member who does a second read. For schools where students do not evaluate applications, the first read is done by an admissions board member and then passed on to another board member. By the second evaluation, a decision is made to reject, wait-list, further review, or admit the student. Candidates in the admit pile typically are extended an interview invitation. A few candidates may be "rescued" from the reject pile for various reasons (for example, their unique perspective based on their backgrounds and experiences). Those that are in the wait-list pile will be held until applications are reviewed from the next round to see how strong they compare to the next batch of candidates. Some candidates will come off the waiting list (this number varies from year to year based on how competitive the overall pool is). Applications in the further-review pile will be reviewed by another board member or discussed at committee before their fate is determined.

Some MBA programs make decisions by committee. Yale School of Management is an example of such a program. At Yale, applications are reviewed individually by board members and then discussed in committee. In this situation, batches of applications are debated, and no final decisions are made until after board members have had a chance to discuss—or should I say dissect?—each candidate's merits. Each board member seems to have a lot of power in "making a case" for or against a candidate. This is why it is important to create a distinctive brand that the MBA admissions board can identify and remember. This makes it easier for the person who is arguing for your candidacy to make a compelling case on your behalf. Schools without committee involvement typically rely on board members to review candidates. The admissions director then makes the final decisions on who is invited for interviews and, later, who receives a letter of admission.

THE POST-APPLICATION PROCESS

Once the MBA application is submitted, it certainly isn't the time for applicants to relax and rest on their laurels. Underestimating this phase or taking missteps can hurt your admissions objectives.

After you have submitted your application, there are a few things you can do to prepare yourself for business school. This may include registering for one or two business classes if you feel you need a refresher or if you have not taken such coursework in the past. This could be helpful if you have been out of school for a long time. At the very least, such coursework is excellent preparation to ensure that you are not too rusty when you begin the business degree. Additionally, should the admissions board admit you under the condition that you take business courses, you'll already be prepared to meet that requirement. You may also want to consider these frequent questions that applicants often have during this phase of the application process.

How Should I Quit My Current Job?

One of the decisions facing applicants once they are admitted is when to quit their jobs, if they choose to do so. This decision warrants careful consideration. Most importantly, it is critical not to leave your job unless you have received an official acceptance. Do not make the mistake of one overly confident applicant who did not heed this advice. She believed that the admission "was in the bag," so she subsequently quit her job before getting an admission offer. She was a top-rated investment banking analyst at a top-five investment bank in New York. She had received interview offers from Harvard Business School, Wharton, and Columbia and was confident after each interview that she would be admitted to one of them. Unfortunately for her, she was denied admission by all the schools she applied to. Exiting before you receive an admission offer is a risk not worth taking.

It is also important to remain sensitive to your employer during this transition. If you choose to remain at the firm, it is important to convey unrelenting commitment to your job. Should you decide to leave, however, you should have an exit strategy that you can ease your boss into. A candidate I know frantically contacted me after her current boss threatened to call the admissions board to rescind his recommendation for her at a top business school where she had applied. His reason? He felt that she had not shown good faith by choosing to quit several months ahead of when he expected her to leave. Clearly, she had not managed her boss's expectations effectively, and this put her in a precarious situation. As you can see, it is important not to burn your bridges. You never know when you will need that former boss again. Consider offering to train your replacement when quitting your job. Of course, every situation is unique, so you will have to decide what course of action is right for you.

What Happens After a Decision Is Made on an Application?

Once a decision is rendered on an application, it is entered into the application database. The outcome is then communicated to the applicant at the notification deadline. A huge pet peeve for the admissions board is when candidates call to find out their decision before the notification date. Not too long ago, overeagerness led several candidates to illegally access a database in an attempt to discover their admission outcomes prematurely. They were caught and paid a steep price: some schools rejected them despite having initially admitted them. I understand the pressures candidates are under to find out their admission outcome, especially after waiting several months. I feel your pain! The best thing to do after you submit your application is to stay busy to keep your mind off of the admissions forums and resist checking your email obsessively for the interview invitation. But, of course, this is easier said than done.

The day before the notification deadline is a crazy day for all applicants, with many camping next to their computers, awaiting news of their admission decision. These days, many admissions directors call admitted candidates to congratulate them before or shortly after the notification email has been sent. Geographical region sometimes dictates who receives calls first. International applicants who reside abroad may get calls first, given the time difference.

Even after you have been admitted, keep in mind that your application can be rescinded should you demonstrate poor judgment. Remember that you are viewed as someone who will reflect positively on the brand of the MBA program. Your admission offer can be withdrawn should anything negative or scandalous be associated with you. So exercise wisdom both in what you say in online chats and blogs as well as in your life in general.

What Is the Application Verification Process?

After a candidate has received his or her admission offer, the admissions board verifies the information presented in the application. Verification of applications isn't new. Admissions boards have typically verified admitted students' official transcripts and GMAT or GRE scores. More recently, however, the MBA admissions boards have expanded their verification to the candidate's career track record and will scrutinize information involving employment dates, history, bonuses, and salaries. Wharton has been doing verifications far longer than most schools, but the trend today among top MBA programs is to verify applicants' information at some level. The approach used by each program varies, however. So while some use an actual verification firm, others may opt to do so themselves by calling your former employers. Schools that do not have the bandwidth to verify every single candidate may focus on candidate information that seems far-fetched.

Candidates should take the verification process seriously and ensure that all information provided in their application is accurate. I know of instances where admission offers were revoked due to inconsistency in the candidate's information. This was even the case with an applicant from China who falsified his grade in one class from a B to an A. The outcome was that his admission was rescinded. He would have been admitted anyway with the B grade, but his dishonesty cost him a spot at a top business school. Candidates are not immune after they are enrolled, either. If a school should receive a late verification report indicating that the candidate provided false information, the already-enrolled candidate can be kicked out of the program. Even casual or unintentional mistakes can be problematic, so be extremely careful when inputting your information, and if you are not sure of something, spend the extra time to get the accurate information. My advice to all applicants is to resist the temptation to embellish or exaggerate your story. Falsifying your achievements, career impact, or any other information can lead to your admission being overturned. Don't take that chance.

The following words from Harvard's website summarize the MBA admissions board's view of verification:

> The School will verify application information and reserves the right to withdraw any offer of admission already made if there is any discrepancy between the self-reported information and information provided through verification.

(Source: HBS admissions website)

FINAL THOUGHTS

The application to business school is a marathon, not a sprint. It takes years of "training" and careful execution to yield the desired results. Taking this approach and devoting appropriate time and resources to each stage of the process will give you a better shot at getting into a top institution. Given the significant benefits of an MBA from a top school, it is a missed opportunity to leave any part of this process to chance—and to avoid doing so, you must have a thorough understanding of the admissions criteria that every candidate is evaluated on. I examine these criteria closely in the next chapter.

CHAPTER FIVE

Understanding the Admissions Criteria

B EFORE I GO ON to discuss the specific application components, I want to review the overall admissions criteria that are used to evaluate candidates. A lot of questions surround exactly how candidates are evaluated and which aspects of the admissions criteria count the most. This chapter focuses on the three admissions criteria used by the MBA admissions board in evaluating all candidates. I also go into details of the specific components of each criterion to ensure that you understand how the admissions board views them and how you can maximize your chances of being admitted. After you understand the admissions criteria, you should be able to objectively evaluate your candidacy. This chapter also provides suggestions of steps you can take to address any gaps in your application.

Top business schools evaluate candidates across three core areas, namely:

- Academic ability and intellectual aptitude
- Leadership impact and managerial potential
- Uniqueness (diverse experiences or perspectives and differentiated personal characteristics)

Some of the greatest myths surrounding the application process are related to candidates' misconceptions of the admissions criteria. When writing the first edition of this book, I emphasized the fact that all three criteria are important, and they are. However, it is important to clarify that, without a solid academic record, the rest of the application is all for naught. While all of the criteria are important in securing an offer of admission, you must have a strong academic foundation to substantiate the remaining elements of your application.

It is important to understand how these three admissions criteria are viewed by the MBA admissions board. Ideally, candidates should try to be strong in all three areas. Given an extremely competitive admissions landscape, the stronger you are across all three criteria, the better your chance of being admitted. So although we all know someone who was admitted without excelling in the three criteria, I encourage every applicant to present his or her strongest suit and submit an application that presents a compelling case across all three.

Each top MBA program refers to the admissions criteria in a different way, but ultimately, they all evaluate candidates based on these three categories. These statements taken from MBA admissions websites illustrate this point.

Stanford

   1. Intellectual Vitality

   2. Demonstrated Leadership Potential

   3. Personal Qualities and Contributions

Harvard

   1. Habit of Leadership

   2. Analytical Aptitude and Appetite

   3. Engaged Community Citizenship

The committee values academic performance and seeks candidates who demonstrate superior intellectual ability...have developed a strong foundation and/or essential skills for their future professional goals...have proven themselves as both leaders and team players, who are well rounded and interesting, and who have demonstrated the will and ability to actively contribute to the well-being of their community.

Chicago

The Admissions Committee looks for people who have demonstrated the ability to succeed through work experience, academic endeavors, and extracurricular or community service involvement.

INSEAD

We expect intellectual curiosity coupled with a desire to learn and stretch yourself in a rigorous academic programme, as well as personal qualities to contribute to the many activities of the Institute.

HKUST

We seek high-quality students from a diversity of backgrounds with a broad spectrum of valuable experience... We are looking for outstanding candidates with leadership potential who have the capacity to make lasting contributions to the region or industry in which they are working. Our students are dynamic and talented individuals who balance an ethical, responsible approach to business with the ability to move ever forward in their pursuit of success, contributing to both their professions and the community at large.

Tuck

What makes a candidate successful? There is no formula for admission to Tuck. Each decision hinges on the interplay of five principal factors: Demonstrated Academic Excellence, Demonstrated Leadership, Demonstrated Accomplishment, Interpersonal Skills, and Diversity of Background and Experience.

IMD

Intellectual ability (your ability to grasp complex concepts and synthesize new knowledge rapidly)... Leadership potential (your knowledge, vision, courage, and ethics; your empathy and ability to motivate and orchestrate teams and individuals)... Interpersonal skills (your ability to work well in diverse teams).

Stern

We seek students who are confident in their ability to master the required material and have the courage to ask challenging questions...who have a proven track record and clear professional goals, both short-term and long-term...who will contribute to the Stern community. We seek students with proven leadership ability, maturity, character, and strong communication skills, who will be active participants at Stern and have a great passion for, pride in, and commitment to Stern.

Let's take a look at each of the three core areas.

ACADEMIC ABILITY AND INTELLECTUAL APTITUDE

The curriculum at MBA programs is challenging. It is therefore important that admitted candidates have the appropriate academic preparation to handle a rigorous environment. Candidates do not need a business degree from an undergraduate university to apply to business school. In fact, the majority of MBA programs report that business majors make up only about 20 to 25 percent of their class. What's more important is that candidates show that they are intellectually sharp and have the discipline to engage and contribute in a rigorous educational setting.

Whether candidates can handle the rigor of the MBA program is assessed in two ways: their standardized test scores on the GMAT or GRE and their college transcripts. Both of these variables are reviewed in the context of the candidate's life: what opportunities have they had? Are they the first in their family to go to college? How do the GMAT/GRE and GPA overlap?

Ideally, you want both the GMAT/GRE score and GPA to be very strong. For some applicants, although the test score may be lower than the median at the school, the GPA may be significantly higher. The reverse can also be the case. If you find yourself in this situation, there are practical steps you can take to convince the MBA admissions board that you are intelligent and able to handle a challenging program. In such circumstances, the recommendations become even more critical, because they can add further reinforcement of your intellectual ability, curiosity, and analytical and quantitative strengths. Coursework can also alleviate some of the academic concerns, as does retaking the standardized test and earning a higher score. Let's take a closer look at the GMAT, GRE, and your transcript.

The GMAT

The GMAT is the entrance exam that is required by all top, full-time two-year business schools in America. It has been around for almost sixty years and is accepted as the official test at almost six thousand schools worldwide. Once a paper-and-pencil exam, the GMAT has become primarily a computer-administered exam. It is also adaptive in nature: the computer generates questions based on your skill level and your performance on previous questions. After a candidate takes the GMAT, the score is active for up to five years, so it is important to take the exam as early as possible. The test itself is administered six days a week, with the exception of holidays. Applicants can take the exam up to five times in an academic year (waiting thirty-one days between exams). Business schools do not penalize candidates for taking the exam more than once. In fact, most schools accept the highest score (check with your school to make sure that this is applicable).

Candidates who are unhappy with their GMAT results the first time should definitely retake the exam. However, the fact that MBA programs accept your best GMAT score isn't license to take the GMAT half a dozen times. Two or three times is acceptable. The fifth and sixth times may be overkill. The important thing here is to invest in adequate preparation ahead of time to avoid having to take the exam too many times. Remember that the test itself is not cheap. Each exam costs $250, so it is to your advantage to fully prepare for the exam before taking it. (You can learn more about the GMAT by visiting www.mba.com, where you can register for the exam.) On the other hand, if you take it once and you are dissatisfied with your score, and if you think trying a second or third time can significantly improve your score, then that is fine. If your score doesn't improve after two or three times, I personally feel it is more effective for you to focus on other parts of the application where you may have greater control in shaping your candidacy.

Timing when to take the GMAT is vital since you have to wait thirty-one days to retake it. Avoid taking the exam too close to the application deadline. I know candidates who have scored unexpectedly poorly on the first GMAT, and because of the thirty-one-day waiting period, they missed applying within the first round.

I'm often asked about the ideal GMAT score an applicant needs in order to be admissible. Unfortunately, there are many misconceptions surrounding this subject. The truth is that there is no magic number to guarantee admission. MBA programs often state that they do not have minimum GMAT scores or cutoff requirements for admission. Although that is true, a GMAT of 300 will not earn anyone a spot at Stanford or any top-ten MBA program; on the other hand, a GMAT score of 800 won't guarantee a candidate admission to a top MBA program either.

The best way to view the GMAT is to recognize that, on its own, it is a necessary but not sufficient component of the application. Getting a strong score can keep you in the running for a coveted admission spot, but a mediocre score can end your admission aspirations. Check out the websites of the MBA programs you are interested in to find out where your GMAT score falls compared with the median GMAT score of the entering class. If your score is significantly below that of the median—640 compared with 706, for example—you should postpone applying and devote more time and resources to improving your score.

The GMAT scores standardize the academic components by providing a benchmark to assess different candidates coming from varied professional and personal backgrounds and experiences. This is especially so when candidates come from schools that admissions boards are not as familiar with. Even for well-known schools, majors and grading systems vary. A 3.7 GPA at one school may be closer to a 3.4 at another school. The GMAT score, on the other hand, is a variable that provides the MBA admissions board with perspective on how the candidate scored compared with others who took the test. The other reason MBA admissions boards care about the GMAT score is that some of the ranking agencies rely on this information when ranking MBA programs. The GMAT has considerable weight in the application process, so give it the attention it deserves.

GMAT Components and What They Mean to the Admissions Board

The GMAT was revised in June 2012 to include an integrated reasoning section, after faculty at business schools highlighted the need for MBA students to have strong analytical and problem-solving skills to succeed both as students in business school and beyond. The GMAT is made up of four components: the analytical writing assessment section, the verbal section, the quantitative section, and the integrated reasoning section.

GMAT TEST SECTION	NUMBER OF QUESTIONS	QUESTION TYPES	TIMING
Analytical Writing Assessment	1 Topic	Analysis of an Argument	30 Minutes
Integrated Reasoning	12 Questions	Multi-Source Reasoning, Graphics Interpretation, Two-Part Analysis, Table Analysis	30 Minutes

Quantitative	37 Questions	Data Sufficiency, Problem Solving	75 Minutes
Verbal	41 Questions	Reading Comprehension, Critical Reasoning, Sentence Correction	75 Minutes
Total Exam Time			3 hours, 30 minutes

(Source: www.mba.com)

The analytical writing assessment (AWA) is made up of one essay question that asks you to analyze an argument. You will be given thirty minutes for this section. The AWA score ranges from 1 to 6, with 6 as the highest possible score. The integrated reasoning (IR) section is comprised of twelve questions made up of four parts each: table analysis, two-part analysis, graphics interpretation, and multi-source reasoning. You will have thirty minutes for this part of the test. The IR is scored on a range of 1 to 8, with 8 as the highest score. Neither the AWA nor the IR is factored into the overall GMAT score, and neither is overly emphasized in the evaluation of candidates. But that doesn't mean that applicants should blow these sections off. While high scores won't necessarily give you a significant advantage, scores that are extremely low can raise concerns for the admissions board. The remaining two parts of the GMAT are the verbal and the quantitative sections, each of which is scored from 0 to 60. The verbal section is made up of forty-one multiple-choice questions that include sentence correction, critical reasoning, and reading comprehension. You will have seventy-five minutes to complete this section. The quantitative section is also allotted seventy-five minutes. This section is made up of thirty-seven multiple-choice questions covering data sufficiency and problem solving (covering such topics as algebra, geometry, and arithmetic). Total GMAT scores, which combine the scores from the verbal and quantitative sections, range from 200 to 800.

In addition to the raw number ascribed to each section, there is a percentile figure associated with it. Admissions boards pay very close attention to the percentile figures for the verbal and quantitative sections. So not only is it essential to have a strong overall score and percentile, but it is also important to perform strongly across both these sections. An applicant to business school, Chad, illustrates what a great GMAT result looks like. He has a score of 760. Following is the breakdown of his scores:

Overall Score:	760
Overall Percentile:	99%
Verbal Score:	42
Verbal Percentile:	95%
Quantitative Score:	51
Quantitative Percentile:	99%
Integrated Reasoning:	6
AWA:	5.5

The first thing the MBA admissions board will review when evaluating the GMAT score is how the person performed overall. So the first note would be that Chad scored 760 and that his score is higher than that of 99 percent of test-takers. But they will not stop there. They will then check to make sure that there are no issues between the verbal and quantitative sections. Scoring highly in both sections is important. Chad's verbal and quantitative breakdowns of 95 percent and 99 percent show that his GMAT is fine—both scores are above the 90th percentile.

Besides the overall GMAT score, a candidate's performance in the verbal and quantitative sections is important to the evaluation of his or her application. At a minimum, candidates should aim to score above 80 percent in both sections. But what if there is a discrepancy between the two? Being weak in either the verbal or the quantitative section can raise red flags for the MBA admissions board. For instance, an international applicant who has a 99 percent in the quantitative section and only a 60 percent in the verbal section will surely face questions concerning his or her verbal abilities. Candidates in such circumstances should plan to retake the exam and improve their performance in the verbal section. Conversely, a nontraditional applicant whose work experience is devoid of quantitative exposure and whose quantitative score falls in the 66th percentile will have a tough time convincing the admissions board that he or she has a strong enough quantitative background to thrive in a business school. Such a candidate can address this issue by retaking the exam and by taking quantitative classes and performing well in them.

The admissions board looks at the AWA score, but historically, it hasn't been a major factor in the admissions decision. AWA scores of 4.5 and above are considered fine. A high AWA (5.5 or 6.0) will rarely earn the applicant any major points. However, a low score (3.5 or lower) will raise questions regarding a candidate's writing ability. Although important, the AWA has traditionally been the least scrutinized component of the GMAT at most top business schools. This is changing somewhat as schools become more concerned about inconsistencies between applicants' AWA scores and the writing abilities demonstrated in their application essays; in cases like these, they may pay more attention to the AWA score, especially when the applicant is a nonnative English speaker. Anyone who chooses to use an advisory firm should maintain the integrity of their writing: never resort to hiring writing professionals to write your admissions essays. A candidate with an AWA score of 3 whose essays read like those of a Pulitzer Prize–winning journalist will have a major problem explaining the inconsistency.

Integrated reasoning is still quite new, and it's unclear how much emphasis admissions boards will put on candidates' IR scores. The test-prep giant Kaplan conducts the annual Business School Admissions Officers Survey to get insight into how admissions boards make decisions and the factors that are taken into consideration. The 2012 survey covers perspectives from 265 business schools, including seventeen of the twenty-five top-ranked MBA programs from *U.S.News & World Report*. In the 2012 survey, 41 percent of those surveyed said that they think the addition of the integrated reasoning section makes the exam more reflective of the business school experience. Schools recognize that there are still quite a few applicants who took the GMAT before June 2012 who don't have IR scores. Over time, however, I suspect that schools will use the IR more if there is evidence that it is a good indicator of how students will handle analytical courses in business schools. Even outside of the admissions circle, employers like Bain, a top-tier consulting company, are toying with the idea of incorporating the IR in the evaluation of job candidates. Applicants should therefore prepare for all the parts of the GMAT to make the right impression when evaluated on this academic data point.

BASIC GMAT TIPS

- Start early. Plan to take the test at least a year before the deadline.
- Take a couple of practice tests to see how you perform.
- Invest in a GMAT prep course if your practice score is below the median score of your target MBA programs.
- Consider taking the GMAT while you are in college. It is easier to take an exam while you are still in studying mode. The GMAT score is active for five years.
- Retake the exam if you are not satisfied with your score. A majority of MBA programs accept your highest score. (Check the specific programs to make sure their policy doesn't change.) The Graduate Management Admission Council, which administers the GMAT, reports that more than 20 percent of GMAT test-takers retake the exam in a given year.
- The GMAT range of admitted students at the MBA program should serve as a guide. Scoring below this range does not automatically disqualify your application. The strength of the rest of your application will be taken into account.
- You can take the GMAT once every thirty-one days, so plan accordingly to ensure that you don't miss your application deadline.

Many test-prep programs are available to help applicants boost their scores. Some that have been around for a while include Princeton Review, Kaplan, Veritas Prep, Bell Curves, and Manhattan GMAT (which has been bought by Kaplan). But new ones have joined the market, and one in particular, Knewton, is transforming the way students are preparing for standardized tests, even though the company was only founded in 2008. Started by Jose Ferreira, this company is changing the way applicants have traditionally prepared for the GMAT. Instead of the standard classroom format, Knewton instruction is 100 percent on-demand and online teaching at a fraction of the usual cost for test instruction. MBA applicants are also guaranteed all their money back if they do not improve their scores by at least fifty points. Not a bad deal if you are someone who learns well through an online medium. MBA candidates should do their due diligence to assess which test-prep program would best provide them with the support and preparation they need in order to nail a strong score. I encourage you to also read the GMAT interview of Veritas Prep at the end of this book.

The GRE

The GRE revised general test has been around for more than sixty years and has become very popular as a test for graduate school admissions. Many top business schools didn't accept the GRE until a few years ago, when MBA programs like MIT Sloan Business School and Stanford Graduate School of Business began accepting it. Other schools followed suit, and today, nearly all top MBA programs in the world accept the GRE. The cost of the GRE ($185 worldwide) is cheaper than the GMAT ($250), which could be a factor for applicants concerned about keeping their costs low.

The GRE assesses graduate school applicants' verbal reasoning, quantitative reasoning, and analytical writing skills. Each section of the GRE evaluates applicants' specific abilities. Here's how ETS, the company that issues the GRE, describes the three components of the GRE:

- **Verbal Reasoning**—This section of the test has two thirty-minute verbal questions. It assesses applicants' ability to "analyze and evaluate written material and synthesize information obtained from it, analyze relationships among component parts of sentences, and recognize relationships among words and concepts."
- **Quantitative Reasoning**—This section of the test has two thirty-minute quantitative sections. It "measures problem-solving ability, focusing on basic concepts of arithmetic, algebra, geometry, and data analysis."
- **Analytical Writing**—This section of the test has one seventy-five-minute analytical section comprising two essays. It "measures critical-thinking and analytical-writing skills, specifically your ability to articulate and support complex ideas clearly and effectively."

(Source: www.ets.org/gre)

There are two options for how you can take the GRE: computer-based or paper-based. Deciding on which one to take depends on what is available where you live as well as the mode of testing that is best suited to you. Are you more of a paper-and-pencil test-taker or are you comfortable with the computer-based test? The answer to this question should drive your decision on which type of test to sign up for.

You can take the test once every twenty-one days and up to five times on a continuous basis in a year. The paper-based test is available up to three times a year at locations where the computer-based test is not available. Business schools accept applicants' highest GRE scores, so feel free to retake the test at least one additional time if you are unhappy with your initial test score. The GRE is valid for up to five years and is offered at test centers around the world. Registration for the GRE is done at www.ets.org. You will also find test preparation resources such as *POWERPREP II* (online software that includes two free full-length practice GRE tests) and *Practice Book for the Paper-Based GRE Revised General Test.*

The GRE was revised in 2011, introducing some key changes. The test takes an hour longer to complete (four hours instead of the original three). The table below (adapted from ETS's website) outlines the different score ranges for tests taken before August 1, 2011, and those taken after.

	GRE TESTS TAKEN ON OR AFTER AUGUST 1, 2011	GRE TESTS TAKEN BEFORE AUGUST 1, 2011
Measure	Scores Reported	Scores Reported
Verbal Reasoning	130–170, in 1-point increments	200–800, in 10-point increments
Quantitative Reasoning	130–170, in 1-point increments	200–800, in 10-point increments
Analytical Writing	0–6, in half-point increments	0–6, in half-point increments

Although the types of sections have remained the same in the new GRE, the content has changed. The verbal reasoning section places more attention on critical reading and less on vocabulary. The quantitative reasoning section places more emphasis on data analysis and problem solving. The analytical writing section has not undergone a major change, although the allotted time for the analytical essay has been cut down from forty-five minutes to thirty minutes.

The GRE score also comes with a percentile rank that represents the percentage of test-takers who took the test and scored lower than your score. ETS has also created a GRE-GMAT score comparison tool to help compare the GRE score to the GMAT. MBA programs have a mixed view of the score comparison tool, and it isn't fully embraced by all MBA programs that accept the GRE.

By now you are likely wondering which test to take, the GMAT or the GRE. The simple answer is that it depends on your particular situation and on the schools that you are targeting. A few programs like Oxford Saïd Business School have held off from accepting the GRE. However, many of the top MBA programs do accept the GRE. Even programs like Chicago Booth Business School and Berkeley's Haas Business School, which had initially resisted accepting the GRE, have caved in. Every MBA program is seeking ways to grow its applicant base, and the GRE is a natural pipeline to recruit students from such backgrounds as science, technology, engineering, and mathematics, applicants who traditionally target masters programs instead of MBA degrees. There can still be variations in how admissions boards view the GRE test.

MBA programs report their GMAT statistics, including average, median, lowest, and highest scores, but so far, MBA programs do not report GRE data. This could be of slight advantage to candidates who have taken the GRE test and not done as well on it as they'd hoped. In such instances, the MBA program may be more willing to admit the candidate with a nonstellar GRE score, since his score won't be factored into the overall score statistics that the school reports. But there can be a downside to taking the GRE over the GMAT. Applicants from backgrounds where a high number apply to business school (such as bankers, consultants, private equity analysts, etc.) may raise a few eyebrows if they opt for the GRE over the GMAT. On the other hand, someone coming from a nontraditional background who takes the GRE isn't likely to raise any eyebrows. If this individual decides to take the GMAT and manages to get a very high score, his application could very well secure a slight bump ahead of another candidate with a similar profile who opt not to take the GMAT.

Ultimately, your decision to take the GMAT or the GRE should be based upon how you will perform on these two tests. Applicants should take practice exams and select the test on which they are more likely to do well. If you are not sure which one to take, you can also take both tests and submit your highest score.

ENGLISH LANGUAGE ASSESSMENT (TOEFL, IELTS, AND THE PTE ACADEMIC)

International candidates who studied at institutions where English isn't the main language are required to take an English assessment exam. There are two major language exams that international students take for admission to business school: the TOEFL, formerly known as the Test of English as a Foreign Language, and the International English Language Testing System (IELTS). TOEFL is the more common and accepted test, although some MBA programs accept the IELTS in lieu of the TOEFL. Both exams assess an international candidate's ability to speak and comprehend standard English at a college level. Because the precise requirements for exempting from this exam vary from school to school, international candidates should visit each program's website to confirm which test is required. For instance, at Wharton, international candidates need to take the TOEFL, whereas Chicago Booth GSB and UCLA's Anderson School accept either the TOEFL or the IELTS.

The TOEFL, the older test, has its roots as far back as the mid-1960s and is more widely accepted in the United States. The test is offered both through a paper-based and computer-based format. The TOEFL PBT (paper-based test) has three sections (listening comprehension, structure and written expression, and reading comprehension) and is made up of multiple-choice questions. The test takes four hours, including thirty minutes for the Test of Written English (TWE). TOEFL PBT scores range from 310 to 677; the TWE is reported separately and the scale is 0 to 6. The TOEFL iBT (Internet-based test) is the computer version of the test and is scored based on the following four areas—reading, listening, speaking, and writing.

- Reading   0–30
- Listening   0–30
- Speaking   0–30
- Writing   0–30
- Total Score   0–120

The TOEFL PBT is being phased out as the online version becomes more common, so if you're considering taking the PBT, it is important that you confirm whether your target school accepts it. Harvard Business School, for example, only accepts the iBT. The TOEFL iBT and the TOEFL PBT are both valid for two years. MBA programs do not accept expired scores, so make sure your scores are valid when you apply to business school. You can also arrange to have your scores sent directly to the school by providing the program's test code. For more information on the TOEFL, visit www.toefl.org.

The International English Language Testing System (IELTS) is a relatively new exam started in 1980. IELTS test-takers can select between the academic and the general training formats of the test, depending on their objectives. The academic-training option is required for those pursuing graduate school, while those seeking a visa select the general training option. Applicants can register for a computer-based exam on its website (www.ielts.org) or sign up to take the exam at a test center, although only a limited number of locations are available. Test scores range from 1 to 9, with scores north of 7.5 required at top business schools that accept the IELTS. The test lasts for two hours and forty-five minutes and comprises four parts—listening (thirty minutes), writing (sixty minutes), reading (sixty minutes), and speaking (eleven to fifteen minutes). The three sections, excluding the speaking section, are administered at one sitting. The speaking section can be done on the same day or seven days before or after the original test date.

Another English language test that is accepted by more than four hundred MBA programs is the Pearson Test of English Academic (PTE Academic), which assesses applicants' English-speaking abilities through twenty different tasks that reflect real-world situations. The components of the test include an introduction of yourself (which isn't timed) plus a speaking and writing section, a reading section, an optional break, and a listening section. The test is three hours in length and is broken down into timed sections. The test scores range from 10 to 90. Like the IELTS, the PTE Academic can be used for visa assessment for the UK and Australia.

Top MBA programs vary on their cutoff scores for English language exams. Refer to each program's website to confirm the requirements for the specific programs that you are targeting. Harvard Business School explicitly states on its website, "The MBA Admissions Board discourages any candidate with a TOEFL score lower than 109 on the iBT, an IELTS score lower than 7.5, or a PTE score lower than 75 from applying." In contrast, Yale School of Management's assistant dean and director of admissions, Bruce DelMonico, stated in an interview with Poets & Quants that Yale has done away with tests of English ability and instead will be relying on its new video interview to assess international applicants' English abilities.

The Transcript

The college transcript plays an important role in the MBA admissions evaluation. In Kaplan's 2012 Business School Admissions Officers Survey, 49 percent said the standardized exam was the most important factor in the admissions process, followed by 31 percent who rated the undergraduate GPA as the most important part of the evaluation process.

The academic profile of a candidate reveals his or her performance over a period of time and paints a picture for the admissions board about how the candidate has managed his or her time in school, intellectual curiosity, and willingness to embrace challenges. The cumulative GPA isn't the only thing that matters when assessing a candidate's transcript; the trends of the grades are examined for consistency. So for instance, someone with an overall GPA of 3.5 who has straight-A grades in the first three years and C and D grades in his or her last year can raise major flags for the MBA admissions board. Equally problematic are situations where the candidate's academic performance is like a rollercoaster, where they perform well in one year and poorly the second year. Transcripts with consistently strong grades over the course of the entire academic experience are ideal. If you are still in college, then you should do everything you can to make sure that your performance is on an upward trajectory. One thing is for sure: finishing weak is one of the hardest issues to overcome with the admissions board. Therefore, MBA candidates should avoid having their weakest grades in their last year of college. It is easier to explain a weak start than a weak finish.

The rigor of the academic experience is also taken into account when evaluating candidates' transcripts. No admissions board wants to admit a candidate who would flunk out of business school. Therefore, the college transcript is carefully scrutinized to ensure that the candidate has taken a challenging academic program and performed well. The GPA of each candidate provides the MBA admissions board with a general sense of how the applicant has handled academic challenges; this is then used to extrapolate how the applicant will perform in business school. A strong GPA enables the board to answer the question, "Can this candidate cut it academically?"

But the admissions board also looks beyond the GPA. It takes into consideration the academic difficulty of applicants' majors. For instance, the MBA admissions board recognizes that some majors, such as physics or computer engineering, may typically offer fewer 4.0 GPAs than less rigorous majors. Also, the board is aware of the significant differences between schools when it comes to grading. As a result, the admissions board is sensitive when evaluating a 3.0 GPA from a school with little grade inflation versus a 3.7 GPA from a school where a significant population earns high grades.

You demonstrate commitment to your area of study when you have taken challenging courses and even pursued independent study or honors research. However, it is equally important not to be too narrow. By taking courses outside of your major, you can show that you are not just a physics or computer geek. This will help differentiate you from other candidates with similar majors. The admissions board can also see through candidates who have taken easy classes just to pad their GPAs.

Applicants should educate admissions boards when they have pursued an unusual academic program, especially if it is highly selective and rigorous. Mention unusual education or accomplishments in your résumé or interview. Some examples are being the first in your department to complete a dual degree in an unusually short time frame, or being one of the two people from your school to be inducted into an honor society. Equally interesting is taking the initiative to track down a professor from another institution and convincing her to oversee your senior thesis if it is in an area that isn't covered by faculty at your school. Being willing to step beyond your academic comfort zone is a differentiator that can give you an edge in the admissions process. At the end of the day, MBA admissions boards want to go beyond the letters and numbers of your transcript and aim to understand the motivations that drive you to pursue knowledge, the thought process behind your academic decisions, and the insights that have molded you into the person you are today.

Context is a major factor in the evaluation of candidates, and it plays a major role in evaluating a candidate's academic history and profile. Make no mistake about it, where you went to college or university matters a great deal in the application evaluation—but not necessarily in the way most candidates may think. A very intelligent student who could have gone to a highly selective school but instead attended a moderately rated institution will raise some questions immediately in the minds of the admissions board. Why did this candidate not go to a more rigorous school? Was it as a result of an inability to pay, a lack of opportunity or awareness, or because he is a slacker who coasted through high school and didn't challenge himself enough to get into a highly selective school? The family you come from is factored into this assessment. This is why schools ask candidates about their parents' occupations, whether they are alumni of the school, and the level of education that they have. These data points all add up to paint a picture of the backdrop behind each applicant's story. A candidate who is the first in their family to go to college and whose parents were unskilled workers may not have had the resources to apply to academic institutions that are viewed as top notch. On the other hand, a candidate who is the son of a CEO and whose parents both have graduate degrees but who ended up at a local, nonselective institution will raise a few flags. Recognizing this factor, applicants must be proactive to address any unusual circumstances that have shaped or impacted their decisions.

If this happens to be you, don't worry. You can still apply successfully if you play your cards right. I'm reminded of a client of ours who was an international student who left her country to attend a U.S. school. Despite coming from a privileged background, she made the choice to enroll at a modestly selective school, but she maintained a perfect GPA at that institution and through sheer determination was able to land a coveted position at a top firm. She then applied and secured admission to her MBA dream school. The admissions board cut her some slack because she was as an international student who didn't grow up in the United States. Had she been born and raised in the United States, she might have had a tougher time explaining her educational choice.

MBA programs differ in terms of whether they explicitly ask for GPA cutoff marks. Schools like Cambridge Judge MBA put it this way: "The precise qualification varies according to country and university, but as a general guide, we are looking for the equivalent of a first-class or good upper-second-class honors in the British system, or a GPA of at least 3.3 (out of 4.0) from a major American university." INSEAD's MBA program does not have a GPA cutoff and even goes as far as stating in the frequently asked questions section of their website that "INSEAD does not have a minimum GPA requirement as the GPA system is not a globally used grading methodology. We primarily look at the courses taken and the grades received in each course, in addition to the overall academic performance."

Internationals

Many top business schools invest a lot of time in visiting different countries during their marketing cycle. They use these trips to learn about the schools and companies that employ the applicants from that region, and as a result, they are well versed on the academic differences among many of the international universities. Internationals coming from schools that do not give GPAs or class ranks do not need to worry; the MBA admissions board will not penalize your application for this. If in doubt, check with the MBA program to find out how it wants you to handle this situation (whether to leave the GPA blank or provide an estimation). The admissions board is familiar with the grading systems at non-U.S. schools. They understand that a first-class honor is rare and signifies exceptional academic achievement, while a third-class performance obviously raises significant concerns about a candidate's academic ability. They also appreciate the academic rigor of a degree in engineering from a school like Imperial College in the United Kingdom or Indian Institute of Technology in India.

Explaining Transcript Inconsistencies

Health issues (on a personal level or involving a family member) are often the reason for a candidate's academic decline. A candidate I know had two tough semesters when her mom was struggling with a life-threatening illness. This resulted in a big dip in her transcript her sophomore year. Luckily, she was able to turn this trend around, and for the remaining two years of college, her grades were consistently above a 3.5 GPA. Other candidates have spotty transcripts because they worked full-time to support their education. Then there are situations where a candidate has low grades as a result of not effectively balancing academic studies and leadership involvement. Regardless of what the scenario is, candidates need to address any gaps or hiccups in their transcript. Using the "additional information" section on the online application or the optional essay to address academic missteps is the ideal strategy. The way you describe the situation can be telling. Demonstrate maturity by owning up to what happened and avoid making excuses. But don't go to the other extreme by groveling and overemphasizing the issue, which could cause the admissions board to fixate on it.

BASIC TRANSCRIPT TIPS

- Low GPA? Take two or more quantitative classes.
- Use the optional section of the application to address weak grades.
- Don't make excuses about weak transcripts.
- Have a recommender highlight your professional quantitative, analytical, and/or technical expertise.
- A very strong GMAT/GRE score can help mitigate a low GPA.
- Strong performance in a graduate program can also help offset a weak transcript.
- But don't pursue a graduate degree simply as a way to offset your weak undergraduate records.

Addressing the academic component of the admissions evaluation is a necessary part of the application. But once you have scaled this hurdle, you still need to address the remaining two admissions criteria: your leadership track record and uniqueness.

LEADERSHIP IMPACT AND MANAGERIAL POTENTIAL

You cannot read through the website of a top business school without coming across the word "leadership." Admissions boards are all looking for leaders with a track record of effecting change and improving any environment where they are.

Leadership isn't limited to formal titles such as vice president or manager. Leadership is measured based on the level of impact a candidate has. This is why admitted early-career candidates, those with less than two years of work experience, can still show remarkable leadership despite very junior titles at their jobs. The MBA admissions board wants to learn about situations where you initiated something that hadn't existed before, convinced your superiors about an opportunity, created a tool or product that improved the way business was done at your firm, or managed a process, project, or person with a fair share of challenges and delivered a successful outcome at the end.

Leadership can also be demonstrated in your knowledge arena. For instance, becoming a resident expert at something (above and beyond your job responsibilities) that creates value for your group or firm shows thought leadership. Although many candidates may not have had formal management experience, their exposure to leading small teams can offer interesting insights about their leadership potential. It is always important to show self-awareness of your strengths as a leader and the areas you could further develop as you grow in your management responsibilities. But equally important for a candidate is to show self-awareness of why a particular leadership impact or experience is personally meaningful. The why and how are as important, if not more so, as the what.

The MBA admissions board evaluates leadership on three dimensions that I call "the 3 Cs of Leadership," namely:

1. College leadership
2. Community leadership
3. Career leadership

College Leadership

Although it may have been a few years since you graduated from college, your college leadership is an important variable in your candidacy. In the ideal admissions world, candidates should be strong across all three leadership areas. From my experience, however, most admitted candidates are strong in two out of three of these leadership dimensions. What I've observed is that college leadership and career leadership are often very strong, leaving a gap in community leadership. The main reason for this is limited time. Many candidates are working eighty-plus hours each week, making committing to community service activities on a regular basis impossible. This is where college leadership comes into play. Many candidates had an excellent track record of leadership while they were in college. These candidates will have to rely on their college leadership and career leadership track record to impress the admissions board.

But what if your college leadership was weak? Some candidates with weak college leadership track records may have a compelling reason, such as having to self-fund their education. For some, it could be a result of partying too much in college. Regardless of why, candidates with a deficit in their college leadership must focus on strengthening their community and career leadership before applying to business school.

Do keep in mind that college leadership isn't simply about formal titles in student organizations. Although those are fine and represent the bulk of college leadership examples candidates have, many acceptable leadership examples at the college level are a result of someone taking initiative. An example is the student who has to work to fund her education and sees an underutilized system or a potential market that her employer isn't capitalizing on. By stepping up to present this idea to her bosses and helping to implement it, she will demonstrate a strong leadership track record.

For many candidates reading this book, college is in the distant past, so you can't do anything to change your college leadership (but you can focus on community and career leadership). However, for those of you who are still in college, it is never too late to start creating leadership impact. Are you an athlete? Could you serve in a leadership role on the team? How have you helped your team become stronger and closer? You don't have to be the captain of the team to do this. Is there a problem that you can resolve even without a formal title? Is there an interest you have that matters to you for which there is no formal organization at your school? If so, don't hesitate to start this organization. If you enjoy teaching or tutoring, is there a way to move beyond your typical tutoring role to one where you can manage the other tutors? Perhaps the opportunity to teach a class could present itself? My point here is that you need to raise your game. Don't be shy to step up and put your leadership stake in the ground at your school. And focus not simply on title, but on impact—that's the true test of leadership!

COLLEGE LEADERSHIP EXAMPLES OF SUCCESSFUL MBA CANDIDATES

- Strategic director at a college credit union, where he instituted new initiatives that led to expanded services for students
- Manager of student employees in an on-campus position
- Founder of an art organization that gave students opportunity to showcase and express their creative talent
- Teacher for a freshman seminar that pushed and stretched her students to develop new ideas and explore alternative conclusions
- Portfolio manager of student fund with 20 percent return

- Captain of varsity sports team
- Creator of regular dinners for international students at parents' home to help create a sense of community for classmates
- Latin dance instructor at old people's home
- Founder of tutoring program for at-risk kids

Community Leadership

To strengthen your community leadership, you can join a nonprofit organization and assume a leadership role in it. Most nonprofit organizations are in great need of human resources and money. You can have a major impact as a volunteer. Be careful that your involvement isn't seen as trite. Simply participating in an event once every few months does not qualify as strong evidence of leadership. Opt for tangible contributions. A concrete and significant leadership example could be applying your marketing experience to write the marketing plan and launching the marketing strategy for a nonprofit organization. Another example could be using your professional business development experience to help a community-based organization establish strong relationships with partner firms as a way to build revenue.

Do not underestimate the power of getting involved at your alma mater. By initiating recruitment activities for your college, you can demonstrate your leadership skills by establishing relationships, leading a team, and executing a plan. This is exactly what Stacy, a candidate, did. She noticed that many students from her alma mater did not pursue careers on Wall Street. Since it was a nonselective university, top banks did not recruit at her school. Stacy created a career support program that educates and mentors students and alumni from her university about career opportunities on Wall Street. This experience stretched Stacy's leadership abilities, as she had to attract and manage disparate alumni from varied industries. She learned how to sell her idea with conviction as she dealt with her school's administrators and career services personnel. She also honed her negotiation and communication abilities. To crown her involvement, Stacy received an alumni award for extraordinary service.

Applicants can also opt to serve on the board of a nonprofit organization to help provide strategic leadership advice. A great organization that places talented young professionals on the boards of nonprofit organizations is BoardNetUSA (www.boardnetusa.org). I don't recommend joining a nonprofit board simply to check the box. The admissions board can see through this. You want to be authentic. So, should you decide to pursue this option, make sure to select an organization that ties to something you are passionate about. And while you are on the board, it is key that you initiate activities that yield real solutions to improve the organization.

If you don't find an organization that appeals to you, then consider creating one. Starting an organization, even a nonprofit, can enable you to build an excellent leadership track record. Juan returned to his home country, and after noticing that there was no formal internship program to employ smart college students during the summer, he set about creating one. Not only did this experience provide interesting content for his essays, but more importantly, it gave him an opportunity to give back in a meaningful way. Juan had moved to America when he was young and had benefited from many formal internship programs. He wanted to give other students from his country a similar opportunity. The passion with which he spoke of his project was infectious, and it was easy to see how this was a labor of love for him. This leadership experience influenced his positive admission outcome.

I often hear candidates lament over their limited time for community service. As a busy entrepreneur, mother, and author, I recognize the time constraints that most professionals face. My advice to applicants is to be picky how you spend your time and choose things you are truly committed to, not just selecting activities because you wish to earn brownie points for business school. However, it isn't about quantity, but quality. Pick something that really speaks to your heart and find a way to make a meaningful contribution. For example, given the importance of my faith to me, I often choose to spend a significant amount of any free time that I have in my church. An applicant I know wanted to deepen his community involvement and chose to partner with a group of internationals who had a mission to commit $100 a month for one year, with a goal of raising funds that would be disbursed to two selected organizations in his home country. It worked. He fulfilled his commitment, got his friends to join, and had the satisfaction of seeing two nonprofit organizations expand and offer more services to the poor.

Regardless of which path you choose to take, it is more important to have one community involvement where you have significant impact and depth than to have a lot of activities with no impact. It is not enough to be a member of an organization. MBA programs are looking for leaders and want to see evidence that you have had an impact on people's lives and on an organization. Even if you are applying this year, it is never too late to get involved in community leadership. What is important is making sure that whatever you choose reflects your passion and brand.

COMMUNITY LEADERSHIP EXAMPLES OF SUCCESSFUL MBA CANDIDATES

- Board leader of a nonprofit hospital
- Business development and marketing volunteer for StreetSquash (an inner-city sports nonprofit organization that builds up the self-esteem of teenagers through squash)
- Founder of tutoring program in an inner city
- Board leadership of the Asian Task Force
- Leader of Women's Initiative for National Domestic Violence Organization
- Sunday school teacher and accountant for church
- Member of executive leadership team of an international business forum
- Publicity chair of a national association
- Founder of first-ever scholarship program and alumni fund at alma mater
- President of the Nigerian Business Forum
- Founder of philanthropic private equity enterprise
- Organizer of fund-raiser to help family member battling life-threatening disease

Career Leadership

Career leadership carries the most weight when boards evaluate a candidate's leadership experience. That is why most top MBA programs request that applicants provide recommendations from supervisors who can attest to their professional experience and trajectory. For early-career candidates, college and community leadership can be taken into account—especially when they have limited leadership experience in their career.

When considering career leadership, you should always focus on the actual impact you have had, not simply on your title. Go beyond your job description to demonstrate your contribution, and make sure to address why you chose to take the leadership steps in the first place. If the leadership role involves working with people, that's great. Opportunities where you managed a team allow you to clearly show your leadership abilities. It isn't just about how many people you have on the team; the important thing is that you demonstrate your insights into how people operate, how to motivate them, and what your leadership strengths and developmental needs are.

The MBA admissions board wants to know that you have challenged yourself and that you take initiative. They are interested in understanding your motivations and the type of leader you are. Team dynamics are pivotal to leadership. How do you handle conflict? How do you deal with disappointment and failures? Many of the top business schools will demand that you address these questions. At the heart of these questions is a desire on the part of the MBA admissions board to make sure that you are mature enough to learn from tough situations, have a healthy emotional intelligence, and can work well with people regardless of the circumstance.

I often hear MBA candidates complain that their jobs make it tough to show leadership. Investment banking analysts who work in a hyper-hierarchical environment are a good example. Let's look at a few ways an investment banking analyst can demonstrate career leadership.

- An investment banker who sees an opportunity to create a new training program can stand out in the applicant pool based on her commitment to others and her ability to transfer her knowledge to improve the experience of her peers. If the program is already established, she can seek ways to improve it and could be selected to lead training as well.
- Another example is the investment banker who sees opportunities where others see obstacles. For example, by using his Spanish language skills and knowledge of Latino culture, he can add value when working on projects in Latin America, an area that the company may not have much exposure to.
- Then there is the investment banker who raises her hand to work

on that tough project that seems mired in challenges, or to work with the difficult managing director who everyone avoids, and is able to successfully "manage up."

- A commitment to excellence and a strong track record of delivering impeccable results can capture the attention of the admissions board, as seen in the investment banker whose work experience is significantly accelerated because he is hand-picked, as a result of having developed a reputation of excellence, to work on high-profile deals with significant responsibility.
- Equally interesting and differentiating is the investment banker who steps up and operates as an associate and manages her peers and new analysts to greater success.

I think you get the point. In each of these instances, the focus is on how the person used her particular situation to achieve something, as opposed to the circumstance itself. The preceding leadership examples are not just for investment bankers but are applicable to candidates from any industry. It is important to figure out the unique experiences you bring to the table and then capitalize on them to differentiate yourself from the pack. The following are a few examples of the types of leadership track records one can have to stand apart in the application process.

CAREER LEADERSHIP EXAMPLES OF SUCCESSFUL MBA CANDIDATES

- Starting a successful medical products business and providing a livelihood to employees
- Initiating and leading the business development that landed the firm a client that increased revenue by 20 percent
- Conducting the entire valuation of the highest profile transaction at firm worth EUR 1.1 billion due to strong analytical track record
- Operating in the role of an associate while still an analyst
- Building a training program, hiring a team of international analysts, and creating a formal analyst culture at firm
- Co-establishing the leveraged finance practice in another country

- Managing the consulting team that introduced and implemented an automated management tool for clients worldwide
- Investing in a struggling employee and helping that person develop into a confident and successful leader
- Creating a utility tool to improve the tracking system of a shipping company
- Managing employees on an assembly line and improving efficiency by 25 percent
- Reducing human product errors from 10 to 4 percent at pharmaceutical firm by introducing a new tracking system and training employees to use it

International applicants may feel that they are at a disadvantage when it comes to extracurricular and college leadership. You can breathe a bit easier knowing that admissions boards are fair and tend to look at each candidate in the context of his life. So, for instance, if you are an international student who was schooled outside of the United States, chances are that your educational institution probably stressed college leadership less than your U.S.-educated counterparts. Variations will also exist in terms of opportunities for extracurricular activities in different countries, and admissions boards take that into account when evaluating candidates. The other thing to note is that international MBA programs also place less emphasis on community and college leadership and more emphasis on your career leadership, work progress, and promotions than their U.S. counterparts.

So with the academic and leadership criteria out of the way, candidates are left to tackle the last of the admissions variables: their uniqueness. Unlike the other two admissions criteria, the uniqueness admissions criterion allows the greatest flexibility for candidates to market themselves in a powerful way.

UNIQUENESS

The third admissions category that MBA admissions boards use in evaluating candidates is the uniqueness of your brand. Business schools are looking for individuals who are a fit with their brand. And nowhere is this more evident than through your personal characteristics and unique perspectives.

This aspect of the evaluation is by far where applicants have the most flexibility and influence. To a large extent, applicants' academic histories have already been formed. Their leadership track records and management experience have been established. The insights that applicants offer into who they are and why they have made the choices they have made to date can land them a coveted admission spot in a top business school.

A good way to illustrate this point is by looking at investment bankers, a group of candidates who are overly represented in the application pool. The following fictional example speaks to the power of the unique perspective applicants bring to their application.

Five hundred investment bankers apply to an MBA program. Ten percent are accepted. That means that 450 investment bankers will be rejected. What is unique and interesting about the fifty who are admitted? It is the personal characteristics and unique perspectives that they offer that often set them apart from their competition. All candidates, regardless of their industry background, should ask themselves how they are different compared with other candidates from similar backgrounds.

The personal characteristics and unique perspectives are different for each candidate. Some applicants are interesting in that they are the first in their family to get a college education. Their initiative, vision, and "bootstrapper" background differentiate them from their competitors who have had a lot more opportunities available to them. For other applicants, it is the innovative nature in which they approach their work that is distinctive. Even candidates with the more unusual examples of having been raised on a farm in Iowa or growing up in Alaska or Chechnya can offer interesting and different viewpoints to the class based on their diverse personal life experiences.

This is an application to business school, so you should highlight the different perspective and experience that you bring in the context of how it can add value to the class discussions and student community. Uniqueness for its own sake isn't what MBA programs are after. Rather, what is attention-worthy is how growing up in Mongolia and working in the United States in the pharmaceutical industry has influenced your desire to return to Mongolia to open the country's first health- and nutrition-focused business (like GNC). The unique vantage point you have of the economic landscape of Mongolia and the subtle cultural obstacles that you will need to overcome are the types of stories that will allow you to present convincing and differentiated essays.

But the reality is that most candidates do not come from exotic backgrounds and do not have profound experiences such as experiencing combat in Syria, Afghanistan, or Libya. If you happen to fall into one of these unusual applicant backgrounds, that's great. Leverage it to show how you will offer a different viewpoint to the MBA program. However, if you find that your background is more along the beaten path, there are tangible things you can do to stand out in the pool as well.

For instance, have you traveled abroad or lived in different countries? You can capitalize on your international experiences, lessons learned, and insights drawn from working in diverse environments. Are you an avid sports person who enjoys challenging yourself? You can describe your experience training for the marathon or the process of climbing Mount Kilimanjaro and the team dynamics of that experience. How did this situation change or shape you? Drawing lessons from these types of experiences and connecting them to what you will bring to the particular business school can be appealing to the admissions board.

If you come from a privileged background, it is important to know how to present your experience. Be careful not to sound spoiled or entitled. Also, when recounting experiences, you are better off choosing things that do not play into a stereotype. For instance, if asked about a mistake you made, you are better off selecting an example that shows personal awareness (realizing you are fallible), instead of one that simply shows bad judgment (crashing your parents' Bentley after a night out).

Here are some additional examples from candidates who have succeeded in branding their way to their dream business schools:

- Raising five siblings without parents allowed a candidate to demonstrate his initiative, management skills, and maturity.
- Health problems led a candidate to develop his knowledge of pharmaceutical industry/health policy issues. As a result, he became passionate about the business side of drug development and transferred this interest into thought leadership at his firm.
- Being raised by entrepreneurial parents gave a candidate exposure to running businesses and an appreciation for the discipline, creativity, and innovation required to start a business in the future.

- Witnessing her mother's domestic abuse fueled one candidate's commitment to empowering women.
- A hunger for a global education led a candidate to leave her home country, attend college in the United States, and convince her firm to send her to Europe to gain international work experience.
- A thick skin developed as a door-to-door sales guy helped a young man develop tenacity, a willingness to take risks, and a "don't accept no for an answer" attitude, leading to a very successful career.
- A hunger for adventure drew a young woman to seek out opportunities to live in emerging countries and to take a risk by accepting a job in Africa at a young company where she was given unprecedented leadership responsibility.
- An entrepreneurial streak and bold ambitions drove a reapplicant to reassess his life experience and pursue an education to create his own start-up.
- A candidate who marched to the beat of his own drum was able to capitalize on the joy of his "global village" group of friends and his willingness to pursue opportunities that most people run from to secure admission at a top program.
- A fashion-forward candidate with a strong quantitative foundation was able to rebrand herself as a fashion/retail candidate and succeed in her reapplication bid.
- A candidate was able to scale a small school into five schools, providing education to individuals in remote villages who would otherwise have remained illiterate.

Successful candidates do not fall within prescribed categories or profiles. Rather, they have understood the admissions criteria and have successfully presented their own unique experiences to show how they will add value to the MBA program. The good news is that most of your competition is not perfect. They have gaps or weaknesses that they have to address as well. It could be weak GMAT or GRE scores or GPA, lack of exemplary leadership, or a vague sense of their brand (what is distinct or unique about them). Investing time in assessing and addressing any gaps that exist in your application will strengthen your MBA candidacy. And in no place is the brand more telling than in the essays. The next chapter explores the MBA application essays in detail and offers insights on how to tackle them effectively.

CHAPTER SIX

Essay Fundamentals

I HAVE COVERED THE THREE main admissions criteria used to evaluate MBA candidates and will now focus on the different components that make up the application. The first is the MBA application essays. MBA admissions boards have historically stressed the power of the essay in the application process. Stanford puts it this way:

> Your Stanford MBA Program essays provide you an opportunity to reflect on your own "truest interests" and "highest aspirations." While the letters of reference are stories about you told by others, these essays enable you to tell your own story… Our goal is to understand what motivates you and how you have become the person you are today… We want a holistic view of you as a person: your values, passions, ideas, experiences, and aspirations.

(Source: Stanford GSB website)

In short, what Stanford and other top business schools want is simply to get to know the candidates really well. Who are you? What is your brand? What do you stand for? The description above is at the heart of what all MBA programs are looking for. The essays afford applicants a wonderful opportunity to share their story, their brand with admissions boards of the leading business schools in the world.

A lot has been written about the importance of the MBA essays, and many applicants have drawn the wrong conclusions about them. The first incorrect assumption that has emerged is the view that the essays are a panacea for an overall weak application. Let me be clear: no amount of brilliant essay writing will wipe away a mediocre academic profile. Rather, the value of application essays is that they can differentiate you from the competition by revealing your salient and interesting brand. They are powerful in getting your application to stand out when your academic and work profile is already relatively strong. The second misconception about the application essays is that they are writing contests. Some applicants have gone as far as hiring editors who craft entire essays in perfectly worded prose in an attempt to game the system and secure admission.

In light of this, admissions boards at top business schools are becoming savvier about pinpointing essays that have been written by the applicant and ones that are overcrafted and polished at the hands of hired advisors. Attempts to game the system will backfire, and applicants who have outsourced their applications end up getting rejected. The appropriate role of an admissions consultant is to help applicants to conduct the deep introspection required to define their brands, review their work, and provide objective feedback. Taking over the writing of an applicant's essays is unethical. I encourage applicants to invest in the soul-searching that is needed to gain clarity around their brands and to then commit to writing the application essays themselves. You've already taken a great first step by getting this book.

The main fallout from overpolished essays is that many leading business schools now question the authorship of essays more than they did in the past. Some have responded by reducing their admissions essays' word counts and number of required essays. Harvard Business School has taken the lead on this by reducing its essays from two to only one and making it optional for applicants. This decision came on the heels of its change the previous year to reduce its essays from four to two 400-word essays. UCLA's Anderson School has dropped its essays to only one. Other MBA programs have followed in Harvard's footsteps, with schools like Stanford reducing its essays to three, Wharton from three to two, and London Business School from six to three. Other programs have focused on reducing their essay word counts, as in the case of Columbia.

What do these changes spell for MBA applicants? Applicants shouldn't be intimidated by them. After all, the fundamental strategy for writing successful MBA essays has not changed. What has changed is the size of the canvas space. If anything, the reduced number and word counts for MBA essays place greater pressure on applicants to be more aware of their personal brand; since applicants have to do more in less space, there is little room to ramble or present an incoherent brand message. I'll emphasize the fundamentals of incorporating personal branding into your essays. Do keep in mind that my focus remains on equipping applicants with strategic tools to ace their MBA essays and is less about the technical nuts and bolts of essay writing. Applicants who are struggling with the mechanics of essay writing will need to look to other resources that focus on essay-writing techniques, such as Paul Bodine's books.

Business schools will likely continue to change their essay requirements and topics each year, and applicants will have zero control over this. Therefore this book doesn't focus on specific essay prompts, which will likely not be relevant in a few months. Rather, my goal is to get applicants to become more aware of how to approach any essay question that they face in a way that allows them to introduce their key brand messages into their story and win the heart of the admissions board.

I'll remind you that, unlike any other part of the application, the essays are the one area where candidates have the most control in representing themselves. After all, undergraduate grades are already predetermined, and there is a limit to how much a GMAT or GRE score can improve if you are not a great test-taker. With the exception of in-person or video interviews, the essays are the best way for candidates to reveal their brand. Essays are blank canvases that provide candidates with an incredible opportunity to create a Picasso painting. Through my admissions experiences at Harvard and Carnegie Mellon, I have observed numerous instances where one candidate's application stands apart from others with identical backgrounds based simply on the treatment of the essay topics and the type of information the essays reveal about the candidate's brand. These successful candidates understand that presenting their experiences in the form of stories allows them to paint a vibrant picture of themselves, as opposed to simply stating facts in a dry way.

Applicants to business school must be comfortable going into depth when describing who they are and what matters to them. It is impossible to submit a powerful application without revealing personal aspects of who you are. That said, applicants need to be wise about the personal stories they share with the admissions board. Not all personal experiences are appropriate to discuss in your application. A good litmus test to determine whether a subject is worth including in your story is to ask yourself what it reveals about you as a future business leader. Helping to raise your five siblings shows maturity and "management" ability. But you would be hard-pressed to make a convincing case that overcoming a rough breakup with your first love reveals something meaningful about your leadership. The essays for business school are a test of an applicant's judgment. Make sure that whatever personal insights and examples you provide do not raise red flags about you. A sure way to guarantee that your application gets dinged is by exhibiting poor judgment and choosing the wrong topics.

Unlike other graduate programs where the standardized scores drive the admission outcome, to a large extent, business school essays can significantly influence the admission decision.

MBA ESSAY OVERVIEW

Time is a major factor in presenting a winning application, so start early. Allocate enough time to tackle each essay thoroughly. While some applicants can complete multiple applications in just two months (I've even had a client submit as many as five in less time), to be on the safe side, you should give yourself at least four months to complete two to four applications. You can also stagger your applications by submitting some in the first round and the remaining ones in the next round. With admission to top schools becoming even more competitive, candidates are applying to a greater number of programs to increase their chances of gaining admission to at least one school. A glance at the application data published by Poets & Quants reveals just how competitive it is to secure admission at some of the super selective programs in the United States.

HOW THE CLASS OF 2015 COMPARES AT STANFORD, HARVARD, & WHARTON			
Criteria	Stanford	Harvard	Wharton
Applications for Class of 2015	7,108	9,315	6,036
Class Size	406	941	845
Percent Admitted	6.8%	12%	21%*
Yield	86%*	90%	65%*

Women	36%	41%	42%
International	41%	35%	35%
Countries Represented	54	60	64
U.S. Minorities	21%	25%	30%
GMAT Average	732	NA	725
GMAT Median	NA	730	NA
GMAT Range	550–790	550–780	630–790
Consulting Background	20%	19%	20%
Private Equity/Venture Capital	17%	16%	12%
Financial Services	10%	14%	27%
High Tech/Communications	16%	11%	6%
Consumer Products	11%	7%	10%**
Government/Military/Nonprofit	13%	12%	11%
Industrial/Manufacturing	3%	7%	NA
Health Care/Biotech	5%	6%	NA***
Energy/Extractive Minerals	5%	4%	NA****

(Source: Poets & Quants website; Class of 2015 profile published by Stanford GSB)

Notes: *Estimate by Poets & Quants

**Wharton numbers include retail, health care, and energy

***Wharton includes health care in the consumer products category

****Wharton includes energy in the consumer products category

Getting started on the essays can be daunting for many applicants. So take a deep breath and exhale. The MBA admissions board does not expect you to write like a Pulitzer Prize–winning journalist. You are not tested on how creative or excellent a writer you are. The main emphasis is on how substantive your leadership impact and potential are, whether you have taken advantage of opportunities available to you, and your awareness of the drivers behind your personal and professional decisions and successes.

That said, you should not present a shoddy essay full of grammar and spelling mistakes. Make sure that you revise your essays as many times as needed to produce well-written finished products. It is generally a good idea to have someone you know who is a great writer—for instance, an English major or an admissions consultant—read through your essays to catch any writing errors.

Before tackling the MBA essays, you should go through a brand audit to identify the most compelling parts of your story. You should also brainstorm to organize your experiences. Successful essays require a fair share of introspection. We encourage applicants to adopt a brainstorming model we refer to as SOARS (Situation, Obstacle, Action, Results, and So What). Investing time in framing your questions in this format will allow you to tease apart your story in a coherent and tangible way, making it possible for you to focus on the more compelling examples in your story. Once you have completed the SOARS model, you will be ready to begin writing the essays. Always do an outline before tackling an essay. An outline is important because you can more effectively focus on the important parts of the experience. When writing an outline, you should always aim to flesh out these key points:

1. What is the situation you wish to discuss?
2. What was challenging, difficult, or unusual about it that is worth mentioning?
3. What steps did you take to address or resolve the issue? How did you do it? What role did you play?
4. What was the outcome of your involvement? Why did you make the decisions you made or take the actions you took? It is important to stress specifics of the result. If it is quantifiable, then don't fail to show the before-and-after outcome you were able to create as a result of your involvement.
5. So what? Be clear on why anyone reading the story should care about it. What was meaningful about this experience? What did you learn about yourself? Why does it matter to you? This is where you reveal your insights and self-awareness to the MBA admissions board.

Candidates to business school are not limited to following this outline. If another process works for you to effectively outline your essays, then that's great and you should use it. What's important is that you take the time to assess whether the story you have selected is compelling enough to feature in your application. Using the SOARS model to brainstorm essay topics will quickly reveal to you whether the story is strong enough or whether it lacks substance. The other point I wish to make about using the SOARS outline for your essays is that you are not limited to using it chronologically. It's a tool that helps you with brainstorming but should not become confining. You can vary the sequence of the story to support whatever creative approach you wish to pursue.

You can see from the SOARS model below how to think through your brainstorming and fill out the form. Take a few minutes to complete it. Feel free to come back to it to refine the story as different ideas come to you.

EXPARTUS SOARS MODEL				
Situation	**Obstacle**	**Action**	**Results**	**So What?**
Student investment fund lost 50 percent of its value; dysfunctional leadership between fund coheads.	Tough financial market making it challenging to turn around the poor investment portfolio; fund leaders quit, leaving a leadership vacuum.	I stepped in, despite limited portfolio experience, created an investment strategy that drove our investment decisions for the next six months.	The fund outperformed the leading index; we recovered all the losses; I built a team to ensure strong succession plan.	This experience confirmed my passion for investing. I also learned a lot about how to adapt to uncertainty and how to trust my instinct better to get people behind the goal at hand.

CHARACTERISTICS OF WINNING ESSAYS

Now that we've established a process to outline the essays, let's review what makes a winning essay. While there isn't a formula to gain admission to business school, there are certainly variables or ingredients that distinguish applications that are admitted from those that are rejected. I will examine those variables closely in the next section.

The PGII Factor

A common question from MBA candidates is, "What sets apart winning essays from bland and ineffective ones?" Having evaluated thousands of MBA essays at Harvard, at Carnegie Mellon, and through my consulting practice, I have identified the fundamental ingredients that successful essays embody. These winning essays have what I call the PGII Factor. They include:

1. Passion
2. Guts
3. Impact
4. Insight

Essay questions that embody these four ingredients create a solid and powerful backdrop from which the MBA admissions board can assess you. Let's take a closer look at each ingredient.

1. Passion

As you are preparing for your essays, ask yourself whether you have clearly identified your passion. Take a few minutes to complete the passion survey from the earlier chapter. Keep in mind that if your essays do not convey your passion, there is a good chance that they will be bland and boring, thus increasing the likelihood that they will put the MBA admissions board to sleep. Do you simply do your job, or do you bring great enthusiasm and energy to everything you do, both at work and beyond? Your attitude reflects your passion. Think about what difference you have made in your company, in your organizations, in your community. Your essay has to convey your passion for what you do (whether in your work, in your personal life, or in your community); your long-term goals have to connect with what you say matters to you. Connecting these pieces to why you are pursuing an MBA is a very important part of the application process.

2. Guts

You can't talk about winning essays without seeing clear evidence of guts and courage to take personal and professional risks. Having guts is not about unplanned, haphazard stunts. MBA admissions boards are an extremely savvy bunch and can see through gimmicks masked to appear like courage and risk taking.

Take two people (Bob and Don) who apply to business school. Both of them have successful careers in the finance industry, and their academic backgrounds are equally strong. Bob has been with the same finance firm for five years. His essay has few examples that showcase him stepping up and having a significant impact beyond what a typical associate does at the firm. Can you imagine how many "Bobs" are in the applicant pool? The Bobs of the applicant pool have made it easy for the MBA admissions board to deny them admission.

Contrast this with Don, who has chosen to leave his firm to start a real estate company, which is his passion. Even if Don's business folds, the MBA admissions board isn't as focused on the failure of the business as they are in what motivated Don to leave a safe job to start a business and the lessons he learned through the process. The board is also interested in learning the impact Don's business had on others. Most importantly, the admissions board wants to learn how his entrepreneurial venture has developed his leadership and managerial potential. His maturity and growth will very well set him apart from other talented candidates vying for a spot in the competitive admissions pool.

I am not advocating that the only way to show guts is through an entrepreneurial endeavor. If you are an entrepreneur, by all means, go for it. However, for the majority of applicants, you can demonstrate your risk taking within your firm by stepping up and going above and beyond your prescribed role. For instance, as a financial analyst, you may realize that your firm falls short in its training and professional development of new analysts, so you volunteer to start an analyst training and mentoring program (if none exists) or to overhaul the existing one. If you are in equity research and have a lean group, you could raise your hand to cover more industries above and beyond what is expected of you. Perhaps you are in the strategy group at your firm, you disagree with the firm's plan to shut down a business unit, and you see it as a missed opportunity. So you take the initiative to conduct a thorough analysis and identify how a counter-approach can add value to your firm. You have the guts to pitch an alternative plan, present data to back up your thoughts, and deliver a convincing argument to your senior management. Behind the scenes, you build bridges and get key people to champion the idea. Your idea not to shut down the group is accepted. The outcome? The group ends up being a major money-maker for your firm.

What if you are an engineer? You could demonstrate your guts by volunteering to lead a system improvement project that involves other departments. Or you could initiate a new safety mechanism that improves the way an assembly line operates. Volunteering to be on cross-functional teams is another good way to showcase your willingness to take a risk by stepping out of your professional comfort zone.

Another way candidates can show guts is by being willing to explore a different business environment. The American consultant who opts for an international project in Singapore will get a broadened perspective that can make him more competitive when it comes time to apply to business school. I know a candidate working in the United States who pushed to be transferred to a European country to work because she knew it would push her outside her comfort level. The same applies to an international candidate living in India who through perseverance secures a job in Europe and is able to gain some global experience, which makes him a more attractive candidate when he applies to INSEAD. I'm not advocating that everyone jump ship for an international assignment; this is an option for applicants for whom such a move is in line with their brand and goals.

Even a simple step of, for example, leaving a lucrative consulting career to become a soccer coach at your alma mater can reflect a gutsy move on your part. But you have to show how this move fits into your longer-term goal. And of course, it also has to fit with your passion for athletics. If your long-term goal is to work for a company like Nike or the U.S. Soccer Federation on the business side, you can make a compelling case for the tie-in with sports and your career move to coaching. You should be careful, however, if you are simply making a move to impress the MBA admissions board. In the event that the admission doesn't pan out, you have to be comfortable living with your decision. So whatever decision you make, be sure to choose roles that you are passionate about and that fit with your long-term goals.

Demonstrating guts is about:

- Raising your hand to take on additional responsibility
- Seizing an opportunity to effect change
- Having the confidence to speak up and sell your ideas
- Taking a path that is untried and different

3. Impact

A major mistake MBA candidates make with their essays is failing to quantify their impact. Impact simply comes down to your track record. What was your specific role in bringing about change or improving a process or product? Note that impact isn't limited to organizations; it also expands to people—taking the intern trying to navigate a large bureaucratic organization under your wing, helping the co-worker who is having a tough time grasping how to read and interpret balance sheets, mentoring the consultant whom everyone views as the weakest link on the engagement team and who is about to quit as a result of his frustrations. These are all individuals that many of us have encountered at some point in our careers. The question is what role we chose to play: Did we engage someone and make a difference to improve his situation when we saw him struggling, or did we simply focus on our own individual success? These types of experiences make for very interesting essays.

The opposite mistake that candidates make related to impact is exaggerating their role. MBA admissions boards can deduce when the truth is being stretched, and this is a major turnoff that will adversely affect your admission outcome. So tell the story with specific details of your involvement, but shy away from stretching your account in attempts to make your essay sound impressive.

4. Insight

The law of writing winning essays in the application process is "show, don't tell." It's not enough to tell the MBA admissions board how great your accomplishments are; you must show them how you have accomplished something and what you learned from the experience. Awareness is king in the admissions process. What you have done is important, but equally important is why you have done the things you have done and how you do what you do that is unique to you.

Be committed to showing the MBA admissions board why the things you have done matter to you. Simply stating that you have leadership and management abilities is not enough. What kind of leader are you? What is your managerial style, and how do you rely on it to bring out the best in the people you lead? Are you a leader who leads in front? Perhaps you are charismatic in your leadership style. Are you more of a "quiet" leader who leads from behind? You need to have a clear sense of your style and have stories to back it up and reinforce your point. It is your self-awareness that sets you apart from all the other applicants who, at a first glance, have the same background.

The Power of the Six Cs

Another essay tool that will empower you to write strong essays is the Six C essay attributes. In addition to the PGII Factor, successful essays tend to be:

- Captivating
- Credible
- Compelling
- Consistent
- Clear
- Concise

When writing your essay, you should always ensure that your essays embody these six characteristics.

Captivating

The essays must capture the attention of the admissions board. It is said that it takes thirty seconds to make an impression (good or bad), and once someone makes up their mind about you, it takes much more time and effort to reverse that impression. The MBA application should be approached from this mind-set as well. The application as a whole and the essays in particular are your opportunity to say, "Hi, my name is Vanessa, and you need to pay close attention to my story." A captivating essay will make the MBA admissions board sit up and remember your story many applications later.

Remember that the MBA admissions board has several thousand essays to read and limited time to evaluate them. So your essay should be anything but bland. The last thing you want is to put the board members to sleep when they read your essays. Let your personality come through. Don't be afraid to take some risks (tempered with judgment) by allowing the different aspects of your personality (brand) to come through. You want the MBA admissions board to identify with you when they read your application. So, simply, the essays need to be engaging, interesting, and personable.

While captivating essays are important, you have to also be honest. There is no room to stretch the truth in an attempt to be interesting. Fabricated stories are grounds for automatic rejection. Given the climate of corporate malfeasance and cases of falsified applications, MBA admissions boards are extremely sensitive to honesty and authenticity.

Credible

Ask yourself whether your story is believable. Given your background, is it reasonable to expect that you will achieve what you outline as your career goals? Avoid grandiose and unrealistic goals. Essays need to maintain a balance: while your vision has to be big enough to warrant an MBA, it still has to be achievable. For instance, saying that you will be the Donald Trump of Africa but having little evidence of real estate passion will leave the MBA admissions board skeptical of your ambitions.

Some career changers fail the credibility test by picking future careers that are a big leap from their current role. If you are an information technology (IT) manager, you will have a tough time convincing an admissions board that you will become a brand manager at Procter & Gamble. This doesn't mean that you can't make major career changes after you graduate from business school. In fact, most graduates of MBA programs are career changers. The challenge is that, at the application stage, you have to show that your goals are realistic. If you select a new career you wish to pursue, make sure you can show that there are some things connecting it to your background, interests, and experiences, to make it believable.

Compelling

Your essay needs to convey a compelling rationale for why you want an MBA. You need to be convincing. What is your long-term vision or goal, and is the MBA necessary to achieve it? Be sure that you have thoroughly examined why you want the MBA and how the degree will help you succeed in your career. If your career ambition is simply a small incremental step, it is unlikely that the MBA admissions board will give you a spot to go into a middle management role when there are candidates who are looking to use the MBA to have transformative impact and change.

Consistent

Essays that are consistent reinforce the brand of the candidate. In the chapter on selling your personal brand, I discussed the importance of doing a brand audit and identifying the brand themes, which are the basis for the essays. By identifying key brand themes to your story, you can write essays that build on each other in a way that reinforces your overall brand message. This is an area where applicants err: they write essays without a unifying story (theme) behind them. The unfortunate outcome is that their application is unmemorable, making it challenging for the MBA admissions board to advocate for their candidacy.

Clear

With limited time, admissions boards need to be able to ascertain the main thrust of each applicant's story. Essays that lack clarity are problematic because the admissions board members will be unable to extricate the brand message of the candidate. To ensure that your essay is clear, make sure you address the who, what, when, how, why, and so what (impact). By getting to the point and using this format, you can eliminate unnecessary aspects of the story, enabling you to present a clear picture of who you are in your essays. When the board reads your essays, who you are should jump off the pages. Also, you should ensure that you have answered the question being asked in the most straightforward and direct way possible. A case in point is the question about describing your defining leadership experience and addressing your strengths and weaknesses. Many candidates address the first part of the question and ignore the second part about their strengths and weaknesses (especially the latter). Make sure you have answered all the questions fully, and write with as many specific examples as possible to ensure clarity of your story.

Concise

The issue of conciseness is related to clarity. Get to the point quickly so the reader can get a clear message of your story. I'm often asked whether the MBA admissions board cares about word count and how far one can deviate from the limits. A majority of MBA programs have reduced their word limits, and some have gone as far as reducing the number of actual essays that applicants have to complete. This is a clear signal that schools are interested in receiving less information from applicants, not more. My advice is to always adhere to the word or page limits. At a basic level, it is a sign of your ability to follow instructions. At a deeper level, it reflects your sense of equity. (Why should you have an edge over candidates who followed the instructions and stayed within the prescribed limit?) In my experience, in most cases, less is more. Rambling, wordy essays rarely engender positive feelings from the overworked admissions board members. This is why it is important to start essays using an outline as opposed to "a brain dump," where you start off writing anything and everything that comes to mind.

And of course, I can't stress enough the importance of revision. I knew an applicant who submitted twenty-plus pages for his first essay to Stanford. Suffice it to say, he didn't gain admission. Extra essays and supplemental documents such as newspaper articles, CDs, and portfolios are inappropriate unless the school specifically requests them. Be sure to use the Six C essay attributes and the PGII Factor to assess the quality of your essays and ensure that you include the information that matters.

ESSAY TYPES AND STRATEGIES TO TACKLE THEM

In this next section, I address the various types of essays covered in the MBA application and provide suggestions on how to deal with them. I have also included some actual examples of essays used by applicants. I recognize that some essay topics may overlap across multiple categories, but for the purpose of this book, I have broken the essays into four groups.

The four essay categories are:

1.   Career essays
2.   Leadership and impact essays
3.   "Who you are" essays
4.   Miscellaneous essays

The Career Essay

MBA programs vary in terms of their view of the career essay question. Some schools, like HBS, have moved away from asking applicants essay questions about their career plans and goals while schools like INSEAD, Tuck, Stanford, and many others still require these types of essays. Some of the questions ask about your standard short-term and long-term career goals and why you've chosen that school's MBA program. Others have added another dimension to the question by asking about your plan B if your original plans fail.

Here is an example of a career essay question with tips on how to tackle it. The Cambridge Judge Business School asks applicants to answer the following question:

> **What are your short- and long-term career objectives? What skills/characteristics do you already have that will help you to achieve them? What do you hope to gain from the degree and how do you feel it will help you achieve the career objectives you have? (Please do not exceed 500 words.)**

The Judge School career essay is more or less the traditional career essay question that you will face from many of the top business schools. It has several questions within one prompt. Applicants should read the question carefully before attempting to answer it to ensure that they address all the questions being asked. Let's break down the Judge career essay question to get a better sense of how we might approach this.

Part 1: What are your short- and long-term career objectives?

The best approach to this essay is to be very detailed as you outline a clear plan of what you wish to accomplish in the short term *and* the long term. You have 500 words for this entire essay, so there is room to build your case. Start by outlining your short-term goal. You want to choose a short-term goal that is realistic. Saying you plan to start a $100 million hedge fund straight out of business school will be a tall order for most applicants. At the same time, you don't want short-term goals that are viewed as too small. Saying you plan to return to your old job at the same level will be viewed negatively by the admissions board. Schools want to admit people who they believe their program will help leapfrog to the next level.

Admissions boards also want to know that your goals make sense. There has to be a strong connection between your short-term and long-term objectives. An investment banker analyst who plans to return to banking as an associate in the short term and to eventually become a managing director at a bank presents a logical career path that will not be questioned. You can also go from investment banker associate to starting a financial advisory firm in the long term. Other career plans can include the pre-MBA banker/consultant who has worked as a private equity (PE) associate and now plans to return to PE. For those with this interest, there are a variety of long-term career paths that they can take after their MBA, including becoming a partner of a PE fund or running a portfolio company. The key is to make sure that your career claim is logical.

Part 2: What skills/characteristics do you already have that will help you to achieve them?

This is where a lot of applicants drop the ball. Don't assume that the admissions board will connect the dots for you. You have to explain the key and relevant skill sets that you have established both from professional settings and from your extracurricular involvements that will prepare you for the career you intend to pursue. Let me continue with the example of an investment banker who wants to return to banking. For this former banker, her skill set will include strong analytical and quantitative skills, ability to work in a fast-paced environment, and strong intellectual horsepower; these are examples of skills she developed during her early days as an analyst, and they will be helpful to her when moving up the ranks in banking. If you wanted to change your location, for instance, then highlighting your language abilities for this foreign region or the ideal experience you wish to have there will help you answer this question effectively.

Applicants who want to make a career change have to be even more careful to convey the relevant skill set that they will draw on to transition into the new position. A computer engineer who wants to transition away from the narrow technical role of being a product developer to become a general manager with profit and loss responsibility has to highlight the skills that have enabled her to succeed to date, like creativity, analytical and quantitative aptitude, project management experience, and technical prowess. But she shouldn't stop there. She also needs to discuss her management experience—perhaps if she had a volunteer role as the director of the board of a nonprofit organization, for example. Even her character traits, such as being ambitious and driven, could be referenced. Beyond describing the skills and characteristics that she will bring, she can also address the additional business skills that she lacks (for example, large team management, people development, budget forecasting, finance, marketing, etc.) and how the MBA will help her to achieve her career plans of becoming a better general manager in the future. This leads me to the last part of the Judge career essay question.

Part 3: What do you hope to gain from the degree and how do you feel it will help you achieve the career objectives you have?

To answer this last part of the Judge career essay question, you need to have done your homework on the school. Let's say you want to become an entrepreneur after business school. You can highlight Cambridge University's location in one of the hottest start-up regions in the United Kingdom. You can also discuss wanting to fine-tune your business idea while you are a student at Judge and then describe how you will take advantage of the program's individual project. Or you may want to mention how the school's unprecedented access to entrepreneurs through its weekly Tuesday Enterprise lectures will help you sharpen your business ideas. You can go on to highlight the school's emphasis on real-world learning and how you look forward to participating in practical business training through its Global Consulting and Cambridge Venture projects.

By showcasing the level of detailed knowledge that you have about the school and articulating how it will help you develop your entrepreneurial skills, you will convey to the school that you are a good fit for it and that you will likely be able to execute on your career goals.

The Judge program isn't the only school requiring applicants to address their career objectives. Duke's Fuqua MBA program also has a career essay. I've chosen Duke's MBA career example to illustrate the differences among schools. Take a closer look at how Fuqua words its question:

Answer all 3 questions. For each short answer question, respond in 250 characters only (the equivalent of about 50 words).

1. **What are your short-term goals, post-MBA?**
2. **What are your long-term goals?**
3. **Life is full of uncertainties, and plans and circumstances can change. As a result, navigating a career requires you to be adaptable. Should the short-term goals that you provided above not materialize, what alternative directions have you considered?**

Unlike Judge, which gives applicants 500 words to address their career goals, Fuqua's essay has only 150 words. The condensed word count poses some challenges for applicants who are forced to write in a tweet-sized manner to achieve this objective. Fuqua's career essay has three parts. The first two are your "usual-suspect" questions—what are your short-term and long-term post-MBA goals—and the third is about how you would handle uncertainty, if your goals do not come to fruition.

To tackle Fuqua's career essay successfully, you must think carefully about each word you write and ensure that it is necessary to convey your goal to the admissions board. The school's fifty-word limit for each of the three parts of the career essay forces applicants to zero in on the most important factors driving their goals.

Part 1: What are your short-term goals, post-MBA?

Here is an example of how you can answer Fuqua's short-term career question:

I plan to become a brand manager for a consumer packaged goods company. This will help me understand the important role marketing plays in growing businesses. Using my ABC Company experience of extracting consumer insights through research, I will be able to respond quickly to changing consumer demands and create winning solutions.

Part 2: What are your long-term goals?

The same brevity with which you tackled the above short-term goal will be required when tackling your long-term goals. State exactly what your long-term career goals are and get to the point immediately. For example:

Long term, I aspire to become the CEO of my family business, ABC Insurance. As one of the largest insurance companies in my country, ABC Insurance is looking into expanding to retail banking, telecommunications, and health care. My ambition is to turn our business into a global diversified company that creates valuable products for its consumers.

You get the point. There isn't an exact answer. It comes down to stating what you are genuinely interested in and making a case for that vision based on your background, experiences, and interests.

Part 3: Life is full of uncertainties, and plans and circumstances can change. As a result, navigating a career requires you to be adaptable. Should the short-term goals that you provided above not materialize, what alternative directions have you considered?

The third part of Fuqua's career question has a twist. Applicants are asked to demonstrate that they are flexible and have a backup plan should the MBA plans fall through. With an economy that is still recovering, it is important that applicants maintain a realistic view of career opportunities, and evidence of this flexibility can come through in their responses to questions about how they deal with uncertainty and their willingness to shift gears and go with an alternative plan. So following up on the above example, you can say something like:

> *Should my goal to become a brand manager of a CPG company not come through, I will pursue an opportunity to work in a rotational program for a multinational company to develop thorough understanding of different business units like finance, marketing, and operations to become a better general manager.*

Since career essays will vary from school to school, it is important not to cut and paste your essay and recycle it for another school's career essay. It would be obvious to the MBA admissions board at Judge, for instance, if you've answered their career essay with the one you wrote for Fuqua. I'm not advocating writing five separate career essays for your five applications. But it is important to pay attention to how the question is worded, and even when you use original content from a previous application, take the time to revise the content to ensure that it answers the specific question being asked.

One of the major things MBA admissions boards also look for in career essays is whether applicants have thought through their career goals and the steps they will need to take to achieve them. Candidates need to be very specific in their career essays. There is little room for vague and broad career objectives. Generic career goals only signal to admissions boards either that you are unsure about what you want to do or that you have not done enough research on the professed career path. In either case, you make it easy for the MBA admissions board to discount your application. So be as specific as you can. A statement such as, "I will become a general manager after business school" is too vague. But saying, "I wish to join a rotational leadership program in an apparel company like Gap after business school, and in the long term, I plan to become the president of a retail company in South America" is a very specific and clear career goal.

Furthermore, all candidates need to make a strong case for why a particular MBA program is the best fit for them, given the set of experiences they have had to date. This is where many candidates fail. Take the time to understand the nuanced differentiation or brand of each MBA program before tailoring your rationale for an MBA accordingly. Campus visits, sitting in on classes, and speaking with alumni and current students will help you zero in on exactly why a particular MBA program is a fit for you. I know a candidate who had applied to multiple schools and visited the programs only after gaining admission. To her horror, she realized she didn't fit in at the programs where she was admitted. She was forced to decline her admission offer and postponed her MBA dreams for the following year.

Finally, no career essay will be complete without showing that you have been successful to date in your present career. The idea is that if you have been extraordinarily successful where you work currently, there is a good chance you will be successful in a new career. One of the biggest problems candidates face in the application process is making the case that they will be successful in a vibrant career after business school when they have worked at a few mundane jobs and have lackluster track records. Should you find yourself in a situation like this, it is critical to hold off on applying to business school and focus on rebranding yourself to build a more compelling professional track record. Doing so will reduce the likelihood that your application will be rejected!

MBA programs that require career essays pay particular attention to them, making this essay vital to your application. Although all the essays are important, I encourage you to devote extra time to making sure your career essay is spot on. That said, keep your audience—the MBA admissions board—in mind as you write. There are a few questions that they will be looking to answer as they're reading your career essay:

1. Is your career goal realistic and achievable?
2. What skills do you have, and do they fit with your professed goals?
3. Are you rigid about your goals or are you resourceful and adaptable if your plans don't pan out?
4. Is your career on an upward trajectory, where you are taking on more responsibility and creating more impact, or has it stalled?
5. What are your career decisions, what steps have you taken, and is there a logical connection between where you are currently and where you desire to go?
6. Are you a good fit for the program?

7.   What will you contribute to the program?

8.   Do you have good interpersonal and team skills that will enable you to thrive in the program?

9.   Are your career ambitions transformative, and will an MBA help you achieve your goals?

10.   Does getting the MBA now make sense? Did you leave applying to business school too late, or are you applying too early and need more work experience?

Answers to these questions will help the MBA admissions board determine whether to admit or reject the candidate. Let's review an actual career essay and examine what makes it effective. There isn't a set formula for writing any of the business school essays, and this applies to the career essay as well. Here are career essays from applicants to INSEAD Business School to give you a sense of what good career essays look like.

Sample Career Essay

Briefly summarize your current (or most recent) job, including the nature of work, major responsibilities, and, where relevant, employees under your supervision, size of budget, clients/products, and results achieved. (250 words)

As the lead investment strategist, reporting directly to the chief investment officer, my responsibility is to maximize return for every unit of risk taken in investing the $2 billion pension assets. To achieve this goal, I develop short-term, medium-term, and long-term portfolio strategies, and I assist the portfolio managers to align the portfolios with these strategies. I interface with investment bankers to develop investment instruments that do not flout the strict ABC Investments* pension investment regulations for pension funds, and I am responsible for defending every single investment at the management investment committee meetings.

*Names of persons and organizations have been changed.

Eight months after joining my firm, I restructured the bond portfolio that had generated sub-inflation returns that year. The impact of this restructuring came through within six months as the bond portfolio realized profits of more than $35 million, generating returns in excess of inflation.

There had been a raging battle for the disposal of the equity portfolio that was valued at $21 million before I was hired. I was able to garner the support of the staff of the investment department, and we worked hard toward retaining the portfolio because we believed it was critical for the long-term performance of the fund. Fifteen months after I was hired, I had the opportunity to make a presentation to the board of directors for the first time. Not only was I able to convince them to retain the equity portfolio, but I also convinced them to raise the exposure by more than 560 percent to $140 million.

Assessment

This essay highlights several achievements that are significant and will catch the attention of the admissions board. The applicant does a good job of outlining his responsibilities—maximizing returns for the large pension fund that he is charged with helping to manage. He comes across as a team player and is quick to give credit to his team—"I was able to garner the support of the staff of the investment department, and we worked hard toward retaining the portfolio..." He could have shed more light on how he did this, but he probably found the tight word limit to be a bit of a challenge.

Sample Career Essay

Please give a full description of your career since graduating from university. If you were to remain with your present employer, what would be your next step in terms of position? (250 words)

Nine months after graduating from university, I secured a twelve-month medical internship at the ABC University* Teaching Hospital.

ABC University Teaching Hospital is the number one teaching hospital in the region, and there is significant delay before qualified doctors are able to secure one of the limited spots in the hospital. After the internship period, I went on the twelve-month mandatory military medical service. In order to get a permanent license to practice as a doctor, or to be eligible for any kind of job in the country, the twenty-four months of internship and military service had to be completed.

After the military service, I switched careers to finance on my journey to fulfilling my dreams. I started my finance career at XLA Brokerage Firm*, the second largest investment bank in my country, as an equity analyst. I was promoted after six months to the role of investment analyst at the peak of the market meltdown. I received another promotion after six months to the position of senior portfolio manager in charge of a $35 million portfolio. I left XLA Brokerage Firm for ABC Firm,* the largest pension fund administrator in my country, where I was given the position of senior research analyst. I was promoted to lead investment strategist after fifteen months. If I remained with ABC firm, I would be promoted to the position of chief investment officer.

*Names of persons and organizations have been changed.

Assessment

The writer does a good job describing his career since graduation. One thing he could have done differently is to cut down on the first paragraph a bit and introduce a sentence that sets the tone about the fact that he is a career changer who switched from medicine to investment management. Because admissions board members have too little time, setting up the essay or providing a road map for them, instead of launching into the story and then having them connect the pieces based on the facts shared, can be more effective.

TIPS ON HANDLING CAREER ESSAYS

- Answer the question directly. State exactly what your goals/vision are up front. Then help the reader to understand why you have these aspirations.

- Avoid regurgitating your résumé. Instead of mainly highlighting what you have done, take the time to explain why you made the decisions you made, the key achievements, and how the experiences have brought you closer to your career ambitions.
- Be very specific when stating your career goals. If there is a company you have identified that fits your goals, highlight it.
- Provide evidence to support your career goals. Make sure your work experience and life in general backs up your career goals.
- Of all the MBA essays, this is the one that least lends itself to creativity.
- Demonstrate your knowledge of the industry, including its growth, opportunities, and challenges, and how you plan to make a contribution.
- Make it clear why you need the MBA: show how the goal you have is significant, requiring an MBA to get there.
- Address why each particular MBA program is the right fit for you. Be very specific and avoid generalities.
- Balance talking about what you will get from the program with what you will contribute to it.

Some Recent Career Essay Questions

Columbia GSB: Short Answer Question: What is your immediate post-MBA professional goal? (100 characters maximum)

India School of Business: How does the ISB Post-Graduate Programme tie in with your career goals? (300 words maximum)

Kellogg: Imagine yourself at your Kellogg graduation. What career will you be preparing to enter, and how have the MBA and Kellogg helped you get there? (Please answer in terms of your program choice: One-Year, Two-Year, MMM, JD-MBA) (500 word limit)

Haas: a) What are your post-MBA short-term and long-term career goals? How have your professional experiences

prepared you to achieve these goals? b) How will an MBA from Haas help you achieve these goals? (750 word maximum for 4a and 4b)

Wharton: What do you aspire to achieve, personally and professionally, through the Wharton MBA? (500 words)

Tuck: Why is an MBA a critical next step toward your short- and long-term career goals? Why is Tuck the best MBA fit for you and your goals, and why are you the best fit for Tuck? (500 words)

Rotman: Discuss your personal and professional development over the past five years and describe how these changes have led you to choose to do your MBA at this time. What are your career goals and how will a Rotman MBA help you to achieve them?

The Impact and Leadership Essay

You will be hard-pressed to complete an MBA application without addressing your professional impact. There are specific essays that ask you to describe your impact. Examples of such essays include the following:

- What are your greatest accomplishments, and what did you learn from these experiences?
- Describe an impact you had on a person, team, or organization.
- When did you tackle a situation that was problematic, and how did you turn things around?
- When have you used innovation to solve a problem?

Earlier in this book, I discussed the ingredients of successful essays: passion, guts, impact, and insight. Besides the specific impact essays that you will face in the application process, you should always aim to describe the impact you have had in different situations in all your essays (whenever applicable).

Don't lose sight of the fact that admissions boards are looking for leaders—applicants who have stepped up and taken on additional responsibility or volunteered to improve something that wasn't working effectively. The leadership story doesn't always have to be within the professional context. Applicants should feel free to highlight their leadership record beyond the work setting if they have evidence of that outside of work.

Sample Impact and Leadership Essay

Describe what you believe to be your two most substantial accomplishments to date (if possible, specify one personal and one professional), explaining why you view them as such. (400 words)

I lost my father to chronic kidney disease six months before the end of my medical internship. The hospital gave me the honor of treating him without payment for the two months that he was admitted. After he died, the hospital deducted the accumulated bill from my salary until I finished the internship program. The leftover was just enough to take care of my retired mother and two kid sisters who were still in university. There was a gap of four months between the end of the internship program and the paramilitary medical service. I secured a job within that period with a small hospital that paid me a token salary. This was barely enough to take care of my family. I had to be creative to augment my earnings at this point; I did typesetting and PowerPoint development for final-year medical students who were doing their theses at that time. These two jobs tided me over for the four months until the paramilitary service commenced. This experience is valuable to me because on the day my father died, I promised my sisters, amid tears, that though our father was gone, I would provide for them. I was able to fulfill my promise despite the difficulties, and I am proud that both of them have graduated from university.

My most substantial professional accomplishment was my ability to switch careers from medicine to finance effortlessly. I spent ten years in university to study a six-year course because of recurrent university lecturers' strikes over wages and other working conditions. After spending six years in university only to discover that I still had more years to go, I resolved to graduate with another marketable skill apart from medicine. I took up equity research as a hobby because I was fascinated by the way companies raised funds for their operations and how market prices reflected public companies' performances. I got so involved in the hobby that I became the resident expert on stocks during my internship training, and I started an investment club just before my paramilitary service. Before the end of the service, I had two letters of employment: one as a medical officer and the other as an equity analyst. I am proud of how my hard work and dedication has prepared me to successfully transition to a new industry.

Assessment

These two accomplishments are heartfelt. You get a sense from reading the applicant's essay that he is really proud of them. The fact that he chooses to write essays that cover both his personal and professional achievements is a good decision. It reveals his depth of character in different parts of his life, making him a more interesting candidate. He doesn't try to play the sympathy card with the death of his father—this can easily backfire if not treated carefully. Rather, he tells the story in a matter-of-fact manner, and the focal point is on being able to help his sisters get through college. The work accomplishment is also interesting because it is quite a jump to go from a medical profession to the investment management career. He does a good job of showing the reader the metamorphosis that he went through to develop a hobby into a passionate career. Overall, this is a no-nonsense essay with a good dose of revealing character traits that makes a case for a mature, driven man.

Sample Impact and Leadership Essay

Describe your impact on a person, team, or organization.

After moving to Houston, I was shocked to find no platform for mentoring and developing junior employees, particularly college hires. The pervasive hierarchical system placed little value on investing in junior talent, leading to dismal retention history.

Upon inquiry to create a program for developing junior talent, I was repeatedly told, "It cannot be done! Many before you have tried for years." I decided to try anyway.

Months of deadlocked negotiations followed. I started seeing why others had quit: the bureaucracy was unyielding! Keeping my team motivated was also proving to be challenging. Finally, we convinced the CEO of NXO Corporation* to meet with HR and my team. As we sat at his desk, I drew from every debating experience to persuade them and quell any fears of losing their investment given our low retention rate. Eventually, we won them over. We also negotiated funding, making the employee development program the only fully funded employee club at NXO.

Within weeks, NXO had 400+ members. We oversaw the first cross-site mentoring program for all members, initiated partnerships with community service organizations, and held networking events. The retention rate is also up 20 percent.

I consider building the employee development program significant because I successfully led a team and navigated the seemingly insurmountable bureaucracy to invest in junior talent at NXO Corporation.

*Names of persons and organizations have been changed.

Assessment

This essay is refreshing in that it isn't your typical work-related accomplishment. This applicant's brand themes are innovator, tenacious, and empowerer. The story he shares shows how he creates a program that didn't exist because he saw a need that wasn't being met (lack of systematic mentorship of new talent). Despite little support, his persistence pays off, and he is able to build an employee organization that has created a cohesive community among new employees. He does a good job also of showing the impact he had instead of telling you what he had done. It is always a good idea to tell a story that shows what you achieved rather than simply stating that you are great at negotiation or innovation. Such statements come off as trite to the MBA admissions board. Always show the reader what you did and the motivations to do it rather than stating the obvious.

Sample Impact and Leadership Essay

In discussing Columbia Business School, Dean R. Glenn Hubbard remarked, "We have established the mind-set that entrepreneurship is about everything you do." Please discuss a time in your own life when you have identified and captured an opportunity.

In June, I turned a big problem into a big opportunity. One of my biggest clients was going through a futures delivery cycle and was exposed to very high overnight market risk. Having lost several hundred thousand dollars overnight, he was threatening to take his business away from my firm. His point was perfectly understandable: If the prime broker is notified of his positions at 11 p.m., why should he have to wait until 7 a.m. the next morning to find out? His argument made perfect sense, and I assured my client that I would find a solution.

I took it upon myself to conduct very thorough research; however, the results were discouraging. This procedure took about eight hours to complete, and the same timeline was present at every single competitor. I had to come up with an innovative plan to change such a widely used procedure for the first time, and I had to convince management that it was absolutely necessary. After countless informational conference calls, I came up with a proposal on how to avoid this risk. I suggested that we modify the existing software and staff an employee in our Chicago office overnight to coordinate trades with our Tokyo office.

Now that I had the plan, I needed to get it implemented, and this was the challenging part. As a new associate in the firm, I did not have the authority to hire a new employee or hand out new responsibilities to our team in Tokyo. I strategically chose to approach my manager's manager since he had the authority to implement my idea. Given his experience at our firm, he knew the right people and introduced me to *the global head of futures. Mike D.*, who had more than thirty years of experience with the futures business, directed a lot of questions to me, testing my knowledge of the product, but I had already done my due diligence. I knew all the answers regarding the time spent on each step along the way, the systems used, and the cost/benefit implications of the plan. By the end of this long discussion, Mike was intrigued and wanted to check the feasibility of my plan by talking to his team leaders. I not only persuaded my supervisors but also impressed them with my complete vision from idea to execution.*

I made a substantial impact because I leveraged my connections across the firm, which I have successfully built over the years, and for the first time on Wall Street, addressed the delivery risk with a global approach. I was proud to inform my client that I delivered the results that I had promised and effected change. The new procedure not only helps my client save approximately $1.2 million per year but also gives my firm a competitive edge.

*Names of persons and organizations have been changed.

Assessment

The value of an essay like this is that the leadership impact focuses on seeking out opportunities to create value for the client. This candidate could have given up when she realized there were obstacles in the way and that what her client needed hadn't been done before. Instead, she rolls up her sleeves, creatively identifies a solution, and then lobbies the decision makers to buy her idea. She demonstrates strong emotional intelligence, tenacity, and ability to creatively solve problems. The fact that her solution led to a new procedure at her firm that helps her clients save money to the tune of more than a million dollars is an added boon.

TIPS ON HANDLING THE IMPACT AND LEADERSHIP ESSAY

- Be sure to show the challenge that was involved in achieving the impact. The obstacle could be getting something off the ground; selling/communicating an idea to a skeptical boss; managing people who are resistant to a vision; coming up with a novel business solution to a client's problem; or simply convincing your team to take a different approach to a problem.
- Be sure to be as specific as possible in describing your impact and your actual involvement.
- Do a lot of soul-searching to make sure you select the best representative example. What you may consider great impact may come across as not that impressive. The circumstances surrounding the situation are important. For example, if you are an investment banker with an annual salary and bonus of more than $100K, you may want to rethink whether contributing $5,000 to your brother's education is the best example of your leadership impact.
- The achievement has to transcend your own personal gain. So the impact you had should have a positive effect on your colleagues, customers, or the organization.

Some Recent Impact and Leadership Essay Questions

India School of Business: Pick the most significant achievement (professional or personal) you have had and elaborate on the key learning you took away from it. (300 words max)

Stanford: Answer one of the three questions below.

1. **Tell us about a time in the last three years when you built or developed a team whose performance exceeded expectations.**
2. **Tell us about a time in the last three years when you identified and pursued an opportunity to improve an organization.**

3. Tell us about a time in the last three years when you went beyond what was defined or established.

4. Haas: What is your most significant accomplishment? (250-word maximum)

5. Kellogg: What have been your most significant leadership experiences? What challenges did you face, and what impact did you have? This is your opportunity to explain how you Think Bravely. (500 word limit)

6. Tuck: Tell us about your most meaningful collaborative leadership experience and what role you played. What did you learn about your own individual strengths and weaknesses through this experience? (500 words)

7. MIT: The mission of the MIT Sloan School of Management is to develop principled, innovative leaders who improve the world and generate ideas that advance management practice. Discuss how you will contribute toward advancing the mission based on examples of past work and activities. (500 words or fewer, limited to one page)

The "Who You Are" Essay

Remember that at the heart of the evaluation process is identifying the applications that have a strong personal brand. "Who you are" essays are designed to help the MBA admissions board understand you in a three-dimensional sense. These types of essays introduce your values and passions—what makes you tick—to the admissions board. The board wants to gauge your ability to handle adversity, overcome challenge, and bounce back in the face of failure. Ultimately, the question is whether you are self-aware (whether it's dealing with your developmental areas and strengths or it's connecting the dots together from your experiences). When tackling these types of essays, be willing to reveal your character and the type of student and alumnus you will become.

These types of essays require candidates to reveal a deeper level of insight and information that isn't covered in their résumé. An example is how growing up as the oldest child exposed you to responsibility at an early age, shaping your leadership style and your propensity for stepping up to lead from the front. Another candidate who grew up in a home of entrepreneurs can share insights about why she gravitates to innovation and comes up with creative solutions in her career. Both examples are valid backgrounds that reveal the context that has shaped the candidates' lives. It is less about what your experiences are and more about your awareness of how they have shaped who you are in a personal and professional sense.

Being willing to open up and share stories that present your personal side is the surest way to show the MBA admissions board who you are. But remember: judgment is key. There is a balance between telling the admissions board about hardships that have shaped your character and offloading detailed personal information that may not have much bearing on the application. I once read an application where the candidate described getting over her boyfriend breaking up with her as one of her greatest accomplishments. This may be a struggle that the candidate experienced, but it is certainly not appropriate to write about this topic for a business school application. At best, it calls into question your judgment.

You should also watch out for details that are red flags to the MBA admissions board. For instance, saying that you are highly impatient or prefer working on projects solo does little to endear you to the admissions board, because teamwork is at the heart of business school education. Also, essays that push blame to others instead of taking responsibility for a breakdown of a process or project reflect poorly on the candidate.

"Who you are" essays can be further divided into two groups: self-assessment essays and values and influence essays.

"Who You Are" Essay One: The Self-Assessment Essay
"Who you are" essays are also designed to reveal how self-aware you are. These questions often inquire into your awareness of your strengths and weaknesses, interests, and how you will engage with a program while you are there. What type of leader are you? What attribute has influenced your success? The purpose isn't to identify perfect candidates. However, these essays are tricky in that they require you to provide an honest

assessment of yourself. The MBA admissions board relies on these types of essays to gauge whether you have a realistic perspective of yourself. A major red flag for the board is when there is a discrepancy between how you describe yourself and how your recommenders describe you. For instance, if you say you are conscientious and thrive in fast-paced pressure situations, and your recommenders say you are highly disorganized and need to develop your ability to handle pressure, you have a problem. Be honest with your assessment and make sure your recommenders are on the same page.

Equally important is selecting real weaknesses that you are working to improve. Don't insult the MBA admissions board's intelligence by choosing topics that come off as superficial, for example, saying you need to become less of a perfectionist and then not sharing a real example of how your perfectionism really holds you back. Here's an authentic example: "I have a propensity to overanalyze things. This comes from my natural tendency to be less of a risk taker. Doing intense assessment enables me to mitigate the risk and gives me a comfort level to pursue a new direction. The fallout of this weakness is that there are a lot of business situations where there isn't enough time to do intense research, and I have to become more comfortable with making decisions without gathering all the data I'd like…" You get my point. This is a real weakness; the person understands that it can inhibit his progress as a business leader. What would strengthen this example is going a step further to describe how the weakness is being addressed. Let's look at an actual self-assessment essay.

Sample Self-Assessment Essay

Give a candid description of yourself, stressing the personal characteristics you feel to be your strengths and weaknesses and the main factors that have influenced your personal development, giving examples when necessary. (600 words)

The personal characteristics that have influenced my personal development are patience, intellectual curiosity, and passion for excellence.

I was stigmatized as a child because I did not have the strength to play soccer on the streets with my peers. I was nine the first time I heard that I would die before the age of twenty-one. I was born with sickle cell anemia, an illness that afflicts 3 percent of Africans. The illness is associated with low levels of red blood cells and intermittent periods of crises that last anywhere between a few minutes and several weeks. The pain is so excruciating that most patients are hospitalized for pain control during the crisis period. When I developed these crises, there was very little my parents could do apart from emotional support. Despite this illness and losing a few friends and a cousin to it, I was determined not to die before the age of twenty-one. I knew that I needed to know how to take care of myself if I wanted to live long. More importantly, I understood the pain and I wanted to help others like me. Long before I went to high school, I already knew that I was going to be a doctor and I worked toward it.

My lonely childhood helped me develop my intellect. My parents played a role in this as they bought many books for me; my father bought an atlas that fascinated me. Before the age of ten, I knew almost all the countries in the world and their geographic locations. The Italia 1990 FIFA World Cup was a particularly fascinating period for me as all the countries that I read about came to life when I saw their representatives play soccer. It was because of my intellectual curiosity that I was able to skip an entire year in grade school, delved into the world of finance as a medical student, and passed all three levels of the CFA examination at one sitting each.

I also learned the art of patience during the periods of crises. When the pains washed over me, I reminded myself repeatedly that within a few days, the pains would be gone and I would get back to my life once again. This taught me to appreciate life and to live it to the fullest, molding me into someone with a passion for excellence. I knew my life was a gift and this always brought the best out of me.

My major weakness is my inability to multitask effectively. Because of my desire to bring out the best in my work, I tend to focus on one task and pay less attention to others that I've deemed less important. When I was working on Project Equity, the project that my department carried out to keep equity in the pension portfolio, I was so carried away that I did not prepare adequately for the weekly training program that

I conducted for junior analysts. Although I ended up doing a good job with the training program, I knew I could have done better. When one of my friends brought this to my attention, I developed a way to break other less important tasks into smaller pieces with deadlines. This forced me to keep track of all my tasks as I put all the tiny pieces together. I am still working on this weakness, and I am sure that INSEAD will help me turn it into a strength.

Assessment

The main weakness of this essay is that the writer shares three strengths and only one weakness. It would have been more balanced if he had cut down some of the beginning of the essay to free up room to cover an additional weakness. The introduction about his personal health challenges could also be slightly shorter. Aside from these factors, this essay is effective in sharing some of the reasoning behind his actions. For example, he addresses why he even developed an interest in medicine in the first place due to a life-threatening illness. He also reveals how his awareness of the precious nature of time drives his determination and drive for excellence. Overall, it is a good essay.

Sample Self-Assessment Essay

Provide an assessment of your strengths and weaknesses.

Maturity, adaptability, and leadership are my core strengths. When I was ten, my parents left Africa to work in Saudi Arabia. Living with little supervision in a boarding school in Africa for five years helped me mature quickly. At eighteen, I became responsible for my younger siblings who continually looked to me for guidance and direction as we all tried to adapt to life in the United States. Currently, I supervise people who are twice my age, some of whom have more than twenty years of experience in pharmaceutical production. My maturity has enabled me to successfully lead and manage these experienced line employees while earning their respect.

Living in four different continents has afforded me many opportunities to adapt to different cultures, people, and ways of thinking. Over the past three years, I have had seven different job functions in two different companies. I have worked under different management styles and in different regions of the country. In each position, I have quickly adapted successfully to new hierarchies, situations, and environments.

Throughout my life, I have shown an affinity for leadership. In high school and college, I took on several leadership roles. In my professional career, I have addressed challenging situations at work, leading several teams to success. At Pharma Co. A,* for example, I led a campaign to end the waste of expiring drugs. I also created and led a successful human error management campaign. Recently, I initiated a similar plan at my new company, Pharma Co. B.*

My two main weaknesses are incomplete business knowledge and my learning to balance relationships with line employees and making tough business decisions. To become a successful pharmaceutical business leader, I must get a better grip on marketing, finance, and strategy. But as a line manager, I must learn to keep adequate emotional distance between me and the employees under my watch. While at Pharma Co. A, I once hesitated before reporting an operator who on more than one occasion fell asleep on the job (his mistake, had I not discovered it, would have cost the company $750,000). In hindsight, this was a very expensive mistake that, if not addressed, could have caused the factory to shut down. But because I had befriended a number of the line operators, it was, at first, a tough call to report him. As I take on more management responsibility, I must learn to better balance my investment in the employees and keeping a business productive and successful.

*Names of persons and organizations have been changed.

Assessment

This essay is written by an engineer and is less creative in its style. It is a matter-of-fact essay, representative of the candidate's personality. He provides specific examples when laying out his strengths and weaknesses. He does a good job setting the tone for his experience raising his siblings. One doesn't get a sense that he is looking for sympathy or brownie points. Rather, he uses the experience to show his maturity and strong leadership and management abilities, which are anchored in a series of personal experiences from his family situation. His weaknesses come across as authentic. As an engineer, he conveys the practical business skills that he lacks, which is more a function of his role as opposed to his personal weakness. Had he stopped there, he would have missed an opportunity to show the MBA admissions board a glimpse into who he is and his awareness of his developmental needs. By describing how he struggled with balancing managing people and holding them accountable and then citing a specific example to drive home his point, he presents an interesting essay that shows depth of character. He could have also shared another developmental weakness instead of selecting one about having incomplete business knowledge.

TIPS ON HANDLING THE SELF-ASSESSMENT ESSAY

- Be candid about your strengths and make sure you have substantial evidence to back them up.
- On the weakness side, use real weaknesses, not something trite such as, "I work too hard" or "I need to delegate better."
- Reinforce the main brand message you want to convey about yourself. For instance, if your brand is a perpetual optimist, your weakness could be that you need to temper your optimism because you may fail to devote enough time to anticipating downsides and potential problems when working on projects. And of course, the value of a weakness is to tell a story where it occurred and then acknowledge your awareness of the weakness and show how you turned things around.
- Be comfortable in your own skin. This is an important variable in successful candidates. You want to show that you have a good understanding of why you have made the decisions you have made and have the capability to learn from mistakes as well.

Some Recent Self-Assessment Essay Questions

Haas: Describe a time in the last three years when you over-came a failure. What specific insight from this experience has shaped your development? (250 word maximum)

Cambridge Judge: What did you learn from your most spec-tacular failure? (200 words)

Columbia GSB: What will the people in your cluster be pleasantly surprised to learn about you? (Maximum 250 words)

Wharton: Academic engagement is an important element of the Wharton MBA experience. How do you see yourself contributing to our learning community? (500 words)

Kellogg: What one interesting or fun fact would you want your future Kellogg classmates to know about you? (25 words or less)

Tuck: Describe a circumstance in your life in which you faced adversity, failure, or setback. What actions did you take as a result, and what did you learn from this experi-ence? (500 words)

"Who You Are" Essay Two: The Values and Influence Essay
Similar to the self-assessment essay, the values and influence essay probes what matters to you as it relates to your beliefs, philosophies, and influences. These essays cover such topics as the following:

- Who are your role models?
- What experiences have influenced your development as a leader?
- Which business leaders do you admire and why?
- Describe a situation that has had a transformational impact on who you are.
- What matters most to you and why?
- When were you an outsider?

- Describe a situation when you experienced culture shock.
- What words or adjectives describe you?

These essay questions are trying to understand the experiences that have shaped who you are, your value system, and the people who have shaped your life and worldview. The values and influence essays also aim to ascertain what type of business leader you aspire to become. Don't just focus on what or who. Take the time to express why you feel the way you do. The MBA admissions board wants to know that you have very clearly defined values and awareness around the forces that have shaped you personally and professionally. This gives them a clearer picture of who you are as a person beyond your accolades and job titles.

Sample Values and Influence Essay

Each of our applicants is unique. Describe how your background, values, academics, activities, and/or leadership skills will enhance the experiences of other students.

There are four distinct attributes of my personality that have guided my life: guts, creativity, leadership, and passion. I plan to bring these attributes to X University* program to enrich my classmates' lives and anticipate a two-year period full of growth and development.

Growing up in suburban Detroit, I came to understand there were four major religions in our community: Christianity, Judaism, Islam, and University of Michigan Football. As my friends donned the colors of maize and blue and made plans of who was going to live with whom, my college dreams expanded far beyond the boundaries of my backyard. I wanted a different experience. Y University* presented the opportunity to stretch myself, gain new experiences, and make new friends. In college, I selected engineering psychology, a major few had heard of because it combined the liberal arts discipline of psychology with the mathematical and analytical foundation of engineering, allowing me

*Names of persons and organizations have been changed.

to blend my analytical right brain nature with my creative, expressive left brain spirit. A university experience far from home, an unusual major in the engineering school, a semester abroad in Spain living with an extended Spanish family, and many adventurous trips and outdoor expeditions reinforced my belief in the importance of taking the right risks and pushing myself outside of my comfort zone. I plan to share this free spirit and lessons gleaned from many of these experiences with my classmates at the X University program.

As a child, I had an active imagination and loved performing in shows and dance recitals. I sought interesting and creative ways to entertain myself. I pursued jazz and ballet for eleven years and found creative outlets in college through Y University's Hip Hop Dance Troupe performances. My work at RAA* firm is exciting because of the creative brands I get to work with. I rely on my creativity to create new and innovative product lines. X University MBA program is a dynamic environment that attracts driven, committed, and creative individuals from a wide array of professional and personal experiences. I love that about X University's program, and it is precisely why I'm convinced that it is the perfect program for me. I look forward to starting a dance club for X University program students. I am excited to share my creative background and experiences with other X University program students and teach them how business challenges are best tackled through creative solutions and innovative thinking.

I have always thrived in leadership situations, whether in formal settings at work or in less formal settings in the outdoors. As an outdoor enthusiast, I am faced with numerous situations that stretch my leadership and teach me new skills. I have enjoyed sharing many of these lessons with others. Algonquin Provincial Park in Ontario, Canada, provided a wonderful opportunity to lead youths on canoe trips. I spent many of my summers motivating and leading ten- to sixteen-year-olds through difficult and sometimes dangerous situations. The wilderness of the park was the perfect backdrop to encourage kids to empower themselves through these outdoor excursions while developing their reliance on their team. The external factors of weather and wildlife constantly impose new and various challenges. I embraced the challenge, led responsibly, and found gratification in my ability to competently execute the objective. These lessons have taught me the importance of teamwork, being able to laugh at adversity, have fun, and take a negative and make it a positive. These elements are very analogous to the circumstances one encounters on a regular basis in business. I look forward to joining the Outdoor and Service club where I would lead and coordinate the trips servicing the first-year student community through team-building outdoor adventures. In my professional life, I have learned not to be bound by my early-career status and that being a leader is not about title. I've learned that leadership is about being gutsy, taking risks, influencing teams, and creating opportunities. During my work on developing RAA firm's candy line, I have had experiences to lead teams of graphic designers and candy developers while creating new opportunities for healthier product innovations. I will bring my strong sense of leadership to the X University program community.

During my college experience, I was fortunate to develop my main passion toward children by volunteering at a day care for underprivileged children that was run by the Y University community. Playing activities and reading stories with the children helped me keep my own life in perspective. It was there that I realized that my future career would somehow impact children's lives. Working at RAA firm, I've had a very tangible impact on the lives of kids, and the lessons I've learned will enrich my MBA classroom conversations. I wish to continue my involvement with children through various volunteer organizations at X University MBA program.

It is these four distinct attributes that have made me the person I am today and will help me enrich the learning experiences of my fellow X University MBA program students.

Assessment

This candidate is very outgoing, people-driven, and comfortable in her own skin. Showing your point instead of simply stating it is also important in an essay like this. She does a good job of that when she says: "Growing up in suburban Detroit, I came to understand there were four major religions in our community: Christianity, Judaism, Islam, and University of Michigan Football. As my friends donned the colors of maize and blue, and made plans of who was going to live with whom, my college dreams expanded far beyond the boundaries of my backyard." She could have simply stated, "Pushing myself outside traditional boundaries is a value that matters to me." Instead she shows it by using the preceding illustration. The use of the four religions in Detroit shows her sense of humor, which is done in good taste. Candidates always need to be careful when using humor so that it doesn't backfire. She does a good job of showing how the choices she has made were driven by her natural curiosity and desire to stretch herself instead of playing it safe (whether moving to the East Coast instead of going to U of M like all her friends, or selecting her major, which combines psychology and engineering). Even her industry, entertainment/media, is unique. One gets a sense that she brings passion to anything she does, whether it's working with young people through the outdoor adventure programs or a day care for underprivileged kids.

Finally, by describing her commitment to dance (eleven years of dancing ballet and jazz and performing with the Hip Hop Dance Troupe), she shows her creativity and discipline, traits that would be attractive to the MBA admissions board. The essay is a bit on the long side, but overall, she does a good job of bringing in different things that matter to her without simply listing them. She manages to inject her spunky personality in her essay, ensuring that she doesn't come off as a bland candidate.

TIPS ON HANDLING THE VALUES AND INFLUENCE ESSAY

The trick to writing a values essay is to make sure it doesn't come across as clichéd. Remember, all five thousand applicants to that MBA program will also answer the same question. Can you imagine how the board members' eyes would roll when they read the 255th essay in a row about "How I value making a difference in society" or "My family is the most important thing in my life"? Try to take a fresh angle on the story. Stay away from the beaten path unless you feel it absolutely is essential to who you are.

When writing about role models, also avoid choosing clichéd responses such as "My grandparents [or parents] have shaped my values to become who I am today" (a lot of people will choose the same example). If you must choose this, then offer a unique and interesting angle. For example, instead of the typical story of parents who worked hard and made it, a different take is a story of multiple failures and a persistent spirit that has shaped your worldview. Don't manufacture a story if it isn't part of your experience, but avoid choosing the first "usual-suspect" story that comes to mind. Devote enough time to select a topic that truly represents a differentiated and unique insight into who you are as a person.

When essays ask for a business leader you admire, don't be afraid to select a lesser-known but accomplished business leader. Yes, you may admire Jack Welch, Bill Gates, or Meg Whitman. However, are there other business leaders with whom you identify more closely with who are not as prominent? A young woman whose brand was retail entrepreneurship chose to focus on a widow who was thrust into running her husband's retail business after his untimely death. The business started with a few million dollars in revenue, and she grew the revenue to more than a billion dollars. By eschewing the more prominent business leaders, this applicant focused on a less famous but extremely successful business leader who connected to her retail brand. Her story gave her an opportunity to share new information with the MBA admissions board that set her apart from applicants who were mired in cliched stories. The size of the role model's achievement isn't as important as articulating what you admire about the person.

Tackling the "who you are" essay requires incredible focus. It is tempting to try to dump everything into the story. Given limited word counts, you can ace this essay when you have done a thorough brand audit and can hone in on three or four brand themes that reflect what matters to you. This essay is one of the most challenging application essays out there. It requires the deepest level of introspection, and candidates cannot hide behind any props. It is as bare and open as it gets. Most applicants struggle with this essay because they haven't invested enough time in the self-assessment necessary to unveil the core elements of who they are, nor have they identified the appropriate specific stories to paint a vivid picture of who they are—their brand. Be willing to take a risk and share stories that honestly represent your brand.

Some Recent Values and Influence Essay Questions

Stanford: What do you want to do—REALLY—and why Stanford?

Fuqua: Share with us your list of "25 Random Things" about YOU. (No more than 2 pages)

Haas: If you could choose one song that expresses who you are, what is it and why? (250 word maximum)

NYU Stern: Please describe yourself to your MBA classmates. You may use almost any method to convey your message (e.g. words, illustrations). Feel free to be creative.

Kellogg: Discuss moments or influences in your personal life that have defined who you are today. (500 word limit)

The Miscellaneous Essay

The miscellaneous essay category is the fourth type of essay that candidates encounter in the application process. These essays are broad in terms of specific topics they cover. The MBA admissions board may want you to weigh in on a political situation to assess how you develop an argument and provide evidence to back it up. On the other hand, these essays could also be personalized, providing you with a chance to speak to anything else in your story that is compelling that you were unable to address in other application essays. You can also use these types of essays to explain any gaps in your work experience, academic weaknesses, or potential questions that the admissions board may have about your candidacy. Topics covered by miscellaneous essays can touch on a global issue, what you do with your spare time, or anything else you wish to cover in your application.

I've decided to put Harvard's one and only essay question in the miscellaneous essay category, though I can also see the case for putting it in either the leadership and impact or the "who you are" essay category. The question asks applicants: "What else would you like us to know as we consider your candidacy?" The open-ended nature of this question can be challenging for some applicants. What topic should you choose? Can you write about one thing or multiple topics? How long should this essay be, given that there isn't a word limit?

For a school like Harvard Business School, you don't want to write a full-blown career essay. The reality is that the topics covered in this essay can be drastically different. There may be a handful of candidates who will opt not to submit the HBS essay since it is optional, and some of these students may even get admitted! But I would caution anyone thinking of taking this route to think through their decision carefully. I encourage most applicants to submit the HBS essay. Your topic for this essay will depend on your particular brand and what data has already been covered about you through the other parts of the application, such as your recommendations and résumé. Doing a personal brand assessment ahead of tackling this essay will help you to zero in on your core brand message. You can write a successful HBS essay that is only 300 words. You can also write a successful HBS essay that is 1,300 words. I've seen a successful essay that was more of a story about how the candidate had gotten to where he was today—so multiple points were touched on in the essay. Another effective essay can be focused on one theme, say someone's penchant for seizing opportunities and starting things.

Here are some specific ingredients of a successful HBS essay:

1. Write the essay as if you were sitting across the table from the director of admissions (write in a conversational style; avoid the formal, academic style).

2. Don't try to do too much with this essay; less is more. Focus on a key point or handful of points and *show* through vignettes instead of *telling* them stuff they already know about you from your résumé.

3. Begin with the why—why are you even writing the essay/stories in the first place? What is the big idea? And why will HBS care about it? There has to be a strategy behind the essay. Is your academic story weak? Maybe you can write an essay about your academic journey. You have something you have achieved that stretched you beyond anything you have ever done. Perhaps you can talk about your dreams, motivations, and how you pursued and achieved those objectives. This doesn't always have to be professional.

4. There isn't a formula in terms of topics—you can write about an activity you are genuinely passionate about; you can write about a failure even, and focus on how that pivotal moment shaped how you have subsequently approached life, work, etc. It could be about the biggest "aha!" moment of your life.

5. Your essays should evoke emotions. It may be a smile. It may be admiration. It may be surprise. Avoid the status quo. Most essays will be business-as-usual, conventional essays that will be extremely boring to the admissions board.

6. Do everything in your power to avoid duplicating essays that you wrote for other schools. HBS doesn't want to read Stanford's "what matters most to you" essay just because you want to save time. And remember, both schools are quite different, so you should tailor your message differently anyway. Here's a test: if you can easily copy and paste paragraphs or even entire essays from one application prompt to the next, you should go back to the drawing board.

7. Every candidate has his Achilles' heel. What is yours? Knowing what yours is and writing an essay that directly speaks to the concerns that the admissions board has about your candidacy will endear you to them.

8. Don't try and squeeze "why an MBA and why HBS" elements into your essay just because you think you have to. I've seen essays where applicants have tried to do that, and it breaks the flow of their story and quite honestly adds little additional value to the applicants' story. It can often feel forced and fall flat.

Sample Miscellaneous Essay

My Undergraduate Academic Experience

I was one of three African American females in my class at a small English boarding school and elected to attend X University* because its large, urban, diverse atmosphere represented the opposite of my high

*Names of persons and organizations have been changed.

school environment. At X's School for Communication, I customized my communication major to focus on Latin-American and Afro-American cultures, the former of which I studied during a semester-abroad program in Oaxaca, Mexico. For both cultures, I focused on history with special emphasis on various forms of expression, including folk music and literature. One representative class from my course of study was "Without Struggle," a seminar that required completion of faculty-guided research. My project focused on the benefits and disadvantages of X University's Afro-American-themed college house, for which I designed a survey, analyzed the raw data, and drew conclusions. This experience gave me the strong foundation to excel in "Basic Communication Research—A Quantitative Data Analysis Course." These two classes combined to give me the confidence to serve as a teaching assistant for "Without Struggle" my senior year. As a TA, my leadership style evolved from simply providing my opinion to learning to encourage students to draw their own conclusions.

During college, I did not properly manage academics, extracurricular activities, and employment, spending disproportionate amounts of time on the latter two at the expense of the others. Unfortunately, my grades in some quantitative courses reflect only my misbalanced study schedule, not my true academic fervor. Recalling how I harnessed my study-abroad experience to achieve Spanish fluency, I chose a post-undergraduate employment that would yield "fluency" in another foreign subject: finance. After graduation, I joined ABC Firm* as a sales trader and learned about stock market supply and demand in real time; further, I developed sharp quantitative skills by monitoring the financial markets. Now, as an equity research team analyst, I build valuation models by evaluating financial statements, and I am the lead associate for Online GHI and XYZ Firms,* stocks that respectively trade more than 20 million and 6 million shares daily. I supplemented this comprehension by excelling in a course, "Financial Statement Analysis," this past summer. During this time, I also maintained my volunteer and leadership responsibilities, effectively demonstrating my maturity and improved ability to multitask, juggling real-world duties with scholastic commitment. I will utilize both of these personal qualities to balance leadership positions and academic achievement at HBS, without ever sacrificing one for the other.

Assessment

This essay is written by a candidate who was concerned about her academic track record. She has to strike a fair balance between describing her academic experience and providing evidence that she has the analytical and intellectual rigor to handle a challenging MBA curriculum. She begins the essay by demonstrating her resilient spirit as one of three students of color in an unfamiliar environment. She then introduces examples of her quantitative and analytical skills by describing her data analysis course in college, the financial statement analysis course after college, and her career in a blue-chip firm, where her day-to-day role involves its fair share of quantitative and analytical computations. I like the fact that she owns up to her "failure" in college for not balancing her time well. However, what is important to highlight here is that she strikes a great note between owning her mistake and not groveling. By introducing her work experience in sales and trading and equity research, she is effective in providing additional evidence that shows that she is in her element working in an analytical environment. Finally, she proactively takes a finance course and does well to reassure the MBA admissions board that she has what it takes to handle quantitative coursework.

Let's look at another example of a miscellaneous essay, this time one that deals with a candidate who is reapplying to business school.

Sample Miscellaneous Essay

Reapplication Essay

While I was disappointed that I did not receive an admission offer, my drive and commitment motivated me to reapply. The reapplication process allowed me a period of reflection, enabling me to take a step back to reassess my life. Furthermore, it provided me with an opportunity to focus on my set goal. At work, I have taken on additional responsibilities by managing more people along with centers, which now focus on retail chain strategy. Within the community, I have become more actively involved in a women's empowerment group. I have also increased my GMAT score by 80 points, and in the spring of next year, I plan to build an alternate transcript by taking accounting, calculus, and statistics courses.

One key reason I am reapplying to XLF Program* is the outstanding program in entrepreneurship. In 1965, my grandmother became the first sole distributor of the BYB* brand of liquors in Africa, and my father is a leading African entrepreneur. There is no telling how great a businesswoman my grandmother could have become had she had the proper formal business school education. As an adult, I observe my father's business prowess and though admirable, it would be far superior had he had formal business school education. I am reapplying to XLF Program not to become a moderately successful entrepreneur or to become a good businessperson. I am reapplying to XLF Program for the opportunity to learn how to become a thought leader, an innovator, and a superbly successful businessperson. I am reapplying to XLF Program to major in entrepreneurship and international business and to have the opportunity to take advantage of the Institute of Entrepreneurial Studies.

My first interaction with the XLF culture was at the prospective students information session in November. I also interacted with your students during the planned trip for the dean of XLF in Africa. During my on-campus visit in October, I had the opportunity to attend Professor Smith's* New Products and Services class and Professor Rodriguez's* lectures. Both classes showcased XLF's first-class educational standards as both professors were insightful, challenged the status quo, and pushed the students to think strategically and out of the box. Also during my trip, I had multiple interactions with students and members of the administration. The culture of excellence and collegiality I observed during these interactions was exceptional, and I feel that XLF Program is truly an environment that embraces teamwork, unique attributes, and openness to new ideas. Upon my return home, I took a look at my experiences, and it is unequivocally clear to me that the School of Management is a perfect fit for my personal and professional growth. And this is why I am reapplying to the XLF School of Management.

*Names of persons and organizations have been changed.

Assessment

This essay does a good job setting up the expectations of the admissions board. The applicant immediately outlines what is different with her application the second time around by showing that her GMAT has gone up and that her work experience has expanded, thus increasing the likelihood that the board member reading her application would take her reapplication bid seriously. She then follows up by talking about coursework she plans to take. Although this is fine, ideally it would have even been more compelling had she taken the classes already and had excellent grades to report.

Every candidate to business school has to make the case about what he or she finds attractive about the particular MBA program. As a result, admissions boards read these essays over and over again, a *Groundhog Day* experience. The challenge, however, is keeping the essay fresh and connecting it to your unique background. This essay does precisely that. She connects her personal life (her grandmother's and father's entrepreneur backgrounds) to how she hopes to develop into a better entrepreneur at the MBA program. She also shows that she understands what the program offers by describing specifics of her campus visit, particularly attending classes. The only additional feedback I would give her is to highlight insights she developed from the classes that she can compare to her professional experience working in Africa.

TIPS ON HANDLING THE MISCELLANEOUS ESSAY

- The reapplication essay gives you a chance to make your case for what is different this time around, and with more than 80 percent of applicants being rejected, it is only reasonable to expect that some would reapply at a future date.
- Don't underestimate the importance of the miscellaneous essay, even if it is allocated only 250 words.
- When crafting your response, make sure it is appropriate and doesn't raise any red flags about your candidacy.

> • Use the optional essay or craft your own essay question to address a gap in your story. If you are applying very early in your career, for example, you may want to use this essay to show why now is the ideal time for you to pursue your MBA.

Some Recent Miscellaneous Essay Questions

HBS: You're applying to Harvard Business School. We can see your résumé, school transcripts, extracurricular activities, awards, post-MBA career goals, test scores, and what your recommenders have to say about you. What else would you like us to know as we consider your candidacy? There is no word limit for this question.

ISB: (Optional) Please provide additional information, if any, that will improve your chances of being considered by ISB. (300 words maximum)

INSEAD: Please choose one of the following two essay topics:

  a. **Have you ever experienced culture shock? What insights did you gain? (250 words maximum)**
  b. **Describe the ways in which a foreigner in your country might experience culture shock. (250 words maximum)**

COMMON ESSAY MISTAKES

As you tackle your essays, always ask yourself whether you are falling into one of these traps.

1. Engaging in essay brain dump: Writing your essays without first doing an outline will ensure that you create disjointed and ineffective essays. Use the SOARS model to frame up the outline before tackling any essay.

2. Being bland and generic: Failure to nail down your personal branding will increase your chances of producing boring and undifferentiated essays. Do a brand audit to understand your overall positioning. I can often tell when an essay is written without

a clear brand message: they are boring and don't communicate a message about the applicant.

3.   Being selfish: Focusing too much on "I" can make you come across as arrogant; balance your individual accomplishment with your team involvement.

4.   Going back too far: Selecting accomplishments from a long time ago, for instance, during high school, especially after you have been working for more than seven years, may not come across as compelling. If you must go back that far, it is important to make sure the example is significant and has special meaning in shaping who you have become as a leader.

5.   Using clichés, sermonizing, and stating the obvious: The MBA admissions board knows what conventional wisdom says. They care about what you personally think or believe.

6.   Overusing quotes: There is a place for quotes in these essays, but think long and hard before using up precious words to quote some Greek philosopher or business leader. The MBA admissions board is interested in your original thoughts, not those of a dead poet.

7.   Not answering the question: If the question asks for leadership impact, be sure to tell a story that clearly depicts you as a leader. If the question asks for weaknesses, give examples of real weaknesses. Don't skirt the issue. You will only annoy the admissions board if you do.

8.   Being unmemorable: Choose vivid stories that resonate with the admissions board. Unusual stories or a different take on a common topic can be interesting and capture the mindshare of the admissions board.

9.   Not pacing yourself strategically: Don't try to do multiple essays for different schools at once. Tackle the essays one school at a time and complete them before working on another school's essays. Similarly, you should not underestimate how much time and work are needed to assemble a strong application. Give yourself at least four months to complete the essays and add another month or two when factoring in other parts of the application (including managing recommenders, campus visits, interviews, and so on).

10. Using humor inappropriately: Don't be funny for the sake of being funny. Always exercise good judgment with your essays. Recounting antics that you and your friends found funny will not win you any friends on the MBA admissions board. Subtle humor is more effective.

11. Being too one-dimensional: Focusing all your essays on your professional life misses the chance to show the full range of your personality, character, and motivations. You are more than your job, so where possible, do bring in other aspects of your life experiences to showcase your interests and passions beyond your work life.

12. Trying to be creative for the sake of being creative: Sometimes, less is more. Artificial essays with whistles and bells can backfire. I'm not against being creative, but make sure that your creativity fits with the brand of the school and that it comes off well instead of appearing gimmicky.

13. Being repetitive: It is important to bring up different stories to show the breadth and depth of your personality, experience, and perspective. Using the same example over and over again will suggest that you have limited experience.

14. Not understanding the program's brand: Take the time to understand the brand of the school and what that means for your essays. Kellogg, for example, is a program that is significantly tied to teamwork, so essays that ask about leadership impact should show team partnership instead of focusing on your "lone-ranger" leadership exploits.

15. Having too many people weigh in on your essays: Beware the too-many-cooks phenomenon. It's helpful to get feedback from someone who knows you very well, especially if that person is a good writer. But it's another thing to have your twenty friends, former colleagues, and that relative who happened to graduate from the same business school a decade ago review your essays. At the very least, you will get a hodgepodge of feedback that will yield a disjointed set of essays.

16. Doing a drive-by application: Don't be in a rush to complete your application. Rather, focus on producing excellent applications. The best applications are a result of intense introspection, focus, and multiple revisions.

Applying good judgment when it comes to all your essays will help you get closer to your admission goals. Good judgment means not being stubborn and insisting that you will write the essay about the speech you gave to five people that was the "best speech in this hemisphere." Just because you think the world of something you did does not mean that it is essay-worthy. If you can't point to the tangible impact your actions achieved, you may have to think twice before selecting that topic for your essay.

FINAL THOUGHTS ON THE MBA ESSAYS

One thing you probably picked up from reading these sample essays is that there are different writing styles and that the topics can vary quite broadly. Two candidates can write about a personal accomplishment of buying a house for their parent, and one person's essay soars while the other person's essay falls flat. The difference is in the positioning of the story. Approach your application by writing heartfelt and insightful essays that take the admissions board into a deeper awareness of your motivations and what you care about. This approach will make your application stand apart. You need to use good judgment when selecting your admissions essay topics. The same applies to the treatment of each essay. Your decision to write about how your relationship with your fiancée is your greatest accomplishment needs to be seen through the business school lens. How does that tie into who you are as a leader? Whatever example you choose, make sure it fosters your story that you are a leader and someone who can get things done with and through other people.

It is also important to "own" your story. It can't be manufactured. The essays that grab the attention of the admissions board can be very simple achievements, written in a straightforward style with little creativity and poetry. These essays are successful because they give the admissions board a glimpse into the heart of a candidate. No matter what your life experiences are, make sure you devote enough time to introspection before tackling the admissions essays. Investing in understanding your motivations for your decisions, connecting the dots of your experiences, and proactively communicating what stands out about your brand through your essays can be the difference between a congratulatory phone call from the director of admissions and a depressing email informing you that your application has been rejected.

I've written this chapter to empower applicants with an effective strategy for writing their MBA essays. Whether you are writing one essay or eight, employing these strategies will help you craft strong essays that make a compelling case for why you should be admitted to your dream school. I hope you will take them to heart. Happy essay writing!

CHAPTER SEVEN

The Résumé and Professional Record

T HE RÉSUMÉ IS ANOTHER important part of the MBA application. It is often one of the first things that the admissions board looks at in your application packet. It is a conversation starter. It shouldn't answer all the questions that the admissions board has, but rather should whet their appetite for them to want to read more about your story in the rest of your application.

Think of the résumé as a snapshot of your work, your life journey, and what stands out about you. It reveals to the MBA admissions board your professional and educational accomplishments, as well as any interesting and unusual things you have done or are currently involved in. Remember that at the end of the day, the admissions board wants to assess whether you have leadership potential, good interpersonal skills, and the ability to work well with a team of people.

Top MBA programs require a résumé, so plan to update yours early in the process and invest enough time in it to ensure that it adequately reflects your brand. Unfortunately, many applicants do not pay enough attention to their résumé, thus missing an opportunity to sell themselves to the MBA admissions board.

With MBA programs reducing the number of essay questions on their applications, the résumé presents a great opportunity to highlight important parts of your story that may not be covered in the essays. But this is not a license to dump everything you can imagine into your résumé.

Candidates often question how much work experience is necessary to apply to business school. Deciding how much information to include on the résumé can also be tricky. Those with more years of experience wonder if they should submit their seven-page curriculum vitae (CV) that covers every job they have ever held. On the other hand, candidates with limited work experience worry that they don't have enough information to highlight in their résumés. Although the average number of years of work experience is four to five years for U.S. schools and five to six years for non-U.S. schools, there is no set requirement. Seasoned and early-career candidates are both admitted to the world's top business schools. Regardless of where you fall on the age and work experience continuum, the key is to make sure that your career is on an upward trajectory and that you can make a compelling case for why you need an MBA now. Ideally, you should keep your résumé to one page, two pages at the most (and only for schools like Harvard Business School that accept longer résumés). Be as succinct as possible and focus on the most important impact and contributions you had rather than including ten bullets of each responsibility you had in a particular job. Using active verbs and eliminating any redundancies will help you create a focused résumé.

The résumé for business school is different from the résumé for a job. Unlike job résumés, application résumés should contain limited jargon and acronyms (the person reviewing your application may not know the intricacies of your industry). Also, you don't need to include a reference, summary, or objective section. Neither does it need to have your picture or marital status. The MBA application in general calls for brevity, and the résumé in particular needs to be short and to the point, as it typically gets only a few seconds to about five minutes of the MBA admissions board's attention. I recognize that producing a succinct résumé poses its share of challenges to MBA applicants. I'll focus the next section on the critical components of the résumé.

THE FIVE COMPONENTS OF THE RÉSUMÉ

Determining what to include in your résumé can be difficult for many applicants. Many who struggle with this issue end up including everything they can think of, which does nothing to strengthen their application. Some candidates make the opposite mistake: they make the résumé too short and leave out interesting and unique things about themselves—things that can differentiate them from their competition—and instead focus on solely the academic and career aspects of their résumé.

I will discuss the key things to include in the résumé. For starters, the résumé for business school should have five main components: contact information, professional experience, education, activities, and other (interests, skills, awards, etc).

The Contact Information Section

The contact information section is the shortest one and should contain your first and last name, your email address, and your phone number. I don't think you need to put your mailing address. What will the admissions board do with it? It also simply takes up more space that you can't afford to lose. Keep this section to one line, two at the most.

The Professional Experience Section

The decision of whether to put the professional experience section before the education section is a personal one; you can begin the résumé with either. It's up to you. The longer you've been away from school, the more it makes sense that your work experience is the lead-in for your résumé. On the other hand, if you have recently graduated from college and have only worked for two years or so, then starting with your education section makes sense.

The professional experience section is about achievements you have had in your career and your roles, not simply regurgitating your job description. It is important to communicate your professional career progress by emphasizing the quantifiable aspects of your job.

The types of questions you should be thinking of when creating your résumé for your business school application are: Did I get an early promotion? Was I the only analyst from my group invited to work on a high-value, complicated deal? Did I have an unusual opportunity to manage groups of people, even peers? Did I initiate something that has now become the standard at my firm? Have I had opportunities to lead and work across functional roles? Have I led diverse or global teams? Have I been able to create value at my firm, and if so, exactly how? These questions are designed to help you focus on the tangible contributions you have had at your firms. You will be expected to quantify your achievement in measurable ways, for instance, increasing your firm's sales by 34 percent as a result of a new approach you introduced or reducing the error rate of an engineering project by 15 percent due to a novel system that you implemented.

MBA candidates are challenged with the amount of detail they should cover in the professional experience section. Prioritization is key in this process. Anticipate that you will have about four to five bullets at the most for each job, so think long and hard about the most important achievements you wish to highlight and ascertain whether they reinforce your personal brand. A rule of thumb is that the further removed you are from the position, the fewer bullets you allot to it. Another useful tool in saving space is to provide a sampling of deals or projects you have worked on instead of devoting extensive space to every major project you have worked on. So for instance, an investment banker can select three to four major deals she has worked on to show diversity of industries and breadth of experience instead of every single deal she was part of.

The professional experience section should be in reverse chronology, with the most current job first. If you work for a lesser-known company, consider including a sentence that describes what the firm does, its market size, and what makes it compelling. You should indicate your job title and show whether your role has grown over time. You should also make it easy for the MBA admissions board to follow your progress. Make sure the information on your tenure—your years at the job—is clear and easily identifiable. Ensure that the dates are easy to see.

Internships are valuable work experience that should not be ignored; in fact, they can be critical for early-career candidates with limited work experience. That said, however, the longer you have worked, the less important it is to provide detailed information on each internship you have held. You will need to make trade-offs on what specific information to focus on and what information to minimize. Experiences that reinforce your personal brand should be highlighted (especially if you have strong examples of leadership and impact). If you are branding yourself as someone who is an opportunity capturer and has exceptional relationship management skills, then it makes sense to share that you sourced deals and brought in three new clients to increase revenue by 22 percent. You might then choose to cut out information you have about your excellent computer language prowess in Java and C++.

For those of you with less work experience, the work experience section is even more important, because you have to make a strong case that you have the potential to "hold your own" in business school. You should not only highlight your current work but share information about your internships and show what you were able to do besides what may be considered grunt work. This section of the résumé is where you can show your maturity and initiative. If, for instance, you worked during your school year, you should definitely highlight the work you did and the value you created. If you were involved in an entrepreneurial venture, you should make sure that you communicate the size of the business, the achievement, and your role, so the admissions board can gauge whether you have enough professional insight to be admitted. The good news is that there is no age or work limit, so instead of focusing on the quantity of years of experience, show the impact and quality of contribution you had in the time you have worked.

The Education Section

The education section typically comes after the professional work experience section. The exception to this applies to applicants who are still in college or who have limited work experience. The first point you need to convey in the education section is where you went to school and your graduation year. It is worth including that you graduated early if that was your situation. It is also important to highlight your major, class rank, GPA, and any dual, double, or specialized degrees that you pursued. You should also mention any graduate degrees you have earned, as well as business coursework you have taken (especially if you did not take business classes in college). The education section is also where you discuss your academic awards, such as being on the dean's list or any scholarships and honors awards you received. If you received any unique and highly selective awards or honors, you should quantify this to help the admissions board understand its selectivity. You should also include your study-abroad program in this section.

Some additional points related to your grade point average (GPA): the GPA you reference on your résumé should match up to that on your official transcript. Inconsistencies, especially when the GPA on your résumé is higher than your official GPA, raise questions about your integrity. Education systems vary around the world, so don't worry if you don't have a GPA. If you graduated first class or with a second class upper, in the case of UK schools, then indicate that on your résumé. If you scored 9 out of 10 at one of the India Institute of Technology universities, then you should state that in your résumé. Don't try to convert to a GPA system if you don't have one.

Research papers published in professional journals should be mentioned in this section as well. For example, someone whose honors thesis is selected for presentation at a national professional association should highlight this achievement.

If you transferred from one school to another, it is important that your résumé reflects this change. I'm often asked whether an applicant is obligated to include the schools attended if he or she didn't graduate from there. The simple answer is yes. You don't want to misrepresent yourself. So if you left school after a semester or two and transferred to another school, you should include this information. Many MBA programs ask for all the schools you have attended, so not providing this information can come back to haunt you.

Other unique situations that are worth mentioning in the education section of your résumé can be self-financing your education or being the first in your family to graduate from college.

The Activities Section

This section of your résumé is also very important. Some applicants with very strong leadership track records will call this "Leadership Activities." Others can opt for simply "Activities." Individuals who are branding themselves as entrepreneurs and who have strong evidence of entrepreneurship involvement can choose to call this section "Entrepreneurial Activities." How you name this section will depend on your unique experiences and how you plan to brand yourself. Many applicants can organize their extracurricular activities and interests together under activities. Others may find that it makes more sense to separate them. If you happen to be someone with lots of activities, then you may want to keep them separate, but think carefully around the trade-offs of getting rid of some activities to ensure that your résumé remains one page long.

When you are thinking of your activities, you should think primarily in the context of leadership: Does it highlight your leadership attribute, character, or achievement? Remember the three Cs of leadership discussed earlier. You should keep them in mind when addressing the résumé in general and the activities section in particular. Showing a track record of consistent leadership not only in your career but in your community involvement and during your college years places you on a different level compared to your competition.

The activities section allows you to communicate how you are different from each candidate in your category who works in the same industry or firm. Are you involved in extracurricular activities that matter to you? Pick the ones that reinforce your brand message and where you had the greatest impact. You will be limited by space, so be selective on how far back you wish to go. The longer you have worked, the less far back you should go. A professional with ten years of experience should not go as far back as high school to highlight the summer Habitat for Humanity project he worked on for one weekend. It will raise flags about the absence of more recent community involvement. Your college activities are acceptable.

MBA admissions boards are interested in candidates who have a life outside of work and who are more than academic geniuses. The reality for many applicants is that they will have strong leadership activities while in college, but these often taper off once they start working, especially for those in the financial services and consulting industries. Even if you are no longer involved in a particular activity, if you had significant impact during your college years, you should highlight this in the activities section. Quality is also more important than quantity, so focus on the activities that mean the most to you rather than having a laundry list of peripheral involvement.

Applicants should go beyond listing their activities. They need to provide information that communicates the depth and scope of their involvement. Stay away from activities where your only involvement is as a member. Focus on those where you demonstrated leadership and impact. Applicants to business school often have a lot of leadership activities during college. Many of them showcase their leadership through activities such as managing the student investment portfolio, leading new initiatives through student senate, or supervising more than one hundred students as resident assistants.

Leadership roles can also come from athletics. For instance, you may have been the captain of your soccer team. Did the team's ranking improve? Did you institute any initiative to improve teamwork and training regimens?

Highlight your influence through this formal leadership role. Not all activities include formal leadership titles, however. So even if you were not the captain of your team, playing on a varsity sports team is an accomplishment to be proud of. You can highlight things such as the number of games played, team rank, any awards you received that set you apart (for instance, being ranked fifth in the nation among female doubles tennis players).

Activities can also come from your community involvement. The duration of your involvement is important (highlighting continuity and commitment), but if you do not have a history of long-term participation, you can offset this by focusing on your impact. Some of the exceptional leadership activities that I have come across over the years have been achieved in the span of less than a year. Whether you choose to serve on the leadership board of a nonprofit organization, or you start an organization to help immigrants assimilate into a new society, or you volunteer in an organization that does social good, the important point to convey in the activities section is the quantifiable contributions you have made and why it matters to you in the first place.

You can also do away with the activities section if you don't have many extracurricular activities. If that's the case, you will be better off eliminating this section altogether on your résumé and replacing it with the "other" section. This will allow you to focus on your varied interests, such as your salsa dancing, wine collecting, mountaineering, or whatever it may be. I go into greater detail on how you can capitalize on the "other" section next.

The Other Section

The final part of the résumé is the "Other" section, which can include your interests, skills, awards, or anything else that is important to your brand that you haven't highlighted yet. It is less important what you title this section. For example, you can call this final part of the résumé "Skills and Certifications" to capture your language proficiency skills as well as your technical abilities and certifications (such as the CFA). You can also call this section "Interests" to highlight your hobbies and passions. If you have publications or patents, then you can highlight these particular points in this section. This final part of the résumé can also be presented simply as "Other," which will allow you to cover different things that you want to communicate about your story.

Similar to the activities section, your "Other" section allows you to stand apart from your competition. There are no ideal profiles in this section. The important point to convey is that you are interesting and have a different point of view or perspective you can offer to the MBA class. One of the main admissions evaluation criteria is uniqueness. This information can cover aspects of your brand that differentiate you from other candidates. For instance, are you internationally minded? If you are, you can share your international travels or highlight your multilingual abilities (especially if you have achieved fluency). Don't write that you are fluent in a language when you are not.

This section of the résumé is where you share quirky and interesting things in your brand. Think about what the interest you profile says about you. Ask yourself whether it sets you apart or reinforces a stereotype that already exists about you. A simple example of this can be seen in the case of an engineer who is passionate about salsa dancing. His commitment comes through his four years as a dance instructor. The stereotype of the smart but bland technical individual goes out the window when you envision him gyrating to pulsating merengue music. Why is this important? It shows that this applicant not only has a life outside of work but is highly adaptable and can connect with different people.

Traveling is an interest that falls in the "usual-suspect" category. If you choose to discuss traveling as an interest of yours, make sure you go beyond, "I like to travel and see new cities." This is a major cliché and gets you zero bonus points. A better way to convey this could be leading a trek to a remote area that isn't your usual hot spot. If your travel led to your interest in a particular region and you decided to work there, then it is worth mentioning. Here's an example of this: "Avid Traveler: Trip to Costa Rica during college break led to discovery of eco-tourism and influenced decision to work in Costa Rica for a year after graduating from college."

There are other interesting things about your background that you may wish to address in the "Other" section of your résumé. A few examples are captured here:

- Growing up in an interesting region, especially one where there are ongoing global political issues (for example, Thailand, Egypt, Sudan, Syria, Afghanistan)

- Unusual upbringing can also be interesting to feature in the interests/other section: growing up in a blue-collar family in the Midwest; being the first in your family to attend college; raising your younger siblings because of family issues; living in different countries; growing up on a farm or an Indian reservation
- Running marathons in cities around the world that have a special meaning to you

Skills, awards, and certifications are also important elements to flag in the interests/other section of the résumé. As with other parts of the résumé, you have to determine whether the information you are highlighting will resonate with the brand of the school. Schools that are highly technical will likely appreciate your technical achievements in mastering programming languages or in building a complicated network system more than schools that are not.

If you are a financial analyst, having passed all three levels of the chartered financial analyst (CFA) exams is an important accomplishment to share in your résumé. The same thing applies to other certifications, whether the certified public accountant (CPA) for accountants or the Series 7 and 66 exams to sell securities.

If you have received awards for something you do outside of work, this is also the appropriate area to mention it. For example, I knew a banker who happened to be very dynamic and was selected to be a national spokesperson to promote positive and educational achievements for teenagers. These types of eclectic achievements are worth mentioning in your résumé. A consultant interested in teenage empowerment can highlight her experience launching the first-ever teen-focused television programming in her country. If she received an award for her work, then that is even more compelling.

If you are not sure what should make it into the résumé and what should be cut out, start by writing down everything and then cut down anything that doesn't reinforce your brand, showcase your leadership, or differentiate you from others. Don't be shy about getting feedback from coworkers who are alumni from the MBA programs you are interested in, or getting the opinion of a professional admissions consultant.

But beyond the five résumé components, candidates for business school are often at a loss regarding how narrow or broad they should keep their résumé. This issue goes to the heart of the next section—deciding between breadth and depth when positioning the résumé.

POSITIONING THE RÉSUMÉ: BREADTH VS. DEPTH

I am often asked whether it is better to have worked for one company or in the same industry in similar roles (depth) versus having multiple positions in different industries and/or roles (breadth). The simple answer is that it depends on each candidate's particular situation. There are admitted candidates who worked at the same firm and in the same functional area for several years. These individuals' backgrounds showcase their depth of experience and commitment to their industry. The challenge for applicants with significant depth is to show that they have not stagnated at the same company or job. It is important to show that your responsibility and contribution have grown even though you have remained at the same firm. An investment banker who worked three years as an analyst and then got promoted to associate with responsibility for managing analysts is an example of a candidate with depth of experience.

Equally admissible are candidates with breadth of work experience. These candidates have résumés that reflect different job positions. The roles can be different in terms of function or in terms of industry. An example of a candidate with breadth of work experience is the accountant who worked for Ernst & Young, then joined the Peace Corps after a couple of years, and then decided to work for a foundation. The challenge that a candidate with breadth of experience faces is making sure that the story is cogent and that the dots of the experiences are well connected. Candidates from professional backgrounds with a lot of breadth have to show that their career path has been well planned and isn't haphazard and random.

Regardless of where you fall on the breadth/depth continuum, make sure that your work experiences focus on your brand, demonstrate that you have developed new skills even within a focused role, and that you have had an impact on the organizations, teams, and individuals with whom you have worked. But more than that, you should show that the choices you have made in your career make sense and show logical progression.

The focus should be on the most compelling things about you.

Remember that the résumé is an extension of your brand. Make sure it is consistent with the rest of your application. Are your brand attributes and themes represented in your résumé? When the admissions board reads your résumé, it should confirm the conclusion they have already drawn of who you are. The sample résumé that follows provides a picture of what a winning résumé looks like. This applicant felt strongly about keeping a hobbies section for the résumé instead of calling it "Interests." That's fine. It's less about exact wording of the section and more about what the details covered reveal about you.

SAMPLE RÉSUMÉ

John Greatchance • +2340000000 • JohnGreatchance@gmail.com

EDUCATION

ABC University, City, Country

- Bachelor of Medicine and Surgery, October 2012
- Graduated at the top 8 percent in a class of 200

EXPERIENCE

ABC Pension Fund, City, Country

Lead Investment Strategist, 05/2013–Present

- Develop long-term and short-term investment strategies for a $2 billion pension portfolio
- Restructured the investment department into three functional units, thus improving productivity
- Convinced the board of directors to sell down a sub-optimal $20 million equity portfolio and introduce a new $150 million equity portfolio
- Created an investment policy statement for the proprietary funds that has turned its performance around

Senior Research Analyst, 01/2012–04/2013

- Launched research reports for different investment opportunities for the $1.5 billion pension portfolios
- Developed an internal portfolio benchmark that helped reshape the investment philosophy industry-wide

- Repositioned the $1 billion bond portfolio, resulting in a gain of more than $75 million within six months
- Raised the annual returns of the pension funds from just over 7 percent to more than 11 percent within a year

XYZ Investment Management Company, City, Country

Portfolio Manager, 04/2010–12/2011
- Oversaw the management of an equity mutual fund and discretionary portfolios worth more than $40 million
- Achieved 0 percent attrition rate for discretionary portfolios despite high market volatilities
- Unearthed a relatively unknown listed company that returned more than 200 percent for the firm in less than two years
- Recruited, trained, and mentored junior analysts for the firm

Investment Analyst, 07/2009–03/2010
- Analyzed different investment opportunities and made recommendations to the Investment Committee
- Created a model to determine sources of returns for portfolios, thus enhancing efficient asset allocation
- Influenced senior management to deploy my analytical skills in the corporate brokerage and research units

Equity Analyst, 01/2009–06/2009
- Developed and maintained a model portfolio that formed the basis for all equity investments in the firm
- Structured a two-year note that outperformed the total expected return in six months for a $5 million portfolio
- Launched a monthly report for the equity mutual and discretionary portfolios that enhanced communications with clients

OTHER ACTIVITIES
- Co-founder/Investment Manager, ABC Foundation, 11/2012–Present

HOBBIES
- Traveling, reading, soccer, networking

COMMON RÉSUMÉ MISTAKES

1. Jargon: A résumé for admission to business school is very different from a résumé for an application for a job. Unlike work résumés, which are full of industry terms, résumés for an MBA application need to be short, jargon-free, and clear. Avoid acronyms that have little meaning to people outside your industry.

2. Empty adjectives: Superfluous language without tangible numbers to back it up offers little insight into exactly what you have achieved professionally. Also, speaking in generalities does not reveal your actual impact. Winning résumés always quantify the change you brought about or the impact you had. Here's what I mean: "developed and implemented a new sales marketing plan that lead to a 40 percent increase in sales revenue."

3. Single dimension: MBA admissions boards are looking for candidates who are multidimensional. Don't hesitate to put that quirky hobby or organization you have been volunteering for on your résumé. Being smart or working at a blue-chip firm isn't enough to land a coveted admission spot. Use the résumé to represent what else you have done with your time outside of work.

4. Jumping around: Leaving your job after a brief tenure can be a red flag to the admissions board. Obviously this advice is helpful only if you are planning to make the jump. For those of you who have already left your firm after a brief stint, look for a subtle place in your application to address this issue. But equally important is to connect the dots to show that the next move was a strategic decision that fit within your overall career goals.

5. Dishonesty: This goes without saying, but I can't stress the importance of not inflating your achievements. The MBA admissions board can see through any attempts to "pad" your story. Also, don't be tempted to leave out positions where you worked for a brief period. Hiding the truth has a way of coming back to bite you when you least expect it!

6. Length, clutter, and lack of focus: A five-page CV is not acceptable for an MBA application A busy admissions board member does not want to spend an hour trying to decipher your CV. Keep

your résumé to one page and focus on the impact and results you delivered. Avoid manipulating the font size to try to jam everything into the résumé. Résumés in fonts smaller than 10-point are too difficult for the reader to read. Leave lots of white space to make the résumé attractive and inviting. A cluttered résumé is less inviting to read.

7.   Mistakes: A shoddy résumé will reflect negatively on your brand. Avoid spelling mistakes and grammatical errors. Make sure your numbers are accurate so that you don't have to explain yourself when the school verifies your application after you have been admitted. Inconsistencies in your story can be reason for an admission offer to be rescinded.

8.   No tailoring: Every school is different. For instance, when applying to MIT Sloan, a school with a strong innovation and technical brand, you may be well-served to include information about the highly technical courses you took in college or the technical project you managed during your internship. On the other hand, it may be more compelling to use the limited space to address the marketing projects you worked on if you are applying to Kellogg or Michigan, programs with strong marketing brands.

9.   Failure to educate: If you have an unusual industry, firm, or role, make sure you provide a short description under the professional employment section to educate the reader about your experience and impact. This will help the MBA admissions board understand that your company isn't a hole-in-the-wall and that your impact was significant. This is particularly important for internationals whose companies may not be as well known in the United States.

10.   Being boring: Although the résumé is not an essay, it needs to be interesting and well written to capture the attention of the admissions board. Make sure you use active descriptors and avoid using passive sentences. Action verbs are the best way to describe your experiences.

11.   Poor judgment: In an attempt to make the résumé stand out, never resort to gimmicks; they are likely to fail! Stick to the facts and keep the entire résumé professional. Your email address should be professional; avoid things that will make the admissions board question your maturity, such as spunkychic@gmail.com. Save

those for your friends only. Your résumé will stand out based on the merit of your work rigor, initiative, and impact.

Now that you are armed with a solid résumé, you are ready for your audition, the interview. The résumé summarizes your story, and an interview allows you to expound on it. Next to the essays, your interview is your best chance to "sell" yourself.

CHAPTER EIGHT

The Interview

I NTERESTINGLY, A LOT HAS changed concerning admissions interviews since I wrote the first edition of *The Best Business Schools' Admissions Secrets*. For example, interviews are becoming even more important in the evaluation of candidates due to the decisions by several business schools to reduce the number of application essays. Other changes include Wharton's introduction of small group discussions prior to a one-on-one interview, HBS's decision to require applicants to write a memo to the admissions board twenty-four hours after they interview, and, of course, a new move by a few programs to require applicants to videotape themselves answering questions posed by the school.

You might also find that there is a greater reliance on Skype interviews over phone interviews. Skype has become the "go-to" interview option for applicants who are unable to visit the school.

While developments like these are happening constantly in the admissions process as technology evolves, the purpose of the interview remains the same:

> Your admission interview is both evaluative and informative: it is an opportunity for us to learn more about you, and for you to learn more about Stanford GSB.

(Source: Stanford GSB website)

Applicants must recognize that an interview is a two-way conversation in which you are given a chance to assess whether the MBA program fits your brand; in turn, the interviewer uses the meeting to determine whether you are a good fit for the MBA program.

You have to put your best foot forward and sell your uniqueness. Let's look at a quick example. Susan has an average GMAT score, but her leadership across college, community, and career is significant. She also has glowing recommendations that offset her not-so-stellar GMAT score. In an interview, she is articulate, dynamic, and likable. She knows exactly why she wants an MBA and is able to convey precisely why the particular program fits her goals. During the forty-five-minute conversation, she is able to communicate what is distinctive about her and win over her interviewer. Suffice it to say, she is admitted to her dream school despite having a GMAT score that is below the median of the entering class.

Candidates like Susan understand that the interview does matter. It doesn't make sense to spend all that time on your application and then drop the ball when it comes to the interview. MBA admissions boards use the interview to assess a candidate. Even when the interviews are by invitation only, 30 to 60 percent of candidates who are interviewed receive an admission offer (depending on the school). So you should view the interview as a practical step that brings you closer to your admission goal.

An interview allows the MBA admissions board to verify the authenticity of your "story." It's also a way for the board to learn anything about you (positive or negative) that didn't come through in your application. The main value of the interview is that it can actually sway an admission decision when the board is on the fence about a candidate.

Most admissions interviews at top business schools are based on your résumé. Exceptions to this are Harvard Business School and NYU Stern, which review the entire application of each candidate and generate follow-up interview questions based on the actual application.

It is important for applicants to fully understand each MBA program's interview process and policy.

INTERVIEW POLICIES

Interviews at MBA programs are either open (any applicant can sign up) or by invitation only. Interviews usually last thirty to forty-five minutes, so there is little opportunity to ramble or waste time chatting. Make sure you keep your responses short and to the point. Most business schools interview their entire admitted class. Only a few do not. Also popular is a move from open interviews to invitation-only interviews, demonstrated by schools like Chicago GSB, which went from being an open-interview school to an invitation-interview program. Only a few top MBA programs (for instance, Tuck and Kellogg) maintain an open interview policy, and these interviews have to be conducted early in the application process. To be safe, visit each school's website to confirm its interview policy, since it can change from year to year. Regardless of whether a program has an open or an invitation-only interview policy, or whether the interview is only a few minutes or an all-day affair (as at some of the European schools), you should take the time to thoroughly prepare for it. I will discuss the preparation steps later in this chapter.

Invitation-Only Interview Policy

Most top business schools have an invitation-only interview policy. These programs invite candidates in whom they are interested for an interview. The interviews are typically conducted on campus (by admissions board members, current students, or faculty in the case of some European schools), in your city of residence (by alumni and board members), or over the phone or Skype. Most interviews focus on your résumé. Exceptions exist at schools like Harvard and NYU, where the entire application is reviewed beforehand. The design of the questions allows the interviewers to understand the decisions you have made, your self-awareness, the impact you have had in the workplace, and the way you do what you do that is uniquely you. An invitation to interview is welcome news to any candidate, but it isn't a guaranteed admission. Therefore, you should view the interview invitation as an opportunity to "sell" your story in person to the MBA admissions board.

Open Interview Policy

For an open interview, you should make arrangements to visit the school as soon as possible to take advantage of this opportunity. It's likely that your interview will be conducted by a current student who serves as an admissions ambassador. Because an open interview typically involves a review of your résumé, you should be prepared to walk your interviewer through your résumé and provide him or her with insights into the career choices you have made and the impact you had in each position. Equally important is using the interview to reveal your personality and the activities and organizations you are involved in outside of work that make you an interesting individual. I caution applicants to never pass on the interview, even if the school states that it is optional. Ignoring the interview will likely suggest that you are not serious about the school, which makes it easy for the admissions board to discount your application.

When you interview, you should take every opportunity to impress on the MBA program that you are a great fit and will make a strong contribution to the class. Think of every interaction with the MBA program as a mini-interview. Before your interview, you may wish to attend an information session or student happy hour to learn more about the program. Believe it or not, you are still being evaluated, even when you are out of the interview setting. Outliers will always stand out. So individuals who happen to be extremely articulate or dynamic, or who have unique backgrounds will be remembered from the pack. Also memorable are candidates who are selfish (ask multiple questions during an open-house event), ask inappropriate questions, or seem pushy or arrogant. Even when you are interacting with current students, you are still being evaluated. A former colleague from a top MBA program recounted how a prospective student he had interviewed attended a student happy hour and got drunk, danced on the table, and bragged about how he had the interview in the bag. Suffice it to say, he didn't get the congratulatory admission call. Finally, the proliferation of technology has made it possible for many candidates to interact with each other in online communities. Rest assured that the admissions board is reading the blogs and communication exchanges on these sites. So be very careful what you share. It can come back to haunt you! And while I'm on the subject of watching your online reputation, I need to remind you to make sure that you don't have anything on your Facebook page that may call into question your integrity.

WHO WILL INTERVIEW ME?

There are four groups of interviewers: admissions board members, alumni, current students, and faculty. Applicants often may not get to choose which of these individuals will interview them because it varies from school to school. In some cases, applicants have control over who will interview them—on-campus interviews often mean the interview is by a student or admissions board member, while interviews in the city where you live will often mean that you will be interviewed by an alumnus living in that area or admissions board member visiting the region. If you have the choice, I recommend opting for the admissions board member first and then everyone else. Other MBA programs, like Cambridge Judge School of Business, have professors who conduct all the interviews.

Alumni interviews are very popular among many leading business schools. And some of these schools, like Stanford GSB, do a good job of preparing and selecting their alumni interviewers. The reality, however, is that applicants may not always encounter well-prepared alumni interviewers. I've had several of my clients complain about their experiences. Some extreme cases include alumni blowing off the interview, having applicants wait for long lengths of time, and even saying inappropriate things to the applicant during the interview. Applicants should alert the school if they have concrete evidence of inappropriate behavior on the part of their alumni interviewers.

Interestingly, some MBA programs like Wharton have moved away from using alumni interviewers and now focus more on admissions board and student interviews. HBS now uses nearly 100 percent admissions board interviews, whereas in the past it relied on alumni interviewers, especially for more out-of-the-way regions of the world. Today, HBS and other top business schools have a robust interview calendar, and they visit key cities and countries to conduct interviews.

You will not have the choice to select who will interview you at INSEAD, since their interviews are done by alumni—actually, two alumni. INSEAD's approach to use two different alumni interviewers is intended to ensure more objective and balanced feedback. This can pose even greater stress for many applicants who have an additional interview to prepare for. On the other hand, some applicants can find the INSEAD two-interview option a relief, thinking, "If I don't connect with my first interviewer, I'll have another chance to deliver a better interview with the next."

Student interviews are growing in popularity as well. The value of being interviewed by current students is that they are living the MBA experience and will have a fresh perspective on the school, which can be insightful to prospective candidates. Be ready to ask your interviewer about his or her experiences at the school.

Current students can be protective of their program and, in some instances, may be inclined to act as "gatekeepers." Be aware of this, and don't take offense if you encounter a student interviewer who seems unusually tough. Focus on conveying your brand, achievements, and the specific value you would bring to the program. Stay optimistic and hold your ground when faced with a difficult and belligerent student interviewer.

Faculty interviews are far more popular at European business schools than their American counterparts. The Saïd Business School at Oxford uses either a faculty or administrator of the school who is a sector expert for interviews, while the Judge School at Cambridge relies only on faculty members as interviewers. Applicants should bear in mind that the faculty member is the one teaching at the program and will be paying close attention to the intellectual aptitude of the student beyond the academic data included in their résumés and transcripts.

Regardless of whether you end up with a "save the world" alumnus, an overzealous student, a nitpicky faculty member, or a jaded admissions board member, remain calm and make sure you communicate your personal brand and what you will bring to the program effectively.

WHERE SHOULD I INTERVIEW?

I'm often asked whether there is a difference between on-campus and off-campus interviews. From an evaluation standpoint, there is little difference. Candidates who reside abroad may find it cost-prohibitive to travel to campus for an interview on short notice, given expensive travel costs. They may opt to be interviewed by phone or through an online video method. Regardless of how you interview, all of these interview modes are weighed the same. If you know that you express yourself better in person, then you should choose a face-to-face meeting instead of a phone or Skype interview. The extra money spent for your travel expenses will be worth it if the outcome is an admission offer to your dream school. A phone interview may be a bit more challenging, because the interviewer does not have the benefit of seeing your nonverbal gestures to "fill in" communication. If you opt for the phone interview, make sure you speak clearly, get to the point quickly, and avoid interruptions.

Even if you choose to interview in your city, you still need to investigate the school closely by making a visit. There is no substitute for sitting in class and observing the teaching method, quality of faculty instruction, and interactions between students to better assess whether the program is right for you. A pet peeve of the admissions board is interviewing a candidate who resides in the same city as the MBA program and finding out that he has not taken the time to attend a class. Don't give the MBA admissions board a chance to question your judgment or commitment to their program.

GUIDE TO MBA VIDEO INTERVIEWS

Some MBA admissions boards have expressed concern that applicants have become overpolished to the point that it has become difficult for schools to determine who the real candidate is. This belief, as well as a strong desire to get a better perspective of who each applicant is, has led three business schools to incorporate video interviews as a required part of their application.

Toronto's Rotman School of Management is the leader in video interviews and introduced this medium to its application process in 2012. The school requires applicants to respond to two interview questions drawn from a question bank of about one hundred, which includes such questions as "Who inspires you?" and "If you had a free day, what would you do?" The focus shouldn't be tracking down the actual interview questions. Rather, I encourage applicants to be ready to share who they are and what their brand is and to speak from the heart when answering the video interview questions.

In her admissions blog, Rotman's Director of Admissions, Niki da Silva, describes the value of this new medium: "Both questions are designed to be answered without any advanced preparation and will allow us to get to know the personality, interests, passions, and talents of our applicants much better than we could in a written essay format. This tool actually will allow us to capture video responses in real time, so it is different and more relevant than simply uploading how you might answer a canned essay question in video format."

Some American business schools such as Yale School of Management and Kellogg are following in Rotman's footsteps by requiring all their applicants to complete a video interview. Yale claims that its focus on this format will allow the school to assess language ability (for international students), ability to think quickly on one's feet, and other softer traits such as poise and composure. Kellogg's approach is a bit more laid-back, and it views its new video requirement as a chance for the entire admissions board to meet every candidate. Yale requires applicants to answer three questions that test skills in three different categories—behavior, opinion, and data interpretation. They do not get to retape their answers. The types of questions that you will face will include many of the usual-suspect type of questions, such as how your friends or past colleagues would describe you, your leadership style, how you engage with an organization, a diffi-cult decision you handled, etc. What is new is the open-ended opinion questions like "Without arts, an education cannot be accomplished. Do you agree or disagree? Why?" and "As businesses become more global, the differences between cultures decrease. Do you agree or disagree? Why?" You have to have a strong opinion, and you have to defend it with backup statements. It's less about having the exact answer and more about articulating your opinion confidently and logically.

Kellogg's video interview, on the other hand, includes only one ques-tion, and applicants have three chances to re-record themselves if they are dissatisfied with their responses.

The video format presents unique challenges for which applicants need to be prepared:

- Because you don't always know what questions you will be asked, it is important that you practice a variety of questions but focus more on speaking candidly and supporting your views and less on having the exact right answer, since the questions aren't about the right answer.
- Become comfortable speaking to the webcam, which can be quite awkward for some applicants.
- Time yourself to ensure that you are comfortable speaking within the allotted time. You don't want to cut off the interview too early. You also don't want to be cut off by the system if you are too long-winded. The Yale system cuts you off after ninety seconds, and there isn't a do-over!
- Tape yourself answering the questions and then assess how you performed to see areas where you need further practice.

WHAT WILL THE VIDEO INTERVIEW LOOK LIKE?			
	Yale	Kellogg	Rotman
Questions	3	1	2
Preparation Time	10–20 seconds	1–2 minutes	45 seconds
Answer Time	1.5 minutes per question	1–2 minutes	1.5 minutes per question
Re-record?	No	Yes—3 takes allowed	No
Question type	Behavior, opinion, data interpretation	Personal, "get-to-know-you"	Personal, "get-to-know-you"

For now, most business schools have not introduced a video component to their interview process, but we will continue to watch this trend to see how prevalent it becomes in the future among business schools. Other tips related to preparing for a video interview are covered in the Skype interview preparation section below.

PREPARATION FOR THE SKYPE INTERVIEW

When I wrote the first edition of this book, few schools relied on video interview methods as the main way to assess candidates who are unable to visit campus. Phone interviews were often the standard. Today, most MBA programs prefer Skype as the best way to assess remote applicants. Here are some practical dos and don'ts to keep in mind when preparing for your Skype interview.

1. Confirm the time zone and time; you don't want to find out that you missed your interview because you didn't clarify the start time or correct time zone.

2. Download the most recent version of Skype, and then practice using it. The interview isn't the time for you to begin tinkering with this software.

3. Use a headset. A good option is from Logitech. Test the volume and use the Skype Test Call feature to make sure you are well-prepared. Check your Internet speed, and make sure you have a minimum of 1.2 Mbps of bandwidth.

4. Make sure you have an appropriate Skype username. Needless to

say, beachbabe2010 isn't appropriate. Create a new one if your current one is inappropriate for the interview.

5.   Get your lighting right. For Skype interviews, it is best to have a light directly in front of the computer, facing you instead of behind you. Good lighting makes it easy for the interviewer to see your facial expressions.

6.   Maintain proper eye contact. Avoid looking directly at the screen, since it will appear that you are looking elsewhere. To maintain proper Skype eye contact, you need to look at the webcam lens on your computer, not at your screen.

7.   Choose a tidy room.

8.   Minimize noise. Make appropriate arrangements to ensure that you won't be interrupted by your children, pets, or phones.

9.   Dress appropriately! Avoid the temptation to wear professional attire only from the waist up. I had a client once who accidentally hit his laptop during his Skype interview, turning the webcam downward and revealing his happy SpongeBob SquarePants pajamas.

A FEW WORDS ABOUT INTERVIEW DAYS

If you are targeting European MBA programs like IMD, IESE, or Judge, you will face the all-day interview. In a way, these programs' interview approach is a cross between the traditional interview and a prospective student day that takes place at many top U.S. schools. The European schools want to use the interview experience to sell their programs to the applicants that they are most keen on attracting to their programs. But these interviews aren't just intended to sell applicants on their programs; they are also designed as opportunities for lengthier engagement with applicants as a part of the evaluation process.

Let's take a closer look at IMD's interview day. The school's website explicitly states:

> IMD's unique three-part interview process allows us to assess your intellectual capabilities, emotional intelligence, integrity, and ability to perform under pressure and work with others.

Here is a sample of what a typical IMD interview day looks like:

- Personal interview:

  A member of the admissions committee will take this time to get to know you and develop a better understanding of your career progression and key achievements.

- Impromptu presentation:

  When you arrive, we give you a business topic on which to prepare a five-minute presentation to demonstrate, among other things, your communication and presentation skills.

- Case study:

  A professor leads a mini case study with other candidates, to give you a feel for our teaching methods and us a feel for how you contribute in this kind of setting.

- MBA class observation:

  If possible, you will sit in and observe our MBAs in the auditorium. This helps you to assess us and our teaching style, just as we will be assessing you and your potential.

- Lunch with MBAs:

  Talk to our current participants and ask them any questions you have about their experiences.

(Source: IMD website)

IMD's interview day is one of the most intense and robust interview assessments, and each candidate is assessed across multiple activities. Other top programs have an entire day of activities tied to their interview day, but a lot of their activities are centered around informally getting to know the candidate and providing more of a chance for the candidate to learn about the school.

Here is how Cambridge Judge Business School describes their interview day and process:

Short-listed candidates are invited to an interview day at Cambridge Judge Business School. In exceptional circumstances (for example, if it is difficult for you to get a visa at short notice to visit the UK), we are sometimes able to offer interviews in your own country or occasionally by telephone. We do, however, strongly prefer candidates to visit us in Cambridge, as each interview day comprises a full programme of selection and information events, including:

- a group Q&A session with admissions, careers, and other key staff
- an individual interview with faculty members
- information about funding your MBA
- a tour of the facilities at Cambridge Judge Business School
- coffee and lunch with current MBA students plus meetings with MBA families if required

(Source: Cambridge Judge Business School website)

Applicants interviewing at MBA programs shouldn't make the mistake of assuming that the only evaluative part of the application is the individual interview with faculty. Every interaction you have with a member of the board is a chance to stand out, so be prepared to be on your best behavior the entire time you are on campus.

WHAT DO INTERVIEWS ASSESS?

Understanding what exactly the interview evaluates can help candidates prepare for and ace the interview. The following are the key variables being assessed in interviews for business schools.

Likability

Yes, interviewers want to know that you are someone they can imagine sitting with in class. If they sense any sign of arrogance, awkwardness, or personality issues, they are likely to pass on your candidacy. It doesn't mean that everyone has to fit into a cookie-cutter model. So be yourself, but know that the interviewer wants to admit individuals who come across as positive, inviting, and personable. Even a member of Mensa who is uncommunicative may be denied admission if he or she comes off as arrogant or as a bookworm with little personality.

Intelligence

Intelligence is important. The interviewer will check to see if you grasp things quickly. He or she may spend a good amount of time asking clarifying questions about your academic experience. If your GPA is lower than average, be prepared to speak to the rigor of the coursework and own up to why the grades are not exceptional. You may also be asked about your GMAT or GRE score, so be comfortable speaking about it regardless of whether it is in the high percentile or lower than average. How you address this question is key. If your score is low, you don't want to seem defensive by trying to justify it. Instead, focus on the positives to your story, such as the quantitative courses you took, the A grades you earned, a strong GPA, and rigorous analytical work experience. Conversely, if your score is in the top 95th percentile, don't gloat either.

Candidates may also face questions about trends in the business world or may be asked an open-ended question that forces them to analyze a business situation. Here's an illustration: "Describe in a couple of minutes a trend you see in your industry and tell me how you would go about capturing the market opportunity." What the admissions board is looking for is to understand how you think, whether you are sharp on your feet, and if you have a sophisticated awareness of issues going on in the business world.

Rigor and Impact of the Job

Your work experience will receive significant scrutiny in most interviews. Interviewers usually focus on specific questions about your career that are designed to reveal what your specific role was and the size of the impact you had in each position. Be ready to discuss your exact role and the results you generated. Make sure to quantify your impact whenever possible. When answering career impact questions, be careful not to sound arrogant and be willing to give credit where credit is due.

Leadership

Leadership is a very important aspect of the interview. The three Cs of leadership (college, community, and career leadership) are evaluated during the interview. Remember that leadership is not only about title. It's about initiative, innovation, influence, and expertise. As noted previously, show the impact you had in each position. Use vivid examples to illustrate your points instead of rattling off lists of leadership roles; focus on the most compelling examples and tell short but direct stories to connect the dots between each experience. Don't lose sight of the "why" in the process of discussing the "what." Schools want to understand your motivations for taking on leadership roles and how they shaped and affected you.

Communication Ability

Communication ability is very important, especially for MBA programs that are primarily case-based. Whether English is your first, second, or third language, the interviewer will scrutinize your communication skills. Practicing prior to the interview will allow you to communicate your thoughts in a conscientious and logical way. If you are verbose, it behooves you to really practice a succinct delivery. If you come across as unfocused or, worse, as an incompetent speaker, you jeopardize your admission chances. Nervous candidates can also get into trouble by talking too much and not answering the interview questions. One candidate who was very bubbly rambled so much during her interview for a top program that her interviewer only managed to ask her a few questions during the entire interview. The candidate came across as flighty and was denied admission to the MBA program.

Personal and Professional Maturity

The maturity question is a big one. In an interview, be prepared to express the thoughtfulness that has gone into the decisions you have made professionally and personally. Even if you have gaps in your story (for example, a lower-than-average GPA, limited community leadership, even loss of your job), how you respond to the question will communicate your maturity. Candidates who are just starting their careers are also under significant scrutiny when it comes to maturity. They have to convey that they have thought through their career goals and have a sound rationale for why they want their MBA now.

Self-Awareness

MBA candidates who meet all three admissions criteria can still be denied admission. Such cases are often the result of a lack of fit or an interview that didn't go well. It's one thing to have a stellar packaged story, but how you stand up to the face-to-face evaluation of an interview can determine your admission outcome. A perfect package that doesn't represent who you are will quickly unravel in the interview. Candidates who have all the necessary attributes but lack insight into their goals and the decisions they have made (including the decision to pursue an MBA) will also struggle during the interview. On the other hand, a candidate who may not be exceptional on paper can use the interview to tip his or her admission decision to a positive outcome by demonstrating extraordinary insight and self-awareness. Just as with essays, in which insight is as important as what you have achieved, the self-awareness that you exhibit in an interview is critical in differentiating you from your competition.

When HBS introduced a post-interview reflection component to its application in 2012, there was a lot of speculation about what it meant for applicants and how best to prepare for it. This "memo" to the admissions board is a test of an applicant's self-awareness. You have experienced the interview. You know what happened or didn't happen. You have to accurately read the vibes of the interview and respond appropriately. Your response will be evaluated for the judgment you exercised. For most candidates, the post-interview reflection at HBS will not move the dial one way or the other in terms of their admission outcome. But there will likely be some cases where something that is said in this post-interview memo gets an admissions board that is on the fence to say, "Wait a minute, perhaps this candidate is worth another look."

My advice to applicants is to have your perceptive hat on. What are the questions you were asked, and what information is the interviewer trying to get at? For example, you may go into an interview and find yourself being asked a lot of questions about your work experience. This may be a signal that the interviewer isn't convinced about your role, your impact, or some other aspects of the story. If you feel you were able to answer them satisfactorily, then in a follow-up memo, it would warrant a mere mention. On the other hand, if you felt that there was more that the interviewer was trying to get and that you didn't do a very good job answering the question, then thoughtful but brief statements in the follow-up reflection will be warranted.

A final word of advice on this topic: the post-interview reflection isn't a chance for you to squeeze in a random essay that had nothing to do with your interview. Show good judgment by keeping this short (two to three medium-length paragraphs). Thank the interviewer, recap on the interview, and end with one key point that you want to underscore about yourself. And of course, write in a straightforward way that captures your voice. Read your response aloud. If it doesn't sound conversational, you have likely erred too far on the side of formality.

Team Dynamics

As with likability, you should anticipate that the interviewer will want to assess how you operate in group settings. Be ready to talk about your team projects and how you function in groups. (Are you a leader who steps up immediately, or do you lead from behind?) The important point here is to show that you are not a solo player. Even if your job has limited group interaction, look for ways to introduce how you have sought out that type of interaction (even if it is outside of your job) to reassure the interviewer that you are comfortable when operating in team environments.

Nowhere is the team assessment more relevant than in Wharton's group interview, introduced in 2012. Wharton applicants invited to interview are first emailed a discussion topic ahead of the meeting and on interview day are divided into groups of six, with two student admissions board members observing each team discussion. Each applicant gets to make an opening statement on the topic and then a discussion proceeds. The key thing to keep in mind is that an exercise like this isn't about having "the right answer" but more about giving the interviewers a chance to observe you in a group setting to see whether you can communicate your ideas intelligently, whether you can respect others who disagree with you, and whether or not you are a jerk. The reality of this interview mode, from the feedback I've received from many of our clients, is that most people are on their best behavior. But outliers with poor interpersonal skills do emerge, making it easy to weed those applicants out.

This exercise is then followed with a brief one-on-one interview, in which candidates are asked how they think the group discussion went, whether they interacted in a way that is consistent with how they normally operate in teams, and finally a few usual-suspect questions about their career goals, career progression, and intended involvement at Wharton.

With the exception of Michigan's Ross Business School, MBA programs have not jumped on the Wharton group interview bandwagon. Wharton reported a decline in its application numbers this past year, leaving one to wonder whether the group interview format was a turnoff to applicants, particularly international candidates. This group followed by one-on-one interview format at Wharton is relatively new, and it will be interesting to see how long it continues to offer it.

Composure and Presence

The interview reveals information about who you are in person. It can confirm the brand you presented in your application, or it may completely call it into question. This is why it is important to present an authentic brand in your application. Also, be aware of how you come across in face-to-face interactions. The following story reinforces this point. A candidate was reviewed, and the consensus was that she was a WOW ("walks on water") candidate. But after the interview, her interviewer expressed surprise at how extremely laid-back and almost disengaged she seemed when compared with the vibrant individual who came across on paper. Fortunately, the recommendations the candidate provided were strong enough to lead to an admission offer. Had her recommendations been average, she might not have been admitted. Make sure you are excited, engaging, and interesting during your interview. Try to exude energy when you interview, even if you have a laid-back personality. I'm not advocating being fake. Feigning an outgoing personality when you are an introvert is not wise. But it's important, even while being laid-back, to show that you can be engaged in a dynamic classroom environment.

While composure and presence are important for every applicant, it is even more important for early-career applicants. A candidate with less work experience could shine in the interview by handling the interview with great poise and confidence. With some MBA programs introducing video elements into the application process, the admissions board will have more opportunity to review how you come across in person by simply viewing your taped videos to see how composed you are. You won't be immediately disqualified just because you have a case of nerves. But if you seem very nervous and inarticulate throughout the entire interview, you will likely face an uphill battle convincing the admissions board to admit you into their program.

Fit and Knowledge of the Program

The interviewer will often grill applicants to make sure that they have thought through exactly why they want admission into the MBA program. The more clarity you have about what you need to achieve your long-term goals and the more you are able to connect this with the MBA program, the stronger your case will be for why the program is a fit for you. Candidates who have not visited the campus or sat in on a class leave themselves open to questions about their commitment to the program. Take the time to research the program extensively before interviewing so that you can articulate precisely why the program is ideal for you. Be ready to talk not only about what the program will give you but also about what you will contribute to the program if admitted. Some MBA programs go to the length of asking you about the actions you took to research their program.

HOW TO APPROACH AND PREPARE FOR THE INTERVIEW

Following are some tasks that will help you prepare for the interview ahead of time.

Refine Your Résumé

Remember that the business school résumé is less about job description and industry jargon and more about your potential as a leader and business manager. Refer to the previous chapter on the résumé for reminders on how to craft a strong MBA application résumé.

Talk to Products of the Programs

Most companies have employees who are alumni from top MBA programs. Don't be afraid to invite them for lunch or drinks to learn about their MBA experiences and the subsequent impact on their careers. Current students can also be a huge asset in helping you prepare for the interview as well. Finally, even fellow prospective students can be helpful by sharing their interview experience. (Online communities like Bloomberg's Businessweek.com can give you a sense of the types of interview questions candidates are facing.) I will add one caveat to this: do exercise wisdom when listening to other applicants, because some may be eager to psych out their competition, and not everything they share may be accurate. I once had a flustered client call me at 11:45 p.m. in a panic. A fellow applicant who had interviewed on the same day had gotten in her head by making her doubt her responses and her overall interview performance. It took a few minutes of reminding her of her strengths and what she had to offer before she realized she had been manipulated by the other applicant.

Know Your Story and Sell Your Personal Brand

Reread your application to ensure that you remember all the facets of your story. Make sure your core themes come through as you present your story: passion, guts, impact, and insight. Share with the interviewer tangible examples of impact you have had—demonstrate self-awareness not simply by talking about what you have done but by focusing on why you have made the choices you have made and the lessons you have learned along the way. It is also important to demonstrate that you are confident enough to take a risk (that you have guts) and step up to a challenge instead of simply executing on your job description. Finally, come with great energy and share your passion with the interviewer.

Google Your Interviewer

In a Web 2.0 world where many people have a social media presence, applicants should do their own sleuthing to find out more about their interviewer. Admissions board members often do not put a lot of information on their LinkedIn profiles precisely for this reason. But you could still do a bit of Internet research to find out some information about them. You may find it easier to learn about your interviewer if they are faculty, students, or alumni. In any case, this is not an invitation to stalk your interviewer. In the same fashion as you would want to research the interviewer before a job interview, applicants should try to find out additional information about their business school interviewer. You never know when you can discover a commonality that can be an ice breaker.

You can expect that the admissions board can also exercise the discretion to check out applicants' online reputations. Kaplan's 2012 Business School Admissions Officers Survey revealed that this currently happens in some cases (officers at 32 percent of the 265 MBA programs surveyed admitted to having Googled an applicant and 27 percent to having visited an applicant's social network such as Facebook). While these numbers are relatively low, they may become more prevalent over time. Applicants should take the time to review their online reputation to make sure that there isn't content that could cast a negative light on their candidacy.

Experience the MBA Program Firsthand

Throughout this book, I have stressed the importance of visiting the MBA program you desire to join. Attending classes gives you a firm handle on the MBA program's unique positioning and value proposition. This credible vantage point will enable you to speak authentically about your specific interests and what you will do while in business school. Ideally, you should have already visited the campus and attended classes prior to applying to the MBA program. The interview visit then ends up being a "confirmation" as opposed to a first-time visit, on which you are still gathering facts about the program.

Dress Appropriately and Pay Attention to the Nonverbals

Be conservative when it comes to your interview attire, and go with neutral colors such as black, blue, and gray suits. Female candidates may wear a skirt or pantsuit. Some candidates have asked me about the freedom to express themselves. My response is usually something along the lines of, "This time next year, do you want to be entering your dream school or do you want to be going through a reapplication process?" Given the level of competition involved in applying to a top business school, I would not take any unnecessary risks. When it comes to interview attire, I recommend playing it safe. If you are a creative type and that's a key aspect of your brand, then limit your creative expression more to the accessories you wear for the interview (for example, choose a tie or scarf in a tasteful color instead of a flashy red suit). You want your interviewer to focus on your leadership contributions, not on your fashion-forward style.

Practice, Practice, Practice

I can't stress enough the importance of practicing for the interview. Have someone you know pose interview questions to you, and time yourself. Solicit feedback after the mock interview to identify areas where you need to improve, and be willing to address any feedback you receive. Some people assume they are excellent interviewees and therefore fail to prepare for the interview. This can be a grave mistake. Regardless of whether you consider yourself a "natural" or you dread the interview, you should prepare for it. As with anything in life, the more practice you have, the better. Candidates often tell me that they perform better after their first interview. You may want to interview first at MBA programs where you have an increased chance of being admitted (your safety program) than at reach schools where your admission chances are slim. The more experience you have with interviewing, the more likely you are to improve your interviewing skills.

You should take advantage of interview services that are available. My firm helps applicants prepare for their interviews by providing feedback on their overall brand, mock interview sessions, and detailed advice on how to improve their interview skills. Other resources include companies like Zoom Interview that provide interview assistance to MBA applicants.

Go into the Interview Well Rested

Avoid going to work on the day you have an interview. If you absolutely have to go into the office, then do yourself a favor and set up the interview in the morning. Then return to the office in the afternoon. I can't tell you how many times I've heard of applicants who went into work on the same day of their interview and encountered an extremely stressful day. Being frazzled before the interview is avoidable, so give yourself every advantage possible by going into the interview well rested.

COMMON INTERVIEW MISTAKES TO AVOID

1. Don't be disrespectful to the receptionist or students. Every encounter you have with someone affiliated with the MBA program is a potential interview.
2. Don't try to dominate the interview. This is guaranteed to backfire. Let the interviewer cover all his or her questions.
3. Don't talk too much or ramble. Be concise and to the point.
4. Don't be too forward, and don't ask the interviewer personal questions.
5. Don't be too informal. Address the interviewer as Ms. or Mr. unless they specifically invite you to refer to them differently.
6. Don't forget to bring water to drink. Your mouth may get dry as a result of nervousness, so stay hydrated.

7. Don't interrupt the interviewer. Even if you have an unreasonable interviewer, you'll get no bonus points for antagonizing him or her. Calmly wait for an opportunity to assert your points and brand message.

8. Don't use slang or informal communication, even if the interviewer does. (Remember, you are the one being interviewed.)

9. Don't communicate insecurity and lack of confidence by giving a weak handshake and unsteady eye contact.

10. Don't come off as unfriendly. Smile when appropriate. No one likes a sourpuss.

11. Don't be late for the interview. Aim to be there at least fifteen minutes early.

12. Don't dress inappropriately. Ill-fitting and outlandish attire sends the wrong message about you and your brand.

13. Don't be negative, and never complain or criticize someone you worked with or your company. Ditto for other MBA programs. Do not criticize another competitor program. It sends the wrong message about you.

14. Don't worry too much about the interview. Focus on being yourself.

DID YOU KNOW?

- Did you know that HBS sometimes has two interviewers in the room during the interview (one person interviews you while the second person observes and takes notes)?

- Did you know that you will be asked to speak about yourself for a long stretch of up to thirty minutes at Darden's interview? Get comfortable doing a monologue!

- Did you know that London Business School will give you five minutes to reflect on a real-world situation and then expect you to express your opinions about it?

- Did you know that Stern NYU Business School reviews your entire application before interviewing you?

- Did you know that at Cambridge Judge School of Business all interviews are conducted by a faculty member?

- Did you know that Stanford GSB can select an interviewer who has something in common with you based on what you shared about yourself in the application?

FUNDAMENTAL INTERVIEW QUESTIONS

I have compiled a list of popular interview questions that candidates for business schools will likely encounter. I have broken them into five categories. I recognize that some questions can fall into multiple categories, but for the sake of simplicity, I have them organized in one group. These questions do not purport to be exhaustive. It is more a collection of fundamental questions that every candidate should be ready to face regardless of his or her unique circumstance and experience. Use these questions as a starting point, but I encourage you to also look closely at your own story to assess whether there are gaps or flags that are likely to solicit inquiry in an interview.

1. General

- Walk me through your résumé.
- What will you do if you don't get into business school?
- What will you contribute to our MBA program?
- What do you think will be your biggest challenge at our program?
- Why did you select the recommenders?
- Which programs did you apply to?
- What is your first-choice school?
- Why should we admit you, given the steep competition?
- Why are you interested in our program?
- Is there anything else you wish to tell me about yourself?
- What do you want to be known for in life?
- What do you think about [insert national or international situation]?
- What else do you wish I had asked you about your candidacy?

2. Professional

- What are your short- and long-term career goals?
- Why do you want an MBA?

- Describe your career decisions to date and highlight your greatest impact.
- Why did you select the firms where you have worked?
- How did you actually get your job?
- How has your leadership style evolved over your career?
- How would your supervisor or colleagues describe you?
- What do you think your boss would say are your biggest weaknesses and strengths?
- When did you work in a team, and what impact or role did you have?
- What was your most exciting project at your firm?
- Describe your international experience.
- Describe a professional failure you have had and what you did to overcome it.
- In your career, when have you made a mistake? What did you learn from it?
- What drives you to seek new challenges and opportunities? In your career, when did you take an unusual path or make a decision that was not popular?
- Tell me about a time when you created a product or process that added value to your firm.
- When have you worked in a difficult team, and how did you overcome the challenge?
- What do you believe constitutes a great manager, and are you one?
- What do you like or dislike about your job?

3. Personal

- Tell me about yourself.
- What motivates you to succeed?
- Who do you admire the most, and why?
- How would your former classmates describe you?
- What three adjectives best describe who you are?
- What would you change about yourself and why?
- How do you handle change?
- What is your favorite book, and what do you find interesting about it?

- What has been your biggest self-discovery?
- What is the challenge you've sought that scared you the most?
- What accomplishment are you most proud of and why?
- What are your strengths and weaknesses?
- If you could live anywhere in the world besides where you live currently, where would it be and why?
- If you could be a superhero, which one would you be, and what would you do with your special powers?
- What talent do you wish you had, and why?
- Describe an ethical dilemma you faced and how you addressed it.

4. Extracurricular

- What do you do for fun, and how do you spend your free time?
- What leadership impact have you had outside of work?
- What community service organizations are you involved in, and how have you created value there?
- What clubs do you plan to join if you are admitted?
- How do you lead differently in your career versus in your community?

5. Education

- Describe your academic experience in college.
- Why did you choose your major or school?
- How did you perform academically?
- Which awards did you receive?
- What decisions do you regret making during college?
- If you could change one thing about your education, what would it be and why?

INTERVIEW REMINDERS

- The admissions interview is not optional; you should always interview if the school offers you the chance.
- The interview is a marketing exercise, so go prepared to sell yourself and your brand.
- Know the MBA program thoroughly and communicate what you will bring to the program.
- Dress appropriately—a well-tailored suit is usually the way to go. However, there are MBA programs that have a business-casual dress policy. Also, where you interview can influence how you should dress—an alum interview at a café may require business-casual attire instead of a formal suit.
- Be prepared for the interview; invest time to nail down your responses and get used to answering the interview questions in one to two minutes so that you don't run out of time. If the interviewer asks follow-up questions, then that is your cue to drill deeper in your response.
- The physical résumé speaks to your brand, so make sure it is updated and reflects your main leadership impact; don't forget to use high-quality paper and eliminate errors.
- Wrap up the interview with an intelligent question about the MBA program, but only if you have actual questions. Don't ask questions just to ask.
- Do your homework ahead of time. (Program websites, press releases, and faculty knowledge papers present interesting information about new trends and activities at an MBA program.)
- Always follow up with a thank-you note or email, which should be sent the day of the interview.

DID YOU KNOW?

Did you know that not everyone interviewing has the same chance of acceptance? For example, if a school admits about 50 percent of its interviewees, it doesn't mean that each applicant being interviewed has a 50/50 shot. There are applicants who have a great story and a powerful brand, and are well-liked by the admissions board. Those individuals could be entering the interview with closer to a 70 percent or more admission chance. On the other hand, there are candidates who go into the interview with very low likelihood of getting a favorable admission outcome. For some in this category, their admission chance could be as low as 10 to 20 percent. Someone from this latter group has a lot more at stake in the interview and needs to really knock the ball out of the park for the admission outcome to end up in their favor.

SOME FINAL TIPS ON THE INTERVIEW

Know your story (brand), and make sure you don't leave the interview without communicating key points of why you are unique and interesting: your value proposition. Ensure that you communicate specifically why you fit into the program and what you will bring to enrich the student community. It's possible that you may face an ineffective interviewer. Regardless of who interviews you or whether they ask you productive questions, you have to be prepared to lead the conversation back to major points that reinforce why you are a great fit for their program. Being clear on the four or so brand themes you wish to cover and having specific short stories to reinforce them will help you leave the interviewer with a strong sense of who you are.

But the interview isn't enough to help you close the deal. The MBA admissions board will be looking for a third-party validation of your story (your essays, résumé, and interview) before they admit you. Let's spend some time in the next chapter reviewing everything you need to know about the recommendation to make it a winner!

CHAPTER NINE

Transforming Your Recommenders
into Brand Champions

I HAVE READ NUMEROUS RECOMMENDATIONS in the sixteen years I have been in the admissions industry. The one fundamental difference between excellent recommendations and mediocre ones is that the former are written by individuals who are champions of the candidate, have worked closely with them, and have a clear understanding of the unique value they offer personally and professionally.

To build a powerful brand in the marketplace, you have to have people who are interested and invested in your professional and personal success—in other words, brand champions. More than just recommendation writers, brand champions truly understand what you stand for, your passion and values, and your skills, accomplishments, and goals for your future. They help you refine your brand and act as phenomenal marketing agents of your brand. Most importantly, these individuals are committed to seeing you succeed, are quick to bring you on board for projects with high visibility and importance, and are always willing to speak up on your behalf to promote your career.

Not all recommenders are brand champions. In other words, just because someone writes a recommendation letter on your behalf does not mean that they understand who you are, what matters most to you, and how you envision the MBA to help you achieve your life goals. I have read many recommendations that have had damning consequences for a candidate's admission outcome. Choose wisely and make sure whoever you select is truly an avid supporter.

I'm often asked whether the recommendation is important in the evaluation process. The simple answer is absolutely! The recommendation gives the MBA admissions board a chance to hear from someone who knows you very well to see if he concurs with the story you have shared about yourself in the application. A recommendation letter that is negative or off-track from the story you told in your application at best communicates to the MBA admissions board that you lack wisdom in making decisions, and at worst provides a third-party justification to reject you.

THE POWER OF BRAND CHAMPIONS

Most MBA programs require two recommendation letters as part of the application process. Recently some MBA programs have reduced their number of recommendations. Schools like Harvard have cut down their recommendations from three to two. Georgetown even offers applicants the chance to simply have their supervisor provide a performance review. MBA programs like Stanford are in the minority, since they still require three recommendation letters (one peer recommendation and two professional ones). Business schools tend to prefer recommenders who can speak directly to an applicant's work experience, managerial potential, and leadership.

Because the essays are composed of self-reported accounts, your recommendations are a way for the MBA admissions board to verify the authenticity of your story. All things being equal, the recommendation that stands out can be the deal clincher. For instance, the board may be on the fence about admitting a candidate, but a powerful recommendation that articulates how the candidate is unique, compelling, and a fit with the school's brand can tip the admission decision in her favor. The recommendation adds a rich texture to your story by providing insights (backed by specific examples) of *how* you have done what you have done instead of simply stopping at the achievements alone. Effective recommendations also educate the admissions board about the context in which the candidate works. By learning what's unique about the company, your role, or your impact, the admissions board is in a better position to evaluate your story.

This is why it is critical to cultivate relationships early with individuals who can become your brand champions. Many applicants to business school ignore this important step until a few months before they start applying. I had a client once whose entire application almost crumbled because of her failure to develop relationships with her former bosses. It required some scrambling to track down and reconnect with former supervisors. You can imagine the panic that this applicant felt at the realization that she didn't have appropriate supervisors to write recommendations for her. Luckily, we were able to do significant damage control and she applied in a later round, buying her time to track down previous supervisors who wrote her strong recommendations. Although anyone can find someone to write a recommendation letter for them, cultivating relationships with superiors and colleagues (in both the professional and the community contexts) can be challenging and requires careful strategy. Recommendations that stand out typically come from individuals who are champions of a candidate's brand.

I have also reviewed many rejected candidates' applications, and the recommendations tend to be average at best and weak in most instances. Because the competition for business school admission is so tough, it is important for candidates to manage their recommenders and to select the right people to champion their applications.

FIVE CRITICAL STEPS IN DEVELOPING BRAND CHAMPIONS

1. Know Your Brand

Be clear about your personal brand. You should be able to articulate your brand in one sentence, your personal brand statement (PBS). What you value, your skills and track record, and your passions and goals are all encompassed in this statement. Remember, if this isn't clear in your own mind, then most likely the people you work with have the wrong brand attached to you. Here are two examples of a PBS for a career changer:

"A hardworking Boeing engineer"

"An innovative engineer with a passion for creating business efficiency who plans to turn business problems into solutions through consulting"

The first PBS is limiting and pegs you as an engineer rather than someone who plans to transition into consulting. The second PBS is more robust and positions you as a career changer. You will want to make sure that your recommenders understand that you are evolving into a different career, consulting, and that you enjoy solving business problems, not just executing tactical engineering systems.

2. Choose the Right Brand Champion

For starters, ideal brand champions need to be in positions of power. That doesn't mean that your peers and subordinates shouldn't be aware of your brand. They should! Everyone you come in contact with, both professionally and otherwise, should be able to perceive a consistent message from you about your brand. But for the purpose of the MBA application, your focus should be on superiors, particularly supervisors who can provide tangible and detailed information about you that reinforces your brand.

However, you shouldn't simply go for title alone. Avoid using the CEO or managing director of your firm who can barely remember your name, because their recommendations will offer limited details about your managerial potential and unique, differentiating personal attributes. Rather, it is important to have a relationship with the person that goes beyond interacting a couple of times a year. When it comes to selecting a recommender, ask yourself the following questions:

- How does this person feel about me?
- Have I worked closely with her on a project?
- Has she complimented me based on the results I produced?
- What types of evaluation has she given me in the past?
- Did she go out of her way to assist or support me in some capacity? (The more people have gone out of their way to show a commitment to you, the more likely they are to become your fan.)

A clear indication of whether someone is supportive can be seen in the case of a managing director who specifically requests that you work on her deals and invites you to client meetings. The more exposure she has to *your* work, other than the grunt work that everyone else at your level is involved in, the more compelling a case she can make about your brand and unique value. Assuming that you have had enough regular contact with her and that she has indicated that she does care about your professional success, make sure to keep her abreast of your achievements and goals. Such individuals make ideal brand champions.

3. Regularly Communicate Your Brand

Seize every opportunity to make your brand champions aware of what you are involved in. Update them on your key achievements and plans, and solicit feedback from them. A young man I know is brilliant at marketing his brand to his brand champions. He told me that he sends an email quarterly report to his "board of directors," the name he uses to describe everyone in his network he considers brand champions. The purpose of these quarterly reports is to inform them of his professional and personal life developments. Although the bulk of his work experience has been in investment banking, that does not stop him from successfully position-ing his brand as an inner-city investor. His community involvement and career change have been primarily in venture capital, with a focus on distressed communities. This is what he stresses in his communication. And his brand has remained constant, a "spiritually grounded, inner-city community investor."

Obviously, email communication isn't enough. Face-to-face com-munication is even more powerful. So set up meetings with your brand champions and begin to discuss your brand and vision with them *before* asking them for a recommendation to business school. Waiting two months before application deadlines is leaving it too late.

4. Demonstrate the Value of Your Brand

The fastest way to develop brand champions is to establish a track record of excellence. At your job, you should aim to perform at the highest level possible, regardless of how minute or how grand the project is. Your excellent performance will precede you and begin to get you brand equity. Here is how it works: you are an analyst in the general pool, but you develop significant knowledge in a particular area that most of your peers do not have. You get selected to work on a deal that allows you to draw from that knowledge base, and your performance on the project is without reproach (you work late, you produce results with few to no mistakes). Soon, senior executives at your firm begin to request you when they are working on important deals. By working on these types of deals, you get more visibility and experience. Your reputation grows, and the cycle continues. I've used investment banking to illustrate this point, but the same principle applies to any industry and position. The takeaway is that regardless of your job, title, or industry, you should make sure you produce excellent results. Your impact should contribute to the bottom line of the company or group. You have to walk a fine line between coming across as arrogant and self-promoting and being confident in your accomplishments and not afraid to raise your hand to take on more challenges.

5. Take Action

What do you do if you realize that you do not have brand champions? All hope is not lost. First, take stock of all the potential brand champions that you already have in your network: your former bosses, clients, even other managers with whom you have worked on projects in the past. Once you have developed your list, the next step is to prioritize it. Select five people with whom you wish to develop a stronger relationship, and then design a plan of how to approach them. This is the tricky part. It will require time and a good dose of patience. You need to be subtle about it. Do not approach them immediately to ask for recommendations. You need to capitalize on what you have in common. If you are still working with the person, begin to seek opportunities to work on projects together where he or she will be able to observe your work up close. By working with your potential brand champion on a project and producing excellent results, you will increase your chances of this person's becoming your avid supporter. You should seize every opportunity to share your brand when interacting with your brand champion. For example, if you are a career changer and you are engaged in a volunteer capacity for the new career, discuss your involvement outside of work to help your brand champion better understand your brand.

If you are no longer at the same firm, then touch base to simply find out how your former bosses are doing and to bring them up to speed on your progress. Under no circumstance should you request a recommendation the first time you contact someone you have been out of touch with. It is impolite, and it also is likely to yield a weak recommendation. Ideally, give yourself a year to reconnect with individuals who will write your recommendations. The more time you have to develop these relationships prior to the application, the better.

QUESTIONS TO ASK BEFORE SELECTING RECOMMENDERS

- Do they understand your brand, and are they avid fans?
- Do they have an MBA? If not, do they understand the value of an MBA?
- Have they written recommendation letters before? Are they good writers? Have the people they recommended gained admission to top business schools?
- Are they open to your providing them with information about your brand, accomplishments, and rationale for an MBA?
- Do they have time to write an excellent recommendation letter?
- Are they supportive of your school choice? (I once spoke to a recommender who was writing a letter for a candidate to X business school, and he told me that he thought the candidate was a fit for Y business school and that he didn't see him at X business school. Yet here he was, writing a recommendation for him for X business school. Clearly his recommendation would not be the most compelling.)
- Do they have enough in-depth interaction with you to provide evidence of your leadership?
- Are they senior enough in title to have a broad perspective of what your role is and how it fits into the company?
- Are they optimists? You don't want anyone approaching your recommendation from a "half empty" perspective.
- Are they dependable? Avoid procrastinators who have a reputation of not delivering quality work at deadlines.

If you answer no to any one of these questions, you should think long and hard about whether the recommender is right for you.

THE RECOMMENDATION TIME FACTOR

Timing is very important in selecting a brand champion to write your recommendation. Give yourself a year to eighteen months to begin cultivating relationships with key people who will become your brand champions.

I had a client who really understood the importance of having brand champions. He had actively identified people within and outside of his firm whom he respected and kept in touch with regularly. He was known to put in a call or email when he needed advice on simple as well as major career decisions. Over time, these people became invested in him and accustomed to receiving regular updates from him that reinforced his brand. His ability to get the CEO of his billion-dollar private equity fund to write an insightful, humorous, and glowing recommendation represented the time and investment he had made up front. And I would hazard a guess that this recommendation contributed in some measure to his admission to a top MBA program despite a GMAT score lower than 600.

I have also witnessed firsthand how not having brand champions can threaten one's admission. Another client of mine did not have brand champions behind her when she began the application process. She had a boss who was not particularly supportive of her professional development, let alone her pursuit of an MBA. Further complicating matters, she had not kept in touch with previous supervisors with whom she had great rapport. So when she began her application to business school, she felt awkward tracking these people down after four years had gone by to say, "Hey, remember me? We did great work a few years ago, and I need a 'wow' recommendation from you." After serious scrambling and an aggressive recommendation strategy that involved accelerated relationship building over three months, and after one recommender dropped out as a result of a car accident, she was able to eventually find recommenders who supported her application. The result was admission offers from three out of four top MBA programs.

Although she was lucky (or experienced divine intervention), I wouldn't recommend this approach, because it brings undue strain to an already stressful process, and the outcome could have been quite different.

CHOOSING THE RIGHT MIX OF RECOMMENDERS

So you have developed close relationships with individuals who are invested in your success. How do you narrow it down to the two or three who will write your letters of recommendation for business school? I address the different backgrounds of individuals who typically write recommendations for candidates. Ultimately, you will have to decide what the ideal mix is for you, given your unique situation.

Recommendations from Supervisors

One of your recommenders must be someone who has supervised your work and can speak to your leadership and managerial potential. If you cannot use your current supervisor (because you have worked at the firm for only a few months or because he is generally unsupportive about business school), then consider using a previous supervisor. However, know that the admissions board will be curious why you didn't use a direct supervisor. The additional information section of the application is a good place to address your choice of recommender and to explain any decision that needs further clarification.

The second recommendation ought to come from your professional life as well. It could be from the same firm or from a different firm. The important thing is to balance the perspective being offered to demonstrate the depth of your character as well as the breadth of experience and impact that you have had in the organization. For example, whereas one recommendation may stress your interaction with clients and your confidence, maturity, and performance outside the firm, your other recommendation may go into greater detail to show your work impact, analytical and quantitative acumen, and direct involvement on projects that resulted in success. There isn't one set formula. What's key is showing the different sides of who you are instead of a skewed, one-dimensional perspective.

I'm often asked about the specific examples the recommenders should use. Make sure that the recommenders do not use the exact four examples that you describe in your essays. Not only will this make for a boring and redundant recommendation, it will raise flags that you have limited experience, or worse, that you are the author of the recommendation. You should have some of the recommenders reinforce stories you have highlighted in your essays, but they can add greater "color" and detail to the story. They should also provide fresh examples that you have not covered in your essays (which reinforce your personal brand) to present a rich and convincing recommendation instead of a regurgitation of your essays.

Recommendations from Alumni of the MBA Program

I'm often asked whether alumni recommendations are important. The simple answer is yes and no. Yes, if they know your work from a close vantage point and can attest to the significant impact that you have had. The other situation in which alumni recommendations are preferred is when candidates come from lesser-known companies. In such instances, it is helpful to have a recommendation from an alumnus of the MBA program who can attest to the rigor and quality of the candidate's experience.

But this is not a license to hunt down alumni from top MBA programs for the sole purpose of having them write a recommendation if you have not worked with them in the past. If you use alumni recommenders, opt for those who know your work the best and can back up any assertions they make about your candidacy with detailed examples. If the alumnus doesn't know you very well, then it is not worth using him for a recommendation.

Recommendations from Community Service (Outside of Work)

Equally important is your extracurricular involvement, especially if you have a strong track record of leadership and service. As discussed earlier, MBA admissions boards judge leadership not only in terms of college and career experiences but also in community involvement. For example, if you serve on the board of directors of a nonprofit group and you have managed to develop a strong relationship with your chairperson, you may be better off having him or her write a recommendation for you instead of having all of your recommendations from the same job or from your professional life. Many business schools do not like additional recommendations, so avoid the temptation to have extra "supporting" recommendation letters sent on your behalf. Schools like Wharton that used to be open to additional letters now explicitly request that applicants stick to only two recommendations.

Recommendations from Professors and College Administrators

I'm not usually a fan of professor recommendations, especially if the only point they can make is discussing your intelligence. Unless you did something unique with large impact while you were a student, you should shy away from professor recommendations. Of course, early-career candidates are the exception to this. Even in such cases, however, professor recommendations should speak to your leadership, your initiative, and your maturity. Your transcript and GMAT or GRE score are enough data points to reinforce how smart you are. The admissions board wants to learn more about who you are as a future business leader, so the professor or college administrator should provide information that reinforces this point. Examples that can attest to your leadership potential are your involvement in starting a student organization or in transforming the experience of the student body by lobbying for and changing a campus-wide policy.

Recommendations from Clients or Business Associates

Individuals who work in family businesses or who are founders of their own company will have some unique challenges when deciding whom to use for their recommendations. Do not use a family member as your recommender. If you are an entrepreneur and you are the boss, or a family member is in charge, you should use individuals unrelated to you who are familiar with your leadership, management experience, and impact. These individuals often can be clients or business associates such as your banker, attorney, or accountant. It will be important to manage the process carefully, because they may not have extensive experience writing recommendation letters for business school.

Regardless of whom you select to write your recommendations, the goal always is to make sure they reinforce your brand by showing the scope and impact of your experiences. One sure way to differentiate yourself from the pack is to demonstrate not only your ambition and commitment to your career but also your investment in others' success. The MBA admissions board is looking for well-rounded candidates, and recommendations can reinforce the notion that you are multidimensional.

THE APPLICANT BACKGROUND IN RELATION TO THE RECOMMENDATIONS

I've discussed the different types of individuals who can write recommendation letters. Now let's look at the different MBA candidate backgrounds and the potential barriers they face when it comes to the recommendations.

The Consultant and the Investment Banker

Consultants and investment bankers applying to business school make up a significant portion of the applicant pool. This means that the competition for candidates with this background is particularly fierce.

Individuals writing your recommendation will most likely be writing recommendations for others as well. To a large extent, the skill set that will be highlighted includes your intellectual horsepower and ability to quickly grasp complicated materials, analytical and quantitative skills, decision-making and problem-solving skills, judgment, oral and written communication skills, and confidence.

Beyond confirming your intelligence and analytical skills, recommenders for consultants and investment bankers need to address your emotional intelligence and interpersonal skills, flexibility in dealing with ambiguity, team dynamics, confidence and maturity in dealing with clients and superiors, creativity, and so much more. It isn't enough to talk about how smart a candidate is, because it is already a foregone conclusion, given a solid academic track record, GMAT score, and blue-chip firm. The focus should be on your personal characteristics and the impact you have had that is beyond your job description. Given that most recommenders will have good things to say about their candidates, it becomes even more important to describe not only the "what" of your background but the "how" of what you have done.

As far as recommenders for investment bankers, I recommend using vice presidents (VPs) and higher. It is not that associates can't speak to the quality of your work and accomplishments, but they are too close in position to you. All things being equal, with two analysts with strong recommendations, one from an associate and the other from a VP, the MBA admissions board would likely tip the scale for the VP recommendation over the associate. The caveat to this is that the VP needs to know your work very well and should be a brand champion. There are always exceptions, of course. A lackluster VP recommendation is worse than a stellar associate recommendation. We had a client who had an associate write his recommendation letter. He applied to HBS and got admitted. So yes, you can get in with an associate recommendation, but if you can get an equally strong recommendation from a more senior professional, then you should definitely go with this option.

If you are a consultant, you should consider a supervisor and a senior-titled client who have worked with you extensively. A recommendation from a partner who knows you well because of leadership initiatives you have taken on a project or across the firm would be of value in setting you apart from your competition. The operative phrase is "who knows you well." It isn't useful to have recommendations from highly ranked individuals if they don't know you well.

The Engineer

Engineers are attractive to business schools because they often have project management and hands-on managerial experience supervising employees. This is particularly the case for those who have been line managers. The challenge for engineers is that their recommenders may not always be as savvy as those coming from consulting or investment banking industries. Therefore, to be on the safe side, candidates from engineering backgrounds have to vet the writing skills of their recommenders, who may not be as adept in the nuances of recommendation letters as consultants and banking professionals. Although I never promote writing your own recommendation letters, it is important to sit down with the engineer recommender and remind them of your MBA objectives. While you are at it, it doesn't hurt to provide them with key information about your achievements, work projects, and your overall brand positioning.

The Nontraditional Candidate

Like engineers, applicants from nonprofit organizations, military, government, and artistic backgrounds need to be proactive to ensure that their recommenders understand what is expected of them and the purpose of the recommendation letters. For many applicants from this category, this may be the first recommendation letter for business school that your recommender is writing, so give your recommenders enough information about you, your accomplishments, and most importantly why you want the MBA to ensure that they understand your brand and, in turn, write a glowing letter of recommendation on your behalf. Similar to engineer recommendations, those coming from the nontraditional backgrounds require special care. Make sure to invest enough time setting the expectations and vetting the positioning and information your recommender intends to use for your defense.

So far, I have focused the first part of this chapter on macro issues facing the recommendations. In the next section, I'll examine the recommendation itself, including an actual recommendation rating (grid) and questions. I'll also provide insights into what the MBA admissions board is truly looking for in each of the questions covered. And of course, before wrapping up, I'll go through the common recommendation mistakes applicants to business school should avoid.

TACKLING THE RECOMMENDATION QUESTIONS

The trend in recommendation questions is that less is the way to go. In the past, schools did not limit the word count of recommendations. Many programs now limit their recommendation word counts in an attempt to get recommenders to be more efficient.

Besides the word-count limits, many schools have reduced the actual number of questions contained in recommendation letters. The shrinking of recommendation questions forces recommenders to get to the point more quickly and to cover the relevant information about the applicant.

It goes without saying, but recommenders should make sure they answer every question that is asked in the recommendation form. There is no room for cutting corners by writing one letter of recommendation and using it for different schools. Because each school words its questions differently and the specific information being asked varies, it is important to make sure your recommender fully answers each question while citing vivid examples to illustrate the point. Quantifying the impact the applicant had is more important than using superlative descriptors that come off as trite. Make sure you refresh your recommender's memory by providing him with concrete examples of your leadership and impact at your firm.

Be mindful of the recommender's time. It is unrealistic to ask recommenders to write more than four recommendation letters. Think of the law of diminishing returns. If you overburden your recommenders, they are more inclined to write generic letters that they tailor to the different schools instead of spending a significant amount of time on each recommendation. To be safe, if you must apply to more than four schools, you may want to target a couple of additional individuals to write recommendations for you. This would allow you to focus your star recommenders on the MBA programs that you care the most about.

Recommendation forms typically have a set of questions that ask recommenders to rate the candidate. This grid is an important part of the recommendation, and recommenders should give it adequate consideration when completing it. Your recommenders should give a realistic evaluation of you. But it should also be tempered with sound judgment. A balanced rating is essential. What do I mean by that? Certainly highlighting a candidate's excellent qualities is important. However, recommenders should be able to also identify areas where the candidate can improve.

The reverse can also be a problem. In the course of my time in the admissions business, I have seen too many recommenders hurt a candidate's chance of admission by going to the other extreme and "underselling" the candidate. Recommenders should not view recommendations as performance reviews. Unlike performance reviews that tend to be more critical and have more of an improvement focus, recommenders should not lose sight of the fact that the recommendation should be a tool to "sell" a candidate, not to hurt him in the application process. Lately, MBA programs ask recommenders to provide constructive feedback on the candidate. You need to exercise good judgment here. If your supervisor has provided you with very negative feedback, chances are he will share constructive feedback that can derail your MBA ambitions. So reflect on the feedback you have received from your recommenders in the past before you select who will write your recommendation letter.

I'm often asked by applicants how the grid is interpreted by the admissions board. The board is likely to be skeptical if the candidate is ranked in the highest category across every single characteristic. The view is, "If the candidate is truly that exceptional, does she need an MBA?" On the other hand, rankings that are below average can raise red flags. Therefore, the right approach when filling out the grid is to take a measured stance. If the candidate is truly exceptional, the recommender should rate the applicant in the very top of the grid for characteristics where he or she shines and lower in areas that need improvement. Some international recommenders can be conservative when ranking a candidate. The same goes for some industries. The good news is that the admissions board recognizes these types of differences.

The following is an example of a recommendation grid. This example is only an illustration to show how someone can be rated from "good" to "outstanding," reflecting where the candidate is strong and where improvement is needed. Candidates who are ranked average in some areas but outstanding in other areas can be admitted to top schools. The more important questions are what areas they received an average rating in, why, and what they are doing to address their developmental needs. In the end, there isn't a set formula.

SAMPLE RECOMMENDATION RATING GRID						
	No Information	Below Average	Average	Good	Excellent	Outstanding
Leadership Track Record						X
Motivation					X	
Maturity					X	
Teamwork						X
Oral Communication					X	
Written Communication				X		
Self-Awareness						X
Global Perspective					X	
Interpersonal Dynamics					X	
Intelligence					X	
Analytical Skills					X	
Quantitative Skills					X	
Innovation and Creativity				X		
Sense of Humor				X		

Common Recommendation Questions and Admissions Insights

Each recommendation question is designed to reveal a candidate's professional experience and character. The admissions board's goal, ultimately, is to understand who the person is in a fully dimensional way.

I've organized the recommendation questions into the "usual-suspect" categories and identified the insight the MBA admissions board is interested in gleaning from each question. I've written this section as a sort of "cheat sheet" for recommenders, explaining what the MBA board wants to find out about the candidate being recommended. Feel free to share this cheat sheet with your recommenders once you have them on board to write recommendations for you. It will help them to understand what is expected of them and the ulterior motives behind the set of recommendation questions they have to address.

Relationship with Candidate

The point of this question is to assess the following:

- How well you really know the candidate and whether you have had enough interaction to provide an objective opinion
- The length of time and the capacity in which you have worked together (for example, direct supervisor, mentor, etc.)
- The typical interaction you have had with the candidate and how the candidate compares with his or her peers
- Highlights of distinction and achievements, such as career growth and promotions

Leadership, Teamwork, and Interpersonal Dynamics

This question seeks to address team dynamics of the candidate, including:

- Is the candidate an individual contributor, or does he or she thrive in team situations?
- Does the candidate work well with others (including peers, superiors, and subordinates)? Or does the applicant focus only on how to get ahead?
- Does the candidate manage peer or subordinate relationships well?
- What type of a leader is the applicant? Is this someone who motivates and inspires others?
- Is this someone who has the ability to drive the vision of an organization or project?
- Does the candidate have natural leadership abilities? How so?
- Is the candidate comfortable leading from behind, or is he or she always pushing to be in front?
- Is this a respected leader?
- Is the candidate evolving from being a member of a team to stepping up to more leadership roles?
- Is the applicant becoming the "go-to" person on his or her team?

- How well does the candidate handle conflict?
- Does the candidate think and act quickly on his or her feet?

Unique Personal Characteristics

This is the "why should we admit this candidate" question. The MBA admissions board is looking for the unique or special attributes that the candidate will bring to the class. It is important to address why a particular school should admit this candidate. Given what you know about the candidate, how would he or she fit with the MBA program? Does this applicant have a clear career focus and a natural curiosity to learn and stretch him or herself for the next level? Does the candidate have specific personal characteristics that are extraordinary? What specific examples back them up? Ultimately, the MBA admissions board wants candidates who can help shape the MBA program for the better.

Candidate's Strengths

This section offers a great opportunity to discuss two or three main attributes or strengths that the candidate has. It should support the attributes that the candidate has identified in his or her essays. This third-party endorsement is very powerful in conveying what makes the candidate special and why the MBA admissions board should admit him or her. The board is looking for specific examples to back up the core strengths you highlight. It is critical! The examples should be in sync with the school and the candidate's personal brand.

Candidate's Weaknesses

A very popular addition to recommendations is the question on the constructive criticism or feedback that you have provided to the candidate. The MBA admissions board is looking for specific examples of your providing the feedback and the candidate's actual response to it. Self-awareness and a willingness to take feedback to heart and apply it quickly are important traits to the admissions board.

Constructive feedback questions can be a natural place where recommenders can address an applicant's weaknesses or developmental areas. To remain credible, these need to be real weaknesses. A candidate is not perfect, and the MBA admissions board wants to know that there are areas being developed. Weaknesses that are flag-raisers are major interpersonal skills issues, such as arrogance, shyness, insensitivity to others, "does not suffer fools" attitude, team dynamics issues, and communication weaknesses. MBA admissions boards are loath to see strengths disguised as weaknesses or clichéd answers. Recommenders should always provide specific examples and indicate whether the candidate is open to feedback and criticism.

Intellectual Ability

The MBA admissions board is looking to understand the candidate's ability to handle a rigorous curriculum. They have reviewed the candidate's GMAT or GRE score, GPA, and transcripts with a fine-toothed comb, but will rely heavily on your feedback on the candidate's intellectual abilities, particularly if you can provide specific examples of the applicant's intellectual horsepower and quantitative contributions. The admissions board wants to understand the rigors of the professional context where the candidate has worked. It is important to provide specific examples to showcase how the candidate demonstrated superior analysis or provided an innovative solution to a challenging business problem.

Relevant skills include natural curiosity and an ability to think outside the box, adeptness with quantitative and analytical projects, and thought leadership (which also shows intelligence and intellectual curiosity).

Ethical Issues

Given the corporate scandals of the past few years and the public's skepticism of business, many MBA programs are concerned about the level of integrity and ethics that their candidates bring to their programs. As such, there is a strong focus on candidates' ethical behavior and trustworthiness. Be ready to comment on instances or examples that illustrate that the candidate has a very high moral code of ethics. Always use specific examples to illustrate your point.

COMMON RECOMMENDATION MISTAKES TO AVOID

I end this chapter with the major mistakes applicants make when it comes to the recommendations. Knowing what the landmines are and avoiding them will bring you a step closer to your goal of acceptance to an elite institution.

Show, Don't Tell

Often recommendations are too general and full of fluff. They tell you that the candidate is brilliant and use a lot of adjectives but have very little substance to back up the assertions. If, for example, the recommender says that John is an exceptional leader, it is critical to describe instances when John has stepped up to lead, how he has led, and what impact he has had on his team and the organization. The rule here is to show and not simply to tell. A good way to assess if the point is worth making is to add the phrases "for example" or "in the following instance." If a vivid example does not come to mind to back up the point, or if the example that comes to mind doesn't strongly reinforce the message being communicated, it should be discarded.

Beware the Contradiction Factor

The recommendation is an authentic yardstick by which an applicant's story is measured. So consider what happens in the mind of the MBA admissions board when an applicant positions herself as someone who will start and run a business and the recommender states that the applicant is comfortable only in established organizations. Other examples have to do with industry consistency. It doesn't help a candidate's case when he says that he is passionate about the health-care industry and his recommender says that he will likely end up in a real estate industry as a developer or in some other industry that has nothing to do with the story the applicant has told about himself. This is a common mistake that I often observed while on the MBA admissions board at Harvard. Mistakes like these could have been avoided had the candidate spent the time necessary to educate his recommender on exactly what his position was. Take the time to make sure your recommenders understand your goals and are supportive of them.

A recent experience with one of our clients at EXPARTUS reinforces this point. Dave* had targeted HBS and Stanford. He had written his essays about how he liked jumping in to take risks. The reality, however, was somewhat different. Dave's view of himself was slightly skewed. While he would like to take more risks, he tended to be quite cautious. His recommenders flagged this inconsistency. Fortunately, Dave took

*Name has been changed.

the feedback to heart and adjusted his essay before submitting his application. Had he not engaged his recommenders to understand how they view him, he would have submitted essays that contradicted his recommendations. This ultimately might have led admissions boards to not invite him for an interview.

Recommendation Bias

Recommendations vary according to region and industry. For example, recommenders from certain countries tend to be by the book, blunt, and straight to the point. Their evaluations may be more focused on the areas of improvement and therefore may miss an opportunity to highlight the positives that the candidate brings. Sitting down with your recommender prior to his writing a recommendation for you and discussing any concerns you have as well as what you believe sets you apart will help ensure that your recommendation is balanced. The industry background of recommenders can sometimes influence the recommendation. If you happen to have a nontraditional background and your recommender has little experience writing an MBA recommendation, it is worth sitting down with him beforehand.

Beware the Bland Recommendation

Bland recommendations lack spontaneity and seem too molded and coached. A quick way for recommenders to check if the recommendation is bland is to ask themselves, "If I remove the candidate's name from the recommendation, could this recommendation apply to any other person?" If so, the recommendation could very well lack distinction and will do little to endear the applicant to the MBA admissions board. Ultimately, knowing the brand of the candidate will enable the recommender to move beyond the typical vanilla recommendation and produce a "wow" recommendation that supports your brand.

Recommendation Ownership

The Association of International Graduate Admissions Consultants, AIGAC, conducted an admissions survey that revealed that a large proportion (over 30 percent) of MBA students are being asked by their recommenders to write their own recommendation letters. This survey also revealed that the prevalence of self-authored recommendations can be country-specific, with some countries having a higher incidence. MBA admissions boards are aware of this reality and are therefore more on the lookout for recommendations that are self-authored.

Don't fall into the trap of writing your own recommendation. I know this is a common request from recommenders who either are too busy or are uncomfortable writing a recommendation. It is unethical to write your own recommendation, and the admissions board can tell that you did so, because it will be similar to your essays. Even putting one recommendation next to the other will make it obvious that they were written by the same person. Don't risk it.

If your recommender asks you to write the recommendation and they will sign it, as tempting as that may sound, I strongly suggest you decline tactfully. You can share with them language from the MBA program's website that explicitly prohibits applicants from writing their own recommendation letters. Point out to them that you will make the process as easy and streamlined as possible by providing content to remind them of the detailed projects and impact you had. You can even sit down with them to flesh out your story and the positioning of your application. If they still insist that you should write the recommendation yourself, you should take this as evidence that they are not invested in you. You may have to find a different person if your recommender absolutely refuses to write the recommendation. A practical way to avoid this situation is to give your recommenders enough of a head start that they can devote the necessary time to your recommendation. Also, selecting the right people who are invested in your success and not overburdening them by having them support your eight applications will make it more manageable for them.

Damning Recommendations

There are many ways a recommendation can have a damning effect on the candidate. The most popular is the recommendation that is too short, lacks examples, and is poorly written. For whatever reason (be it a lack of writing ability or lackluster commitment to the candidate), these recommendations call into question the candidate's judgment.

Rushed recommendations also have detrimental consequences because they tend to have spelling and grammatical errors, and in some instances, the wrong school name. And then there is the recommendation that offers back-handed compliments. These also have a negative impact on the admission outcome. Examples such as, "Wesley is very driven and likes to get things done effectively, but this means that he may sometimes step on the toes of individuals who operate at a slower pace" will absolutely mark him as a selfish and impatient person.

Finally, there is the recommendation that intentionally sabotages the candidate's admission chances. "Jaime is extremely intelligent but has difficulty expressing his thoughts in an articulate and clear manner, making it difficult for those who work with him to benefit from his intellect. I have given him feedback to take communication classes and expect he will improve after he does so." Why is this a huge no-no? For starters, business school in general and leadership in particular demand that individuals communicate in a reasonable way in order to lead or manage a project or people. Saying up front that the candidate is a lousy communicator raises an alarm in the mind of the admissions board member evaluating the application. At the end of the day, MBA programs want to admit individuals who can engage in meaningful discussions with their classmates.

Applicants should also beware of that friend who is too eager to write your recommendation. You may assume "it's in the bag" and may not manage the recommendation as closely and effectively as you would if the writer were not your friend. But it is precisely this hands-off approach that may come back to haunt you. Make sure the recommender is not jealous of your aspirations and achievements.

TOP FIVE THINGS A RECOMMENDER SAYS THAT SHOULD MAKE YOU DITCH HIM OR HER

1. I don't think you should go for an MBA.
2. I'm kind of busy at this time.
3. Don't you think you are reaching too high?
4. Why don't you write the recommendation?
5. I don't need any input from you; I'm an expert at this.

You should send a thank-you note to your recommenders after they have submitted a recommendation on your behalf. Upon acceptance to MBA programs, it is appropriate to send gifts to thank your recommenders for their role in your acceptance. When you visit the schools you apply to, it is a good idea to pick up program paraphernalia such as T-shirts or baseball hats that you can give as a small token of thanks to your recommenders. On the other hand, you may prefer to simply take them out to lunch or for drinks to celebrate. The important message here is to convey your gratitude for their time and commitment to your success.

It is important to maintain a long-term outlook on your relationship with these brand champions. Staying in touch with them while you are in business school and beyond is to your advantage. After all, you may need them again in the future.

This chapter has examined the role recommendation letters have in the admissions evaluation. Select your recommenders carefully, because the person you choose can determine the outcome of your admission. Take the time to think carefully about whom to select for this critical role. Chicago GSB puts it aptly when it states: "Whomever you choose to write your recommendation, make sure they know you well and can offer specific examples of your performance and contributions to the organization. Avoid choosing people simply based on their title or status. We are more concerned with content and substance than reputation." Take the time to begin to develop the relationships with individuals in your profession and community to win them over as brand champions. And it isn't too late to start today.

CHAPTER TEN

MBA Applicants' Backgrounds

E ACH APPLICANT TO BUSINESS school is evaluated on his or her academic ability, leadership record, and uniqueness. Keep in mind that each candidate represents a unique background. As a candidate, you should consider whether you are a rare gem in the applicant pool (former Eskimo school teacher with a 750 GMAT) or whether you easily fall into a "usual-suspect" category. Also bear in mind that each applicant has strengths and biases he or she will encounter in the application process. Being aware of this ahead of time can help you strategize and decide on what points to emphasize in your application. You should always be thinking of additional insight or differentiation you can bring to your story to stand out. This chapter reviews the perceptions associated with different candidates' professional backgrounds and offers suggestions of what they can do to turn them to their advantage.

THE USUAL SUSPECTS

Applicants considered usual suspects are primarily consultants, bankers, accountants, and engineers. These applicants are heavily represented in the applicant pool.

1. The Consultant

Consultants come with different types of experience, with strategy consulting as one of the more popular areas. Also, some consultants specialize in industry (financial, retail, or information technology [IT] consulting, for example). Some examples of firms from which candidates with a consulting background apply are McKinsey & Company, Bain & Company, Boston Consulting Group, Strategy&, Deloitte Consulting, Accenture, and Capgemini. There are also consultants who have worked for financial services companies as well as Fortune 500 companies (such as American Express and GE) in an internal consulting role.

Valuable Consultant Skill Set

Consultants are credited for having the following skill set:

- Business savvy
- Strategic thinking
- Analytical thinking
- Excellent communication skills
- Problem-solving skills
- Emotional intelligence and interpersonal skills
- Team engagement skills
- Idea generation

Consultant Detractors

The large number of consultants in the pool increases the competition because they are, in a way, competing against each other. Here are the detractors associated with candidates from consulting backgrounds:

- Talkative
- Can be seen as arrogant
- Viewed as idea people but sometimes lack operational and implementation skills
- Doubt as to whether they are the ones driving their career vision instead of simply following a well-laid plan
- Skepticism as to whether they need an MBA (if you are planning to remain in consulting, the MBA admissions board may question why you want the MBA. Are you simply getting your ticket punched?)

What to Do

- Demonstrate your comfort level taking a path less traveled. It could be a decision you made professionally that wasn't popular or something you did in your community or in college. The important thing is to show the breadth and richness of who you are beyond being a smart, savvy professional who is great at analyzing and creating business solutions for clients.
- Show that you can go beyond developing great ideas; speak to experiences you've had in which you were able to manage people to implement an idea.
- Show that you are the one driving your future and decisions rather than sitting back on your laurels.
- Similar to the previous point, show that you have a clear rationale for why you want an MBA, and not because all your partners have one or because everyone around you gets one after a few years of experience.

2. The Banker

I'm being very broad in applying the "banker" label to include applicants working in investment management, private equity, venture capital, research, sales and trading, and investment banking. In any case, these candidates are overrepresented in the applicant pool at elite MBA programs.

Valuable Banker Skill Set

- Analytical sharpness
- Quantitative strength
- Savvy and polish
- Adeptness at working on challenging projects

Banker Detractors

- Impatient, type-A personality
- Too self-motivated, not necessarily team players
- Limited management experience

- Number cruncher who executes but may not understand the business decisions behind the numbers
- Worker bee
- Unbalanced priorities—no life outside work

What to Do

- Show team mind-set: balance showing your individual involvement and impact with working behind the scenes and helping others become successful. It is important that your story be mixed with "we" and "I" instead of only your own involvement.
- Be sure to convey how your impact at work transcends the financial analysis that you did.
- Don't underestimate the power of initiative and coming up with creative ideas and seeing them to fruition.
- Seek opportunities to lead recruiting and training initiatives.
- Step up to fill a void when the opportunity presents itself. (Don't simply get your job done.)

3. The Accountant

Accountants are also seen as "usual-suspect" candidates to business school. They are often represented in large numbers in the application pool.

Valuable Accountant Skill Set

- Proficiency with numbers
- High attention to detail
- Organization
- Dependability

Accountant Detractors

- Tactical (not strategic) thinking
- Low engagement, with nonstellar interpersonal skills
- Narrow skill set
- Lack of creativity, especially since the work can be boring
- Tendency to be an executor, not a driver of vision

What to Do

- Show an understanding and interest in the bigger picture.
- Demonstrate that you understand business decisions beyond the spreadsheets (how the numbers drive the decisions a business is making).
- Show your understanding of other functional areas; seek cross-functional projects to broaden perspective and skill set.
- Tell engaging stories. Make sure that all your essays are not simply describing financial reviews and reconciling monthly statements.
- Show your personality with appropriate humor and flair.

4. The Engineer

There are a lot of engineers in the applicant pool. They are viewed as a close cousin to accountants. Their roles are often technical. However, many of them are represented in varied industries. As a result, it is not unusual to see engineering candidates from pharmaceuticals, start-up ventures, technology companies, and even NASA.

Valuable Engineer Skill Set

- Strength with numbers
- Advanced technical skills
- Project management exposure
- Implementation experience (doer)

Engineer Detractors

- Poor communication skills
- Rigidity
- Tendency to be an executor, not a strategic or big-picture thinker
- Poor interpersonal skills

What to Do

- Demonstrate that you have vision and that you can come up with an idea, sell it to people, and rally people behind a goal.

- Show personality besides being smart and great at your job. Show that you have a life outside work that is dynamic and interesting.
- Show that you are flexible, can go with the flow, and are not limited by only one approach or idea.
- Make sure you demonstrate your real need for the MBA to get you closer to your career goals.
- Stress your interpersonal and people-related skills and experience.

NONTRADITIONAL CANDIDATES

A growing number of nontraditional candidates are recognizing the value of an MBA. Individuals from nonprofit organizations, military personnel, artists, government workers, and early-career applicants fall into the nontraditional category. Nontraditional candidates are sought after by top MBA programs because of the diversity of rich experiences and perspectives they offer in the class. Admitted candidates from this background usually have three qualities in common: (1) they have an exceptional leadership track record; (2) they have done an outstanding job building a strong case for why they need an MBA; and (3) they typically have a lot of passion for the work they do. But despite the strengths that they bring, nontraditional candidates have major hurdles in the application process: they need to convince the MBA admissions board that they have a rigorous background and relevant or transferable skills, and that the MBA makes sense given their long-term goals.

1. The Nonprofit Manager

One typically does not associate people who "do good" with signing up for the MBA. However, this is a growing phenomenon as more individuals from socially responsible backgrounds recognize that the practical skills taught in business schools are tools that can galvanize their nonprofit organizations. I anticipate that this trend will continue as the lines between sectors blur. Applicants from nonprofit backgrounds provide a different perspective that can enrich the diversity of the student body. But before landing that coveted admission, they will need to show that they have a clearly mapped-out plan for which an MBA is an integral bridge to its accomplishment. Showing intellectual strength and solid managerial accomplishment will help nonprofit candidates mitigate any concerns the MBA admissions board may have about their candidacy.

Valuable Nonprofit Skill Set

- History of operational experience
- Great passion about industry
- Strong interpersonal skills
- Strong communication skills

Nonprofit Detractors

- Weak quantitative skills
- Weak analytical skills
- Unclear rigor of work experience
- Unclear reasons for wanting an MBA

What to Do

- Make sure your academic (GMAT and GPA) data points are sound. Take a class or two in finance or accounting and earn strong grades. Aim for a GMAT score north of 700 to make academics a nonissue.
- Present a crystal-clear vision of your goals and outline how the MBA will help you achieve them.
- Don't assume the MBA admissions board can see the connections and relevance of your work experience to your business school goals. Be proactive in marketing the transferable skills you have.
- Demonstrate that your work experience is rigorous and that you can keep up intellectually with classmates who come from more traditional backgrounds.

2. The Military Candidate

A conversation between two Harvard students captures the perception of military students. Mike: "I'm concerned about how I will do in this class. It's not easy jumping in to make my point in section. I worry about making intelligent comments on the case." Sam: "I know what you mean. Can you imagine what Joe, the Navy SEAL in our class, thinks when he's in class? This is a piece of cake. I'll take many cold calls in section over another mission in Fallujah!" Military candidates have been in remarkably challenging situations and have had their leadership abilities tested numerous times. The challenge for them isn't showing that they have leadership experience but that they can adapt to a nonmilitary environment.

Valuable Military Skill Set

- Excellent leadership record
- Excellent team experience
- Strong communication skills
- Solid interpersonal skills

Military Detractors

- Possible tendency to be rigid and hierarchical
- Difficulty adapting to civilian world
- Disconnect between goals and experience
- Unclear whether the MBA is vital for the career goal

What to Do

- Show that you can be flexible.
- Pick essay topics that show different aspects of who you are beyond your experience in the military.
- Demonstrate awareness and understanding of the civilian business environment.
- Nail the rationale for why you want an MBA and what it will help you achieve professionally. An example can be tying your reconstruction work in war-torn regions with your interest in running an infrastructure development company in the emerging markets. Drawing parallels with your current experience and your future goals can help you create credibility.
- Share stories that show the lighter, softer side of your personality.

3. The Artist

Artists can be performers or managers of arts organizations. They may want to empower future artists by growing the arts lobby organization they started from a regional business to a national one. They may also be performers in a music conservatory but want to transition to the business side of managing one. Perhaps they are recording artists with some recording success but want to manage other artists and start their own label. Even those in the business side of the arts can make a compelling case for why they need an MBA. A case in point is someone who works for Christie's managing South Asian auctions and plans to create his own business targeting the region. Whatever the case, artists will need to show that they have a clear career plan and that there is a business opportunity on which they plan to capitalize. As an artist, even if you are a career changer and want to enter a new industry, it is critical to show that you have achieved some success in your current career.

Valuable Artist Skill Set

- Passion
- Creativity
- Interesting and different perspective
- Engaging and dynamic personality

Artist Detractors

- Weak quantitative skills
- Weak analytical skills
- Experience that may be less rigorous
- Unclear whether the MBA is necessary for their goals
- Skepticism about transitioning to new career (if career changer)

What to Do

- Take the GMAT early and nail a very strong score (higher than 700, ideally). Take business courses and earn A's in them.
- Make sure your vision is clear and map out exactly the steps you plan to take to achieve your career goals.
- Demonstrate that you need the MBA given your goals.
- Share stories from your experiences that show awareness of the

business environment and connect the dots from your track record to show compelling impact.

- Show that you are more than an interesting and passionate candidate. It is important to show your serious side and demonstrate clarity of vision for your future.

4. The Public Sector (Government) Candidate

Talented individuals who work in the public sector and want to find innovative strategies to tackle public issues can make a strong case for their need of a business education. Stanford GSB has been at the forefront of providing leadership to individuals from the public sector through its Certificate in Public Management and the Public Management Program. But Stanford isn't alone in this commitment. Many top MBA programs look to attract public-sector candidates to their programs. Whether you work for the Environmental Protection Agency or serve as the assistant to the prime minister of a country, you can make a cogent argument that developing business skills through an MBA will help you be more successful in your public sector role. Because many issues have a private and public sector connection, you should highlight your awareness of the complexity of business issues facing the public sector today and how global business training can help equip you with the requisite skills to handle them.

Valuable Government Skill Set

- Different perspective
- Insights into the interplay between business and politics
- Management experience
- Great team dynamics and experience

Government Detractors

- Experience that may not be rigorous enough
- Perspective that may be too narrowly defined and may lack broader business insights
- Possible lack of solid quantitative background
- Unclear whether the MBA is a fit, given background

What to Do

- Don't assume the MBA admissions board will connect all the dots of your story. Take the time to connect the dots for them. Focus on the relevant skills you have and how they translate to business.
- Demonstrate that you have a rigorous background (whether through your academic preparation or work experience).
- Make sure that your rationale justifies why you need an MBA in the first place.

5. The Early-Career Candidate

When I wrote the first edition of this book, Harvard had just launched its 2+2 program. This program encouraged college juniors and seniors to apply with the expectation that, if they were admitted, they would complete their undergraduate degree and then work for two years before enrolling at the business school. There was even a push at the time to seek out exceptional college seniors who would enroll directly after graduating from the university. The latter goal has been sidelined, and the school now focuses on the early-career candidates who are expected to work after graduation for a couple of years before enrolling in business school. Stanford GSB has their own version of the 2+2 program where college seniors apply, secure admission to Stanford, and then receive a deferral while they work before enrolling.

Although many schools have become open to younger applicants, the reality is that only a portion of the class will be represented in this demographic group. The average age of an entering class at most top MBA programs will likely remain between twenty-six and twenty-eight years old.

The important message is that early-career applicants who are great leaders, have an excellent track record of making an impact, and demonstrate professional and personal maturity should consider applying to business school whenever they feel ready.

Early-career candidates, like every other applicant to business school, have to make a compelling case for why they need the MBA. For these candidates, there is even greater pressure to make this case. The questions every MBA admissions board member will have are, "Why you are applying now? What is the hurry?" Therefore, if you happen to fall in this category, you do need to demonstrate that you have thoroughly reviewed your career goals, have enough meaningful experience to bring to the classroom, and can show that the MBA is a critical next step for you to achieve your career success.

Valuable Early-Career Skill Set

- Clarity of career focus
- Excellent leadership background
- Drive
- Desire to push the status quo
- Innovation
- Inquisitiveness and natural curiosity

Early-Career Detractors

- Overeagerness, or in too much of a hurry
- Overconfidence
- Lack of relevant experience
- Lack of emotional intelligence or maturity

What to Do

- Take the GMAT and have very strong scores (at least within the range of the program's median score).
- Have an excellent academic track record, which includes a strong GPA as well as some business courses.
- Demonstrate exceptional evidence of leadership in college. The laundry list of club membership will absolutely not cut it. Because you will have limited work experience, you should be able to demonstrate that you are a "natural" leader with real involvement and results you can point to. If you have managed classmates on projects or worked in roles in which you have been given managerial responsibility, then highlight that experience. For instance, if you managed the student union at your college, this example can showcase your managerial potential.
- Maturity is an important trait for all candidates, but it is even more

critical for an early-career candidate, because you need to be able to fit in among classmates who are much older and have more work experience.

- Show laserlike focus when it comes to career goals. Career goals that are ambiguous or general will not cut it. Avoid this by making sure that you leave the board member with an ironclad perception that you are grounded and have a clear but obtainable goal that absolutely warrants an MBA degree.
- Select your recommenders wisely. Although you can likely get away with one recommendation from a professor, having all academic recommendations that stress how smart you are will not work. You need to show your business potential, so look for a recommender who has observed you in a professional situation, whether in an internship or a nonacademic leadership capacity. Student deans can offer strong recommendations if they can talk about how you have impacted the institution through your student leadership roles.

6. The Entrepreneurial Candidate

Entrepreneurs are attracted to the MBA for the practical skills they can gain, access to a broader network, and the opportunity to refine and develop their business ideas. MBA programs in turn are attracted to entrepreneurs for the interesting business experience they add to the class as well as their natural tendency to think outside the box when tackling business issues. If you are running your own business or working for a family business and wish to pursue an MBA, you should take a few moments to learn how your profile is viewed by the MBA admissions board.

Valuable Entrepreneur Skill Set

- High creativity
- Passion
- Dogged commitment to their business
- Interesting entrepreneurial work experience and lessons learned

Entrepreneur Detractors

- Quantitative and analytical gaps
- Question whether they can sit through an entire MBA program
- Question whether the MBA is necessary for their career goals
- Question whether the MBA is an escape plan in the face of a failed venture

What to Do

- Show that the MBA isn't a passing fancy, that it is a calculated decision that will help you grow your business or start another business in the future.
- Select the right program so there isn't any question about fit. There are MBA programs that are more inclined towards entrepreneurship (for example, INSEAD and MIT Sloan), and entrepreneurs should select programs that embrace entrepreneurs. You may also opt for programs that are accelerated or begin in January instead of the usual fall start as they are more geared toward entrepreneurs.
- Demonstrate that the business you started was substantial so the MBA admissions board takes you seriously. Starting a T-shirt business in high school and selling a handful doesn't brand you as an entrepreneur.
- Even if your business venture failed, it is important to share lessons learned, what you would do differently, and articulate how a formal background in business can help you launch a successful enterprise in the future.

JOINT OR DUAL DEGREE PROGRAMS

When it comes to dual degree programs, confusion has existed for a long time regarding the application process, requirements, and deadlines. Fortunately, most MBA programs have streamlined their dual degree processes and have created more clarity about how to apply to them. When applying to a joint or dual degree program, it is your responsibility to convince the admissions boards for both programs that you truly require both degrees and have the background to enrich their programs. If you decide to apply to a joint or dual degree program, here are a few items to keep in mind:

1. Be clear on exactly why you need both degrees. Why is the degree necessary for your career? Address why taking a few classes from the second program isn't enough to meet your goals.

2. Recognize that every program is different. Know both programs very well and invest in the applications; don't assume one or the other is "in the bag."

3. Make sure you meet the deadlines of each program. It is usually the case that you will need to apply to both programs separately as well as submit a dual degree application, which often entails additional essays.

FINAL THOUGHTS

There is no such thing as a perfect profile. Every candidate has to overcome potential detractors, and it is to their advantage to understand how the admissions board views their profile in order to strategically overcome any hidden bias to their story. Becoming aware of the hidden biases against your profile empowers you to proactively address them so that you cast your application in the most powerful light possible.

CHAPTER ELEVEN

Women, Minorities, and International Candidates

T HIS CHAPTER COVERS WOMEN, minorities, and international candidates. You may be wondering why there is a separate chapter
devoted to these three groups. As I grappled with this question, I kept
returning to my observations of the unique issues some individuals in
these three groups face. As a result, I have attempted to provide some
useful perspectives for candidates who fall in any of these three categories.

WOMEN

Women have historically been underrepresented at top business schools,
comprising 30 percent of total enrollment, compared to nearly 50 percent
female representation at the nation's leading medical and law schools.
Many business schools have made growing their female student population a top priority for more than a decade. Significant progress is being
made at business schools like INSEAD (34 percent), Stanford Graduate
School of Business (36 percent), Harvard Business School (41 percent),
HKUST (36 percent), and Wharton (42 percent). Other increases in the
number of women attending business schools in U.S. MBA programs are
also encouraging, with schools like Yale witnessing an increase from the
class of 2014 (35 percent) to that of 2015 (39 percent).

As encouraging as these statistics are, still more work remains to be
done to get a completely gender-balanced class. The reasons fewer women
apply to business schools vary. Here are some of the common reasons
given for why fewer women apply and enroll at leading MBA programs:

1. Lack of female role models in business
2. The perception that MBA programs and business in general are cutthroat and Machiavellian
3. Concerns about quantitative skills
4. Skepticism surrounding the value of the MBA, especially when considering balancing professional and personal life goals
5. The age factor: unlike other graduate programs where female candidates typically enroll right after college, most applicants to business school apply after working a few years. This may create friction between choosing a career and deciding to begin a family. (Choosing the latter option may keep many would-be female candidates from applying.)

The dearth of female MBAs has been a topic of continuous discussions and concern among deans at top MBA programs. As a result, many of these programs have launched aggressive marketing efforts to attract a greater number of women to their programs. It is indeed this same issue that has partly affected the push for early-career initiatives at some leading business schools with hopes of reaching more bright female candidates.

Catalyst, a research and advisory organization, authored a landmark paper, "Women and the MBA: Gateway to Opportunity," in 2002 that revealed a disproportionate number of women were pursuing graduate business education. Organizations such as the Forté Foundation (www .fortefoundation.org) are filling this need. The mission of the Forté Foundation is to "increase the number of women business owners and business leaders and to support their careers through business education and networks." The Forté Foundation, created in November 2001, has members that include individual women, business schools, nonprofit organizations, and large corporations. Today, top MBA programs partner with the Forté Foundation to market their programs to prospective female candidates. I highly recommend the Forté Foundation to female candidates because it offers unparalleled information about business schools from a woman's perspective. The endless resources—a network of talented women, thoughtful leadership articles, female mentors, podcasts featuring accomplished women who provide career advice, admissions events, and, not least, financial support—empower female candidates and help alleviate worries and obstacles that make applying to business school a challenge for them.

The MBA has become much more diverse today. Gone are the days when MBAs were perceived as hard-charging men in pinstriped suits whose sole goal in life was to close the next financial deal. More recently, the message is getting out that MBAs can be socially conscious entrepreneurs or individuals who are transforming the way government operates. In addition, the increasing push for diversity at MBA programs, more active female alumni networks, and growing sensitivity in corporate America regarding work-life balance and telecommuting options make this a great time for anyone to pursue an MBA, especially women. Harvard Business School even created a weeklong executive development program known as "A New Path: Setting New Professional Directions" to help women wishing to return to the workforce update their business skills and reassess their career paths.

MBA admissions boards across top business schools have responded to this scarcity of female applicants by adopting more aggressive recruiting and marketing efforts to attract female candidates to apply. A few examples of such efforts are open-house marketing events held by the MBA admissions boards that target female applicants. At these events, female alumni and students serve on panels and address candidates' questions while sharing their experiences and perspectives as women and the value of the MBA on their career. Female student associations at top MBA programs tend to be active and often partner with MBA admissions boards on marketing initiatives and planning admitted students' weekends to strengthen the yield of admitted female students. I strongly encourage all female candidates to participate in these open-house events as well as attend the Forté Foundation events. They are excellent opportunities to learn about the MBA program from a woman's perspective, but more than that, they give you a chance to make connections with individuals who are closest to the programs.

Many business schools have scholarships targeting women applicants. Here's how the London Business School describes its scholarship for women:

Women in Business Club Scholarships. The scholarship is open to all successful female MBA applicants. The aim of the scholarship is to support female candidates of merit and to help increase the number of women joining the London Business School. More broadly the scholarship seeks to encourage an increase in women considering a management career within the business sector.

(Source: London Business School website)

If you are a woman applying to business school, you should know that business schools are eager to attract talented applicants like you. But keep in mind that the admissions requirements remain the same regardless of your gender. If you meet the admissions requirements and the school offers you a place in its class, you could qualify for some merit-based scholarships that are reserved for highly accomplished female candidates, so be sure to inquire about these types of awards.

MINORITIES

Minority students represent between 10 and 25 percent of the enrolled students at top MBA programs. Expanding the ethnic diversity of their program is important to most MBA programs. And some MBA admissions boards offer minority open-house events to provide a forum for candidates from minority backgrounds to learn about their programs.

Current students and alumni from minority backgrounds also partner with the MBA admissions board on their recruitment and yield events. In many of these programs, annual alumni conferences attract a significant amount of prospective minority students who use this opportunity to assess whether the program is a fit for them. For prospective minority students on the fence, these conferences can be instrumental in the decision to apply to the MBA in general and the business school program in particular. Wharton's Whitney Young Conference (www .aambaawharton.com/current_students.html) and Harvard's Naylor Fitzhugh Conference (www.hbsaasu.com) are two examples of the largest minority conferences at top business schools.

There are also organizations that provide resources and support to minority candidates. Following are a few examples of such programs.

- *Diversity Pipeline Alliance:* The Diversity Pipeline Alliance (the "Pipeline") is a network of national organizations that share the common goal of preparing students and professionals of color for leadership and management in the twenty-first-century workforce.

- *The MBA Consortium:* The Consortium for Graduate Study in Management is a leading organization for promoting diversity in American business. Started in the mid-1960s, it provides an annual competition that awards merit-based, full-tuition fellowships to America's best and brightest minority candidates, as well as non-minority students who are committed to the mission of the consortium. With more than five thousand alumni, fellowship recipients are given access to a robust network.

- *Management Leadership for Tomorrow:* MLT (www.ml4t.org) is a great resource for prospective applicants. Started by a Harvard MBA, John Rice, MLT focuses on introducing minorities to business careers and education by providing one-on-one mentoring, boot camps, and a network from the application process to postgraduation career support.

- *Robert Toigo Foundation:* RTF (www.toigofoundation.org) is another good support group for minorities that provides a combination of scholarship, mentorship, and training, as well as a robust career network for minorities interested in the financial services industry.

INTERNATIONALS

MBA programs outside of the United States attract the highest percentage of internationals, with many reporting statistics of 80 percent or more international enrollment. IESE international enrollment is 80 percent, and London Business School has a whopping 89 percent of nationalities represented. This high trend of international diversity is common among many of the top business schools outside of the United States. Within America, the statistics for international students are lower, with the range from 20 to 40 percent. American business schools recognize that international candidates clearly add to the diversity of MBA programs, and no area has seen as much activity as the international recruitment efforts launched by admissions offices at many top MBA programs.

Today, reviewing the MBA websites, it is quite common to see an extensive list of countries on the admissions' travel schedule. Not only are MBA admissions boards visiting a variety of countries to "sell" their brand to prospective candidates, they are also adding interview schedules instead of relying only on alumni. New York University Stern Business School is one such program that sends MBA admissions board members to China and other countries to interview prospective candidates. Wharton and Kellogg have been leaders in recruiting prospective candidates in Africa in addition to other regions across the globe.

International centers are also becoming quite popular as offshoots of the MBA program, enabling schools to establish infrastructure abroad to develop intellectual capital for faculty, as well as to establish relationships and partnerships in strategic countries.

Alumni returning to their home countries are proving a powerful force in providing networking opportunities for each other and admissions support for MBA candidates. Alumni clubs exist in a variety of countries around the world. If you find that candidates from your country are underrepresented, or that there is no alumni association there, this could be one initiative to which you can help bring attention after you are admitted.

Despite the focus international candidates are receiving from MBA admissions boards at leading business schools, international candidates face several challenges worth exploring. Topping this list is the visa issue facing internationals who reside outside the United States. After September 2001, and with the economic meltdown of 2008 in the financial sector, U.S. immigration laws and hiring quotas have tightened, making it more challenging for international students to receive visas in a short time frame. Therefore, international candidates are encouraged to apply in the earlier rounds to ensure that they have enough time to obtain the visa. Most visa consulate offices require evidence that the candidate can fund his or her education. Before going in for your visa interview, you should make sure you are armed with all supporting materials to minimize the chance of your visa application being denied. The UK conservative government has also tightened its policies around work permits, a policy that is expected to affect the international population.

International students face greater challenges securing jobs during a tough economy, and the economic downturn of 2008 to 2010 hasn't made it easier for them. It can take international students longer to secure a job after graduating compared to their counterparts, depending on the industry they choose to target. My key advice to international applicants is to do your homework early before you enroll at a school. Find out what types of resources the school provides to help internationals like you succeed in the job search. Also look closely at the employment data, and speak to older students about their own recruiting experience. Finally, the best way to ensure that you succeed in your job search is to take a proactive approach to planning for it.

All MBA programs want international candidates because of the diverse perspective they bring to the program. Popular MBA programs such as INSEAD, IMD, and London Business School draw the largest numbers of internationals abroad. U.S. MBA programs will continue to compete with international MBA programs, which often offer language components that make them attractive to international applicants. U.S. MBA admissions boards will have to continue to aggressively target international talent through proactive marketing and by bringing the admissions information to international students' home countries.

On the evaluation front, many applicants have questions about how MBA admissions boards view international candidates in the application process. A common misconception is that boards have different admissions criteria for international candidates compared with U.S. citizens. This is far from the truth. Both groups of candidates are evaluated based on the same admissions criteria described in earlier chapters. That said, an area where I have observed a slight gap among international candidates is extracurricular involvement. In the United States, there is a strong culture of community service and extracurricular activities. Take the college application, for instance. High school students in the United States learn early that they need more than a perfect SAT score and GPA to be admitted to their top schools. Hence, they become savvy about building their extracurricular activities and a track record of leadership. Furthermore, American colleges offer ample opportunities to do internships and participate in student leadership and community service. With the American emphasis on being a well-rounded individual, the average candidate in America has extensive opportunities to develop a strong leadership and community service track record.

This is not to suggest that these opportunities are nonexistent for internationals. However, international candidates have to be more aggressive when identifying opportunities to impact and lead in their communities. In situations in which the opportunities are absent, you should look into creating a volunteer organization from scratch, giving you a great opportunity to showcase your entrepreneurial leadership. I once worked with an international candidate who was reapplying to business school. He had created a brand-new community organization to help university students get placed for internships in his home country. I suspect that this leadership involvement is partly why he was admitted to a top MBA program the second time around.

Obtaining recommendation letters is another area in which international candidates should pay careful attention. I've noticed that international recommenders are not always as knowledgeable about how to "market" candidates. You should pay careful attention to selecting the right recommender if you are an international candidate. Make sure the writing ability of your recommender is up to par and that he or she has a good command of the English language. Remember, you are being assessed on your management potential and leadership, so remind your recommenders to stress these points and not simply state that you are a hard worker and extremely intelligent.

Finally, funding the education is an issue that international students grapple with. MBA programs in the United States and around the world have affiliations with loan programs to support applicants from different regions. You should do your homework prior to submitting applications to identify the resources available for students from your region. I cover more specific funding options for internationals in the chapter on funding the MBA.

CHAPTER TWELVE

Admissions Decisions

A FTER MANY MONTHS INVESTING in the application, the long-awaited decision day has arrived. Decision day—or, aptly, D-day—is a day that is full of angst for MBA candidates. The wait has been long, and candidates have given everything they can to earn a spot at their dream school. Rumors have not been in short supply in popular online chat rooms either. This day is particularly abuzz with final salutations and last-minute encouragements. The clock strikes at the prescribed time and the results pour in.

For about 10 to 20 percent of applicants, the news is positive. Congratulatory phone calls from MBA admissions directors such as Derrick Bolton, Dawna Clark, and Dee Leopold bring good news to anxious candidates. For many, however, the admission outcome is disappointing. These applicants receive the conciliatory email informing them that they are great candidates but an overly competitive year and exceptional applicant pool made it impossible to admit them. I will use this chapter to discuss the different admission decision outcomes and offer suggestions on how to manage each situation.

ADMITTED—NOW WHAT?

Once the euphoria of the good news has cleared, you will have some practical tasks to attend to in preparation for this new chapter of your life. The first order of business is to follow up with your brand champions (recommenders) to inform them of the admission decision and to thank them for their role in making your application successful.

Deciding on which MBA program to enroll in requires thoughtful analysis and research. Often friends and family have strong and conflicting opinions about where you should enroll. But the decision is ultimately yours (unless you have a partner, in which case both of you will need to make the decision together).

As a first step in deciding which MBA program you will attend, jot down the pros and cons of each program. Then visit the programs you are considering for their admitted students' weekend events. One note of caution about these events is that all the schools are going to have their best face on and will have a full-court press to sell you on their program. Therefore, you will need to dig a bit deeper to make sure that your questions are answered and that the program really offers what it says it does.

SOME TOPICS TO EXPLORE DURING ADMITTED STUDENTS' WEEKEND

How comfortable are you with the teaching method at the school? Attending multiple classes during your visit will give you perspective that should confirm or raise flags regarding whether the teaching method is appropriate for you. The current students can also attest to the value and detractors of the teaching method. The faculty can contribute to the quality of your education, so do not hesitate to find out whether the faculty members are accessible to the students and whether opportunities exist to work with them on cases and projects outside the classroom.

Social life is very important. Take your significant other if you have one to explore the culture of the program outside the classroom. How integrated are partners in the overall fabric of the social life? What are things that could be improved upon in this area, and what is currently being done? What social activities do students participate in, and do they appeal to you?

Career services and support have become more important as the economy has gone through downturns in the recent years. Research the level of commitment the career services team gives to students. Talking to students and the career services staff will give you some perspective in this area. Pay close attention to employment statistics of recent graduates. This information is accessible from the career services office.

Once you have made your decision and have paid your deposit, you are ready to tackle the prematriculation process. You will likely be inundated with emails and packets that can quickly become overwhelming. Although it can be tempting to put off going through the materials you receive, take the time to review them carefully to avoid missing any key deadlines. I have identified the major prematriculation topics, although this list is certainly not exhaustive and there may be other issues that you need to address based on your particular situation.

Prematriculation Preparation

The prematriculation process can last for several months until your program begins. Devote the time to ensure that you attend to all matters dealing with this process.

Financial Aid

Make sure you have all the required financial aid forms completed and submitted on time. Now that you are an "insider," you may also be able to identify additional funding opportunities that were not advertised on the program's website. Do not be bashful about contacting the financial aid staff to inquire about further opportunities for scholarships. If you do this, however, it is important to do so tastefully without being annoying. The next chapter covers financial aid information in greater detail.

Housing

Where you will live can have a tremendous impact on your MBA experience, so choose wisely. Is your program on a residential campus? If not, how important is it for you to live close to campus? What about roommates? The MBA experience is not solely in the classroom. In fact, many of the exciting and interesting experiences will take place after classes. Practice enough introspection to decide what matters to you and what kind of experience you wish to have before you select your housing. Since my husband attended business school and we lived both on campus and off, I can offer my personal opinion based on both experiences. On-campus living is all about convenience, and you are truly in the mix of things. Off-campus living gives you a bit more space (if that is what you seek) and can mean that your experience is expanded to the broader community instead of focused on the MBA nucleus of your program. In either case, be proactive. Finding great accommodations is challenging at best and near impossible if you are in a metropolitan area, so start early to sort out your housing situation. Many programs provide on-campus housing based on a lottery system, so plan to take care of your housing as soon as you can, and don't leave it to the last minute, because you can lose out on your lottery if you miss the deadline. Roommates can also pose their own set of problems if you don't select carefully. Some friendships do not survive after the friends have lived together: just because you get along with your friend doesn't always mean you will enjoy living with him or her. If your friend is a certified slob and you can't stand to see a plate in the kitchen sink, you may want to think twice before rooming together. Whatever you decide to do with your housing decision, think long and hard about what your options are and what works for you to ensure a pleasant living experience.

Academic Preparation

Regardless of whether your admission is conditional on additional academic requirements, it is to your advantage to brush up on your quantitative and analytical skills by taking a course or at the very least reading through a well-written text on statistics, accounting, and financial analysis. This is particularly useful for individuals who have been out of school for more than five years. Many MBA programs require incoming students to complete a prematriculation "mini course" offered by the program. These can be in the form of math boot camps or intensive English language programs. The advantage of these programs is that you will have a chance to get to know a small group of your classmates before the semester starts. Many MBA programs also require their entering class to complete a series of analytic and career assessments. These are required and can take time to complete, so although you may be inclined to procrastinate, set aside enough time that you don't jeopardize your admission by not completing the assessment.

Career Preparation

Everyone, particularly career changers, should spend some time thinking about what they wish to study and their career goals. Many MBA programs use Career Leader, a great tool for self-assessment and career guidance. You may also choose to arrange informational meetings with alumni from your MBA program or professionals in the industry in which you wish to work. Consider spending the summer before you start business school working in the role or industry you plan to move into after the MBA. A former client of mine who was a banker but wanted to explore consulting left his job to work for a consulting company in a new geographic location. It was a six-month stint, but it gave him exposure to a new industry beyond the summer internship and also allowed him to explore a new region (which he discovered he loved). This experience confirmed that consulting was the right career for him even before he began his MBA. Investing in working in a new career for a couple of months before you begin business school can give you a bit of a boost when it comes to securing a job. Such positions may be unpaid but will pay dividends when you begin your job search. Besides, you can't underestimate the value of hitting the ground running.

Regardless of your decision, be sensitive to how you exit from your firm. If you plan to explore another career opportunity before starting your MBA, give your employer ample notice before you leave. And please, aim to wrap up all outstanding projects to the best of your ability. It is always wise to leave your bridges intact for the future.

Securing a Visa
For international students outside the United States, begin your visa application process as early as possible (once you receive your admission notice), as the process has become more complicated and requires more time. The same applies for applicants targeting MBA programs around the world; give yourself enough time to apply and secure the student visa to ensure you are able to enroll for your studies. I have seen applicants forced to defer their MBA study for a year as a result of not securing their study visa in time. To expedite the process, have all your documents ready for the embassy or consulate office before you secure an admission offer, you'll be ready as soon as you are admitted.

Have Fun!
Finally, allow time to relax. You may wish to travel to see friends and family or to spend some time on a passion that you have been neglecting. Also, there is ample opportunity to meet your soon-to-be classmates through the prematriculation sites and informal get-togethers in your

city of residence. Some of your closest friendships may be established during one of these trips before the program formally begins. An applicant I know used the summer before starting his MBA to finally earn his pilot's license.

CONDITIONAL ADMISSION

What if you are admitted conditionally? Conditional admission typically has two stipulations: (1) improving quantitative background, and (2) developing English language skills.

Some MBA programs provide summer or prematriculation programs. These programs often cover English language development and analytical and quantitative preparation. In other cases, the admission is conditional on the student's taking courses from a university in his or her home city.

Whatever the case, it is important to view this admission positively. After all, the MBA admissions board would not have admitted you if it did not think you had the ability to handle its program. The additional coursework is to provide you with an opportunity to strengthen any gaps and to empower you to succeed when the program begins. Interestingly enough, much of the feedback I have received on this, especially programs sponsored by the MBA, has been good. To paraphrase one student's view, "The prematriculation program was wonderful as it gave me a chance to meet many of my classmates and form a close bond with them before classes began. It was like starting a program with more than twenty friends."

One point to underscore regarding conditional admission is to make sure that you have read the fine print on your admission letter. The responsibility is on you to fulfill the conditions on which your admission is made. You don't want an oversight to cost you a spot at your dream school.

DEFERRED ADMISSION

Most top MBA programs prefer that candidates apply only when they are ready, and the majority of them do not grant deferrals except under extenuating circumstances. Contact each of the MBA programs to find out exactly what their policy is on deferred admission. Some examples of what the MBA admissions board considers extenuating circumstances include:

- When an illness precludes you from enrolling (you will need medical records from your doctor to attest to this)
- When you are the primary caretaker of an immediate family member who is struggling with a serious health problem
- When you are in the military and have been deployed to combat or assignment
- When you are a college senior whom the MBA admissions board feels will be better served if you gained professional experience
- When you have not been able to secure the visa to study at the program

Unfortunately, at many programs, once-in-a-lifetime career opportunities, although noteworthy achievements, are rarely deemed acceptable reasons to grant a deferral. Be aware that the MBA admissions board reserves the right to make the final call on who they will offer deferred admission to. If your request for a deferral is declined and you choose to reapply in the future, you need to be aware that having been admitted previously does not guarantee you will be readmitted in the future. Admission is always based on the makeup of the class and the rigor of the applicant pool. So if a deferral is not granted, think through your decision carefully before passing up your admission offer. Be sure that the new opportunity is worth it! I have firsthand experience during my time on Harvard's admissions board seeing candidates who did not get in the second time around (even though they were admitted in the past).

WAIT LIST

We have all heard of the wait list wasteland and the many myths swirling around this application outcome. I suspect that to some degree, the myths that surround the wait list are a result of the heterogeneity of MBA programs' policies. Each MBA program deals with its wait list differently, so it is critical to find out the specifics of each program's policy. Contact the MBA program and maintain communication with the MBA admissions board member designated to manage the wait list.

I dealt with the wait list during my time at Harvard, and I saw up close the angst and stress candidates experience while awaiting their admission outcome. The truth with the wait list is that it is hard to crack exactly why you were placed on that list. After all, your application was seen as certainly "admissible," but there is something that didn't quite push it into the admitted pile. A major reason is the sheer quality of the applicant pool. With so many talented candidates applying to business school, sometimes strong is not considered strong enough, given the competition. In other cases, you may have applied in a year when many people with nearly identical backgrounds applied. It can also be a result of numbers, be it a GPA or GMAT score. An applicant I know was placed on the wait list of a top MBA program, and after I read her application, which was very strong, it occurred to me that her Achilles' heel was her GMAT score. It was several standard deviations from the norm. She had retaken the exam and done quite well, but unfortunately the new score was not taken into consideration because the MBA program did not accept additional information after the deadline. Her application was ultimately rejected. It is therefore important to apply to MBA programs when you have the absolute strongest application you possibly can assemble.

If you find yourself in the unenviable position of being wait-listed, here are some practical steps you can take to manage the process:

1.   Immediately express your interest in remaining on the wait list via an email to the wait list manager.
2.   Inquire about the policy, size of the wait list, and timing for the decisions (if this has not been clarified by the wait list manager).
3.   For programs open to receiving additional information, consider sending new and relevant information to bolster your case. A higher GMAT or GRE score, a promotion at work with additional management responsibility, and an award in your community for your volunteer involvement are all good examples of valid information that you can send to the MBA admissions board. The challenge, however, is that each MBA program has a different wait list policy, so make sure you know precisely what's acceptable and what's not. For instance, Wharton explicitly requests that you not send additional information, whereas you *can* send compelling new information to Kellogg. These policies can change from one year to the next, so call the wait-list manager to confirm the program's current policy.

Unfortunately, the percentage of applicants admitted from the wait list is low, so it is in your best interest to keep your other options open. The "bird in hand" theory applies here. It is not unusual to see situations in which fewer than ten people are admitted from a 200-plus wait list. Do you accept the offer of admission while you wait to hear back from your preferred program where you are wait-listed? It is a delicate balancing act. Ideally, you should try to get an extension before you make your decision. In the meantime, you should find out whether there is anything else you can offer to bolster your case where you are wait-listed. Obviously, if it is May and you have been on the wait list for a while, you may have to accept that it is highly unlikely that you will get off the wait list.

If this is the only MBA program to which you applied, or if all your results from other programs were unfavorable, make it clear to the MBA admissions board that its program is your top choice, that you are willing to remain on the wait list to the last day, and that you will enroll at the last minute if an admission offer is extended to you.

What happens if you are denied admission after being on the wait list? The next section will provide you with some options you may want to consider.

DENIED ADMISSION

First of all, if the admission decision is a denial, it is important to keep in mind that this is not the end of the world. After you have gotten over the initial disappointment, you should examine what your application lacked. There are a variety of reasons a candidate does not gain admission. The key ones are:

1. The candidate did not apply to realistic programs but rather applied only to schools where he or she had very little chance of gaining admission.
2. The candidate applied too early or too late in his or her career.
3. The candidate was not a fit for the program to which he or she applied.
4. The candidate was strong, but the overall application pool happened to have exceptionally strong candidates, raising the admission stakes.
5. The candidate's brand was unclear or lacked focus.

6.   The candidate failed to make a compelling case for why he or she needs the MBA.

7.   The candidate's application lacked self-awareness.

8.   The candidate's application had fundamental flags around judgment or interpersonal issues.

9.   The candidate's application lacked strong evidence of leadership or community involvement.

10.   The candidate's application raised concerns regarding academic preparation and intellectual strength.

11.   The candidate's recommendations had a damning effect.

12.   The candidate rushed through the application and did not spend enough time on it.

13.   The candidate bombed the interview.

Take a step back and evaluate your application in its entirety. Better yet, have someone you respect and who knows you very well review your application and provide you with feedback. Current students or alumni of the program are usually effective in giving useful feedback.

Understanding what went wrong with the application can come from feedback from the MBA admissions board. MBA programs vary in their policies on providing feedback. For instance, whereas Harvard Business School offers feedback only to college seniors programs, a handful of MBA programs such as Tuck provide feedback to applicants and even encourage some applicants to reapply in the future.

Feedback sessions are typically offered at the end of the admissions cycle, during the summer. Given the volume of reapplicants, I recommend that you sign up as soon as feedback spots become available since they fill up quickly. Also, because the feedback from the MBA admissions board can be particularly helpful, taking this extra step can play a major role in your reapplication, should you choose to reapply. Most business programs do not provide feedback to applicants whose applications were denied, so you may also wish to have an independent consultant evaluate your old application and provide you with strategic steps you can pursue to increase your chances of admission in the future. At EXPARTUS, we created a program called "The Come Back Kid" to help applicants who intend to reapply to identify what was wrong with their application the first time around and to arm them with a concrete plan to reapply successfully.

FIND OUT WHAT WENT WRONG
WITH YOUR APPLICATION

I have identified some of the common reasons applicants are rejected. Read through them and reflect on your application. Does your application have any of these issues?

- GPA scores inadequate compared to typical class scores
- No brand or differentiation
- Weak academic story (weak grades and/or low GMAT/GRE scores)
- Lack of leadership impact
- Limited compelling professional experience
- Too old and more suited for an executive program instead of a traditional program
- Interpersonal flags such as immaturity, lack of self-awareness
- Bland application
- Not connecting the dots well or addressing gaps effectively
- Essays that lack passion
- Recommendation letters that raise flags about you
- MBA goals that don't make sense or are a mismatch with the program
- Poor interview performance
- Applying late in the application process
- Underestimating how much work is required to submit a winning application
- Bad luck (you happen to apply in the year when more people from your firm or your undergraduate school apply)

These are some of the reasons an application is rejected. Could any of these things have gone wrong with your application? Knowing is half the battle. Then you can begin to put a plan together to reapply successfully. Whether you secure the help of a consultant or you choose to go it alone, you should follow the practical steps that I outline in this chapter to help you become better prepared when you reapply for admission.

REAPPLICATION

After reassessing your application (whether through MBA admissions board feedback, admissions consulting evaluation, or self-reflection), you will be in a better position to decide whether you should reapply in the future.

The chance of a different admission outcome the next time around depends on what the issue was the first time. Academic gaps are much easier to address by retaking the GMAT or GRE and earning excellent grades in quantitative business courses. Weak leadership or community involvement can be addressed by spending a couple of years building a track record in this area before reapplying. However, issues of fit are more challenging, because they reflect incongruity between your brand and that of the MBA program.

MBA programs do not publish percentages of reapplicants accepted, but anecdotal evidence indicates that some reapplicants gain admission the second time around. That said, applying more than two times to an MBA program is overdoing it. The second declined admission may suggest that there isn't a fit between you and the MBA program—your academic numbers may be too low compared with your competition or you are looking to pursue a health-care career and the program doesn't have health-care offerings. There are many other MBA programs where you will be successful, and it is worth expanding the list of MBA programs to give yourself the best shot at being admitted.

PRACTICAL STEPS FOR REAPPLICANTS TO TAKE TO IMPROVE THEIR APPLICATION

- Do your homework and make sure you know the MBA program inside out. Don't apply without visiting the program and attending a class if possible. (This is a common mistake applicants make.)
- Be very specific when discussing why you want to be accepted to a particular MBA program and how it will enhance your career trajectory. Demonstrate a clear fit between you and the MBA program.
- Beef up your career and community leadership, and make sure you have tangible examples of the impact you have made since your previous application.
- Simply reapplying with the same "goods" will likely yield an unfavorable outcome. Be willing to take major action. It may mean changing your job, taking on significant responsibility at work, or doing an international project.
- Increase your GMAT or GRE score significantly by taking a class if

necessary and make sure your score is at least within the median score of admitted students. Take business or quantitative classes and earn As in them to show your intellectual aptitude. Good options are introduction courses in finance, microeconomics and macroeconomics, statistics, and accounting.

- Cultivate relationships with individuals who will become your brand champions, and make sure that they are on board and committed to writing glowing recommendation letters for you. Tactfully request to see your recommendations from previous recommenders if they are open to sharing them with you.
- Invest time in clarifying your brand, and be proactive to make sure your application reflects a powerful brand that is in sync with the MBA program.
- Apply early to avoid running into a situation in which few admission spots remain.
- This can't be overstressed: visit the campus and attend different open-house events and information sessions to make sure you fully understand the program and its brand.

A reapplication is not an invitation to suspend your judgment. Some application situations are lost causes. Some schools do not encourage reapplication, as is the case with INSEAD. Others, like Tuck, are quite reapplicant-friendly. Knowing where a school stands on the reapplication continuum will help you figure out if it's worth reapplying to the program. If, after retaking the GMAT, your score remains below 500, you may have to rethink your school list. Just because a candidate believes he or she belongs to a particular program does not mean he or she will be admitted. I know of a candidate who applied four times to a top MBA program and even after his fourth rejection remained optimistic that he would eventually gain admission. This is clearly delusional and not a good example of persistence. I don't think there is anything wrong with reapplying once to your dream school, especially if you didn't spend much time on your application the first time through.

At the same time, I've evaluated applications where it was apparent that there wasn't anything the candidate could do to change the admission outcome. It may be a fundamental fit issue. Or it could come down to being overqualified for the MBA. Therefore, objective evaluation and honest introspection will help you ascertain whether a reapplication is worth the trouble. The following example illustrates this point. A business associate once asked me to evaluate a friend's application. He was an Asian male with exceptional academic and GMAT scores, he had great evidence of leadership, and he had worked at three blue-chip firms. After reading his essays (he happened to be a very good writer) and entire application, it was clear to me that he was in that category of applicants that had all the "goods" but couldn't make a convincing case for why he needed the MBA. His application was strong enough that he was interviewed by Harvard, Stanford, and Wharton, but all three schools rejected him. This is one of the hardest situations to overcome as a reapplicant. In his case, he couldn't improve his GMAT score or change jobs to get more leadership experience. He already had met these requirements. It came down to whether the MBA admissions board believed that he needed the MBA or that he was simply getting his ticket stamped. Waiting too long to apply to business school can result in a rejected application.

FINAL THOUGHTS

Hopefully, by the time you have made it to this point of the book, you have already gleaned enough insights to ensure that you avoid the landmines that surround the entire application process. I've touched on the less-favorable potential outcomes as well to help applicants navigate effectively should they find themselves in an unenviable situation of a wait list or denied admission. Applying the suggestions I highlight in this section should help applicants to increase their odds of a favorable outcome in the future. Once you are armed with an admission offer, another set of anxieties may take front stage: figuring out how to fund your education. I examine the subject of funding the MBA in the next chapter.

CHAPTER THIRTEEN
Funding the MBA

B USINESS SCHOOLS BELIEVE IT is the responsibility of the applicant to meet the financial burden for their education. With that said, many MBA programs attempt to soften the financial blow to applicants by offering scholarships, loans, and loan forgiveness programs. There is no question that the MBA is an expensive investment. This large financial cost can dissuade many applicants from applying to business school. On the other hand, some applicants pay too little attention to how they will fund the MBA. Members of this latter group tend to focus primarily on the uphill application process with little attention to cost, at least until they have an admission offer in hand. A tardy response to planning how you will finance your MBA may cost you tens of thousands of scholarship dollars.

This chapter attempts to make the funding process more transparent. Strong evidence exists to support the investment in the MBA. However, it is not a license to charge everything without limits. Funding your MBA requires practical planning and discipline to achieve your education dreams. I will discuss the overall cost of the MBA and funding sources. I'll also provide suggestions of how candidates should go about preparing themselves to fund their MBA.

THE MBA COST
One or two years in business school will cost you a hefty amount of money. You will need to cover the cost of tuition, room, board,

transportation, books, medical insurance, special trips, and other mis-cellaneous fees associated with a business education. A few years ago, an MBA at Harvard Business School would have cost you about $110,000 for room, board, fees, and tuition. Today, the cost is nearly $200,000 for a single student and nearly $250,000 for a married student with a child. The total cost of the MBA for a single student residing on campus at Stanford Graduate School of Business is nearly $200,000. These num-bers, although staggering, are consistent across top MBA programs in the United States.

Schools in large cities are not the only ones that have to deal with the high MBA cost. Even programs in small towns, such as Tuck, Cornell, and Darden, have equally high price tags. Tuck's sample MBA fees illus-trate this point.

TUITION AND COSTS		
Tuition and Costs for Academic Year 2014–15		
	T'16	T'15
Tuition	$61,605	$61,605
Program Fee	$4,470	$1,680
Books and Supplies	$1,400	$1,400
Housing	$11,100	$13,632
Miscellaneous and Health Expenses	$13,400	$16,368
Board	$1,575	$975
Total	**$93,550**	**$95,660**

(Source: Tuck website)

You will notice that the Tuck cost for the MBA is broken down into the two years, and when combined, the degree cost is $189,210. The cost is less for MBA programs in Europe and Asia, given their shorter length. Looking just at tuition, London Business School costs approximately £64,000 (equivalent as of this writing to approximately $105,000), INSEAD costs €63,000 (equivalent to $86,000), while HKUST Business School costs HK $545,000 (equivalent to $70,000). Though cheaper than U.S. MBA programs, you can see that the one-year programs outside the United States also come with sizeable price tags.

Regardless of where you choose to pursue your MBA, the cost can increase significantly if you don't create and live within a budget. Some students feel that the MBA is a once-in-a-lifetime experience and use this rationale to justify why they need to participate in every trek around the world with their classmates. The cost of these exotic jaunts can be more than $20,000, adding to the debt students take on when they graduate.

At a glance, the tab for an MBA will leave many applicants with their heads spinning. The good news is that the MBA is an investment in one's career for the long term. In 2013, the median starting salary of Stanford graduates was $125,000 post–business school. These high salaries are not unique to Stanford. Columbia's 2013 data reveals that its median starting salary was $110,000, and Tuck's 2013 results reveal that the mean salary was $115,000. But U.S. MBA programs are not the only ones boasting high compensation for their graduates. The Judge Business School at Cambridge reported a salary average of £66,000 (equivalent to $91,000), and the top-ranking European school, INSEAD, reported median starting salary (including bonuses) of €105,000 (equivalent to $144,000). These career statistics demonstrate that the return on the MBA investment does pay for itself over time.

FUNDING SOURCES

There are five main ways to fund the MBA. Many candidates rely on a combination of these.

Company Sponsorships

Some companies offer to cover their employees' education. In exchange, the employees return to the firm to work for a few years after their MBA. This offer is usually extended to star employees whom a company wishes to retain. Some consulting companies are amenable to company sponsorships. Even if your firm doesn't typically offer sponsorship opportunities, if you have consistently received top evaluations and have brand champions at your firm, don't be shy about proposing this option if you intend to return to your industry.

Loans

Loans are the most common option for funding the MBA. You will need to know what your credit score is, because the loan interest rate will be based on your credit score and history. U.S. lenders determine loan rates based on the three different credit scores: Equifax, TransUnion, and Experian. It is important to know what your score is for all three. Fair Isaac Corp. (FICO) tracks credit histories and scores of all three agencies. Applicants should order a copy of all three scores by going to www.myfico.com. Lending agencies use payment history, how much you owe, how long you have had the credit, how much new debt you have taken on, and the types of credit you have to determine your credit score. You can save a lot of money by cleaning up your credit prior to applying for a loan to fund your MBA.

There are different types of loans available to MBA candidates.

1. The U.S. Department of Education offers two federal loan programs for students, namely, the William D. Ford Federal Direct Loan (Direct Loan) and the Federal Perkins Loan Program. U.S. citizens and permanent residents are eligible for these loans. The Direct Loan program includes the subsidized loans, unsubsidized loans, PLUS loans, and consolidation loans.

    The subsidized loan provides the best rates to students. The subsidized loan is only available to undergraduate students with financial need, while the unsubsidized loan is available to students pursuing undergraduate, graduate, or professional degrees. Unsubsidized loans also do not require students to demonstrate financial need. For more details on eligibility requirements for this loan, visit the U.S. Department of Education Federal Student Aid website (www.studentaid.ed.gov/types/loans/subsidized-unsubsidized).

    The PLUS Loan (www.studentaid.ed.gov/types/loans/plus) is a federally sponsored program that is available to U.S. citizens, permanent residents, and eligible non-citizens with a good credit history. It is designed to help cover financial needs not covered by other loans.

    The last of the Direct Loan programs, consolidation loans, are individual loans that consolidate all federal student loans under one lender.

    The Federal Perkins Loan Program (www.studentaid.ed.gov/types/loans/perkins) provides low-interest loans to offset the cost of education. This loan is open to undergraduate, graduate, and professional students who have high financial need. In this case, the school is the lender, and payments are made directly to the school. You should find out ahead of time whether the school you wish to apply to is a participant in the Perkins Loan program.

2. Private MBA loan programs are available to international candidates at many top business schools. These loans are designed by the MBA programs and the bank with the candidate in mind. Harvard Business School offers a loan program through the Harvard University Employees Credit Union, and international students are eligible to participate in this loan scheme without a cosigner. Wharton has partnered with Quorum Federal Credit Union to provide loans to international students without requiring a cosigner also. Other business schools have similar offerings for international students.

   Lest you think only U.S. MBA programs provide reasonable loan options to MBA students, top international business schools also provide loans to students. INSEAD, for example, has a loan option that is run by the INSEAD alumni community through the popular Prodigy Finance loan scheme. The benefit of Prodigy Finance is that it is open to international students from around the world and, at INSEAD, MBA students from eighty-four nationalities have participated in the program as of this writing. It reports an unprecedented 100 percent repayment history. London Business School offers a similar option, also through Prodigy Finance. IMD offers a loan scheme through two Swiss banks, and international students are eligible for this funding option.

3. MBA programs have created loan forgiveness programs to reduce the financial burden of the MBA on applicants who pursue careers in the nonprofit or public sectors. Harvard Business School, for example, has created a loan forgiveness program for graduates in social enterprise. Stanford also offers a program for both domestic and international students who choose to work in developing countries after business school. Fuqua has a generous loan assistance program that offers financial awards to alumni who work in nonprofit and government organizations. Other top MBA programs offer similar loan forgiveness programs, so take the time to research what each specific program offers.

4. I would be remiss if I did not acknowledge the growing trend of social investment loans. Unlike loan forgiveness programs that apply to graduates who go on to work at nonprofits and in the public sector, social investment loans are available to all students regardless of their industry or sector. These loans are part of a new trend that is transforming the lending industry. Since 2008, a few MBA students have founded social investment lending companies to address the high cost of loans facing graduate students. A few examples include CommonBond and SoFi. CommonBond was started in 2012 by MBA students at Wharton with an objective to offer affordable student loans to students across more than twenty MBA programs. A year earlier, on the West Coast, Stanford GSB students created Social Finance Inc. (SoFi). They started this social investment vehicle as a way to provide affordable loan alternatives to students seeking funding for college and graduate school. Their alternative model targets alumni and investors, who provide borrowers with loans at a lower-than-average interest rate. Alumni offer support to students participating in their loan scheme. Despite its short tenure, SoFi has taken off like wildfire and has provided more than $200 million in loans to students and alumni from more than one hundred universities. These alternatives didn't exist when I wrote the first edition of this book and are another example of the rapid change going on in the business school market.

University Awards

Many top MBA programs offer awards to students to help offset the cost of their education. These scholarships are often merit-based but can be need-based as well.

Stanford GSB, for instance, offers five students Siebel scholarships, awards covering the full cost of attendance for their second year, based on exceptional leadership and academic achievements during their first year. In 2013, Stanford also launched a new program, Stanford Africa MBA Fellowship, which covers the tuition and expenses of up to eight African citizens, who are required to return to Africa after graduation to work for two years to help develop their country. The school offers numerous other scholarships, from the Charles P. Bonini Partnership for Diversity Fellowship to the Reliance Dhirubhai Fellowship for Indian students from economically deprived backgrounds to the Orbis Investment Management Fellowship for first-year students from any background with a passion for investing.

In the case of Chicago GSB, awards are given to students through scholarships that range between $15,000 and $25,000 each year. Tuck offers scholarships that start at as little as $3,000 and go up to a full scholarship for applicants based on merit and need. Cornell's Park Fellowship is usually in the tens of thousands of dollars.

The China Europe International Business School (CEIBS) also offers very generous scholarships to its students. A few of them include an Excellence Award; Merit Award; Women Leadership Award; Entrepreneurship Award; Latin America, Africa, Middle East, and Central Asia Awards; not to mention other awards sponsored by Chinese and international companies.

India School of Business (ISB) offers a variety of awards based on need and merit. The school launched an India Global Scholarship on the eve of its tenth anniversary, and this program offers awards of $6,000 to $30,000 to ten admitted students from ten different geographical regions. Additionally, the ISB awards scholarships of varying amounts to another 110 students. Other scholarship schemes exist through awards given by partnering companies like Novartis and Talentia.

All top MBA programs have some form of award available to incoming students, so take the time to find out what your target programs offer, the requirements, and the deadlines so that you can apply in time for them.

Special Target Awards

These are scholarships that are offered to particular demographic groups. Some MBA programs offer a limited number of Forté Fellowships to female applicants. The Toigo Foundation offers scholarships to minority candidates interested in private equity careers who are studying at Toigo partner schools. Another popular fellowship is the Consortium Fellowship, which is now available not just to underrepresented minority candidates but to any U.S. citizen or permanent resident with an interest that is aligned with the Consortium's mission. Specific companies are also involved in offering fellowships and scholarships to incoming business school students. Banks such as Goldman Sachs, JPMorgan Chase, and Credit Suisse First Boston (CSFB) provide fellowships to MBA candidates. Even Fortune 500 corporations offer scholarships to candidates with industry experience and interest. There are enough options that applicants can take advantage of to fund their MBA—it just requires careful research and adequate preparation.

Personal Savings

Applicants to business school have an expected family contribution (EFC) that they need to make toward covering the cost of their education. Applicants need to start a couple of years before applying to business school to save money and cut down on their expenses. MBA financial aid officers expect that you will contribute sizably to your MBA costs.

I can't stress enough the importance of hustling to find scholarships and financial sponsorships. Unfortunately, you can't always count on every single award being on the MBA program websites and catalogs. You will have to be a bit of a detective and dig discretely to find out if other scholarships are available under the radar. Current students are a good resource to glean such information from.

MATERIALS REQUIRED FOR FINANCIAL AID APPLICATION

- An application to the MBA program submitted in time for the financial aid deadlines (verify each MBA program's deadline ahead of time)
- A completed FAFSA (Free Application for Federal Student Aid) form (www.fafsa.com)
- The financial aid forms for the MBA program
- Your most recent federal tax returns
- Evidence of salary (pay stubs)
- Documentation of assets and bank statements
- Other forms or documentation may be required—confirm this with the financial aid office at your MBA program

---

PREPARING YOURSELF FINANCIALLY
TO FUND YOUR MBA

Applicants are expected to have some savings that they will use to offset the cost of their MBA. The reality for many candidates, however, is that this isn't always the case. If you are already in the application stage, then you will need to focus your strategy on finding as much "free" money as you can to help you bear the financial burden. But don't expect the financial aid office to throw loads of money at you. If, on the other hand, you haven't applied yet but are thinking of doing so in the future, there are steps you can take today to prepare financially.

KEY STEPS TO PREPARE FOR
FUNDING YOUR MBA

- Establish a good credit history. Your credit history determines the interest rates that you will receive on loans. Devote time to establishing good credit. If you have poor credit, take the time to clean up your credit history. Someone I know had a horrible credit history (560 credit score), and after devoting a couple of years to cleaning up his credit, his score jumped higher than 700. Strong credit scores can make a difference of tens of thousands of dollars saved on lower interest payments.

- Build a cash reserve. Planning early gives you the opportunity to save money toward your MBA. Loans and scholarships are not the only way to fund your degree.

- Establish relationships with cosigners. This is particularly useful for international students whose interest rates can be reduced several percentage points when they have a cosigner for their loan rather than applying for the loan on their own.

- Invest time up front to research private scholarships and fellowships. Many private organizations set aside awards that often go unused because people didn't apply for them.

- Look into alternate sources of funding. With the advent of loan schemes like SoFi, more applicants will have access to loans at a cheaper interest rate.

Worrying about funding the MBA should not prevent you from applying to your dream school. It is an investment in your future and a worthwhile one at that. Getting in is the hardest part. Once you are admitted, you will find various outlets to explore for financing your MBA. Diligence, planning, and a little bit of ingenuity can go a long way in helping you secure financing to offset the cost of your business education.

CHAPTER FOURTEEN

Final Thoughts

I HOPE THIS NEW EDITION of *The Best Business Schools' Admissions Secrets* has dispelled your concerns about the application and has made the process more transparent and less stressful. I have given you a glimpse into how the admissions boards at top business schools perceive candidates. I've also shared with you specific and practical tips on how you can avoid making mistakes that can cost you admission into your desired MBA program. But most importantly, I have emphasized the importance of seeing yourself as a brand and managing your brand successfully throughout the application process. Regardless of whether you decide to pursue an MBA, I encourage you to invest in your personal brand.

Practical takeaways from this book include the following:

1. You are a brand! I've heard back from many readers of this book who ultimately decided against applying to business school but were still able to apply the branding lessons covered in this book and reap the benefits. I want to encourage you to invest in conducting a brand audit and begin today to manage your personal brand. Not only will it help you land admission into a top business school, it will also help you navigate your career better while living your life in a meaningful, focused way with passion, guts, impact, and insight.

2. Research and understand the brands of the MBA programs you're interested in and make sure they're a good fit for you.

Give yourself permission to deviate from the path you may have originally assumed was for you. Now that you've done serious soul-searching and have a clearer sense of your brand, you may discover schools that are a better fit or other paths that you would not have dared to pursue before.

3. The essays are critical to gaining admission to elite business schools. Successful applications have well-executed essays that have the following six characteristics: compelling, captivating, consistent, credible, concise, and clear. Because many schools have reduced their number of required essays, it is even more critical to know your brand, zero in on the key elements of your experiences, and share these important points in your essays. There is less room to ramble; with less space to tell your story, you have to keep it simple and share the things that really matter.

4. Brand champions can make or break an admission, so choose wisely and invest in cultivating recommenders who will become raving fans.

5. Don't underestimate the importance of the interview; whether in person or by video, it is your chance to make a strong impression on the admissions board. Preparation and practice will enable you to sell your brand successfully. Devote enough time for preparation, and you will be able to ace your interviews.

6. Understand the three admissions criteria: academics, leadership, and unique brand differentiation. Know what your strengths are and where you fall short. Commit to plugging the holes in your candidacy, whether it is gaining more leadership experience, taking business classes, retaking the GMAT or GRE, or simply developing your personal brand to become a more appealing candidate.

The good news is that you don't have to be a rock star to get admitted to your dream school. Getting in involves doing your research, tailoring your story to fit the program's brand, and capitalizing on your unique brand differentiation. Embrace your brand, give yourself enough time to market your story, and do it right the first time. I wish all of you significant success as you brand your way to an MBA!

APPENDICES

Admissions Board Application Insights

JEVELYN BONNER-REED, Former Associate Director of
Admissions at Kellogg

When should candidates begin planning their application for business school?

Their senior year in college: they should take the GMAT while they are
still in studying mode (especially since their peers will be working on
their LSAT/MCAT exams). The GMAT score is valid for five years, so
taking it their senior year allows candidates to focus on the other aspects
of their application once they are ready to apply to business school.

What key qualities stand out in applicants who are admitted?

Balanced individuals who put energy into their academics, work, and
extracurricular activities. A trend toward pushing yourself and not
settling is important. If you were a history major, why didn't you challenge yourself by taking quantitative courses? If you started off as a
member in clubs, what stopped you from moving into leadership roles?
If you took the GMAT once and your score was just okay, why did
you not try to improve it? MBA admissions boards do not like to see
candidates taking the GMAT twenty times, but it is okay to retake it
once or twice. These are the types of questions on the minds of MBA
admissions boards.

What is the most important part of the application?

The whole package is important, but the essays are critical, because the applicant has total control over them and can constantly revise them, unlike other parts of the application. In a pool of similar-looking candidates, they can be the differentiating factor that persuades the reader to admit you. Additionally, you can use them to explain gaps in your background (if you have low grades or employment gaps, you can address these issues in a mature manner).

What steps can career changers take before applying to an MBA program?

They can do informational interviews for the new career to understand skills they will need and make sure it's a fit. They should also highlight skills they have that are transferable to the new career. Some admissions people may be uncomfortable if it's too big a career jump or if the candidate has unrealistic expectations of what it might take to successfully switch careers.

What are the most common admissions mistakes you have seen applicants make?

Applicants worry too much about what the admissions board wants to hear instead of representing themselves. Applying to too many schools can lead to application burnout. Another mistake is not doing the research before you apply, resulting in a missed opportunity to convey specifics about the school.

What advice do you have about selecting recommenders?

Choose someone who knows your work very well: a manager or professional mentor who has worked at the company and knows you. You can also use a client. The first time they hear you are applying shouldn't be when you are sitting with them to ask for a recommendation letter.

What characteristics are found in excellent recommendations?

They are succinct yet detailed with real examples. If it is too long, you lose the reader's interest.

How important are age and years of work experience?

Having two to three years is helpful (you can contribute to classroom discussion), but too much work experience makes it harder to switch careers. The bottom line is whenever you think you are ready for business school. You may have to determine whether a full-time, part-time, or executive MBA is most appropriate.

How do admissions boards view reapplicants?
It depends on why you were denied admission in the first place. If it is anything but environmental fit, you have as good a shot as anyone else when you reapply. If it's a fit issue, there is nothing you can do about it. Candidates should consider fit not only in terms of the different two-year MBA programs but should assess whether they would be best served in a different type of program such as an executive or part-time MBA program. You should request feedback from the school about your candidacy when it's offered! Unfortunately, most schools do not offer this service.

What should applicants do to address a weak test score or GPA?
Whatever you do, you can't have both. The GMAT or the GPA has to be at least in the median ballpark for the school. If one is below average, you can point to the other to show your academic competency. Candidates can also take specific courses at local colleges and universities to address any academic deficiency.

What advice do you have for wait-listed candidates?
Find out how the program likes to handle wait-listed candidates and follow the requirements. Some schools allow for candidates to submit additional information about their candidacy while others want you to just wait.

What should candidates do to nail the interview?
Practice!!! Some people have been at their jobs for a few years and haven't interviewed for a while. Practice and prepare as if you were going into a job interview. Share work and life experience examples and do your research on each school beforehand.

What should rejected candidates do to improve their application next time?
Step back, evaluate why you didn't get in at all, do a feedback session if offered, and potentially reapply to the program. You should also expand

your school choice list. Have something different to bring to the table (e.g., higher GMAT score, new coursework with strong grades if your GPA is low, or a promotion or more responsibility at work if you were stagnating in your current role).

You have an MBA. What did you value about your MBA?

Learning the language of business. My undergrad was in engineering, so the MBA opened my eyes to areas I knew little about (marketing, finance, etc.). I grew up in the Midwest with little to no international experience, so I was most impressed with the level of international exposure I found in business school, from living in the International House with international students from all over the world, to trips around the world with classmates, to doing an exchange program at London Business School. My MBA was truly global and opened a whole new world to me.

CONRAD CHUA, Head of MBA Recruitment and Admissions at University of Cambridge Judge Business School

Cambridge Judge Business School is a top global MBA program. What makes it unique?

I believe that the most important distinguishing factor about Cambridge Judge is its close association with the tremendously diverse and vibrant community of Cambridge University itself. Some business schools are either self-contained or distanced from the university that they are associated with, but that is not the case here. Cambridge's college system promotes interdisciplinary learning and living, and our students are constantly exposed to cutting-edge research and cutting-edge people from a huge range of disciplines. Whether hearing a Nobel Prize–winning faculty member speak, learning from PhDs at the top of other fields, or simply conversing with fellow members of their college, our students can learn so much about topics far outside of the business school and apply those ideas to their education and post-MBA careers. Quite a number have gone on to start companies with others that they have met at Cambridge. It is an environment that truly encourages interdisciplinary success, as everyone here wants to be at the top of his or her chosen field, whatever that might be.

What types of students do well at your program?

First, students must have the academic strength necessary to cope with a very challenging and fast-paced one-year program. Secondly, collaboration is a strong part of our ethos here. To thrive at Cambridge, students must be able and eager to work with a wide variety of people, some of whom might be very different from themselves. Our students feel that collaboration is a vital part of their experience here and also key to what they would like to do later in life. I also believe that unusually curious students tend to do very well here. Our students want to learn about topics outside of the business school, and each year, I am surprised and delighted by their creativity. We have seen students stage operas, excel in sports, create pop-up restaurants, and in general embrace all there is to do at Cambridge. That being said, such curiosity must be coupled with a certain focus and resilience. Life in Cambridge can easily distract unfocused students, so it is important that incoming students have the discipline necessary to see their studies through.

What advice do you have for applicants to succeed in their MBA application?

Students should take the time to make all elements of their application strong, from studying for the GMAT to selecting strong recommenders. We do call up references quite often, so students should select recommenders who thoroughly understand what they have accomplished and are willing to speak to us about those accomplishments. Most importantly, though, students should take the time to learn more about our school and our MBA program. We are very active on social media and on our admissions blog, both of which are great ways to get a feel for what goes on here. We want people who will feel comfortable in the environment that we have to offer. If a student does not feel that comfort level or does not want such an interdisciplinary environment, then Cambridge might not be the best fit, and that is okay. There are many other great schools that could be a suitable fit, and it is important to think carefully about what type of experience you are looking for.

What is the biggest surprise students find at your program?

I find that our students are often surprised by just how difficult the program is and how hard it is to balance the rigorous academics with their extracurricular activities, social life, and in some cases, family life. Each year, it takes incoming students about five to six weeks to recover from the first onslaught of classes and to find their own equilibrium. There is certainly an adjustment period, but for my part, I am always pleasantly surprised by how well strong students manage to strike that balance and achieve so much during their time here.

LISA PIGUET, Associate Director of MBA Admissions and Marketing at IMD

IMD is a top global MBA program. What makes it unique?

Several elements differentiate IMD from other top business schools. To begin with, our class size is a bit smaller than most MBA programs, because we only accept ninety MBA students per year. In our admissions office, we have a saying that "We do not accept the best ninety, we accept the best group of ninety." We work very hard to create a dynamic, challenging, globally diverse class. Secondly, IMD's eleven-month program is extremely intensive because it packs the teaching hours of traditional two-year programs into a much shorter time frame.

In terms of class composition, IMD has a very strong focus on industry. Many of our students come from industry backgrounds and return to industry jobs after graduation. This does not mean that we do not accept students with a financial or consulting background; it simply means that we have a diverse student body with a wide range of work experience. Our students are also slightly older than those of a typical MBA program. The average age is thirty-one, and applicants must be twenty-five with a minimum of three years' full-time work experience. Again, this slightly older age range contributes to the diversity of our class, as our students have a rich history of work and life experiences to share.

IMD's focus on leadership is another important differentiator. We do not just set aside a few classes for leadership. It is a regular part of the eleven-month IMD experience, and in addition to coursework, our students each attend twenty sessions with a licensed psychoanalyst as part of their training. Technically this is an elective (the twenty sessions), but 95 percent of the class ends up taking it). We firmly believe that you cannot be a good leader of others until you truly understand yourself.

Finally, we have a very unique interview process that helps us pull together a strong class each year. All applicants must come to our campus for a full day of assessment, beginning with a formal one-on-one interview with a member of the admissions committee. The rest of the day includes an impromptu applicant presentation, a group presentation, lunch with current MBA students, and participation in a case written by an IMD professor. This day helps us to get to know applicants much more personally and to carefully select those who we believe will thrive at IMD.

What types of students do well at your program?

We are a very international program, typically with at least forty different nationalities represented within any given class of ninety students. To do well in this environment, students should embrace these diverse perspectives. We also look for people who are dynamic, who like to be challenged, and who have significant work experience to share with their peers. Group work is at the core of most of our classes, so our students must be strong teammates with excellent interpersonal skills. They should also be very committed to leadership development and ready to embrace our intensive training in that area.

What advice do you have for applicants to succeed in their MBA application?

IMD is very achievement-oriented, so prospective students should make sure to clearly bring out their achievements throughout their application. The best applicants are concise and creative, and show drive and passion. They are also self-aware and honest. We are not looking for cookie-cutter applicants—we want students who are unafraid to genuinely be themselves.

For advice about our unique on-campus interview, I always tell prospective students to get in touch with recent alumni. They will have plenty of helpful tips for preparing for that day. For the interview itself, students often find the CAR acronym helpful—Challenge, Action, Results. Use this acronym as a framework for expressing your achievements. Students should also be ready to participate and talk about their ideas. In a class of only ninety, we cannot afford to have students who sit back and do not contribute to the discussion.

What is the biggest surprise students find at IMD?

Many of our students are initially attracted by the tremendous concentration of international business in Switzerland but, by the end of the program, find themselves falling in love with the country and wanting to stay. Also, students often tell me how surprised they are by how much they transformed during the program, beyond anything that they expected beforehand. I attribute this to IMD's integration of hard and soft skill training and to the emotional intensity of our leadership training. It is not an easy program, certainly, but our alumni consistently report that it is well worth the effort.

SEAN O. FERGUSON, Associate Dean of Master's Programs and Director of MBA Programs, HKUST Business School

What is the most important thing you want applicants to know about HKUST?

We believe HKUST is a great business school for students who are looking to capitalize on the economic growth taking place in Asia. HKUST is strategically located in Hong Kong, which is less than a five-hour flight to most of the major business hubs in Asia. Hong Kong is a gateway to the immense opportunities in China; alternatively, it serves as a platform for access to Southeast Asia.

Our student body is very diverse, with 97 percent of our students coming from outside of Hong Kong; more than thirty nationalities were represented in our most recent incoming class. For a class of about 110 students, this is an exceptional ratio. The diversity of our student body makes for a rich in-class learning experience. The international exposure of our students in tandem with the diverse background of our faculty will challenge your thought process and force you to have a more comprehensive view of global business.

What types of applicants do well at HKUST?

We take a holistic approach to admissions and value diverse points of view in the program. As such, we don't have a preferred profile. We look more for students who have a global mind-set and want to pursue a career in international business.

As do most schools, we look for strong academic credentials and professional progression in one's pre-MBA career. However, we are particularly interested in high-impact candidates who have left their imprint on their organizations. Also, we are looking for individuals who can work in and influence multicultural environments.

What advice do you have for applicants on how to apply successfully to your program?

We evaluate candidates based on their academic and professional accomplishments as well as interaction during the interview. Overall, HKUST focuses on three admissions dimensions:

1. **Contribution.** We believe that the most valuable learning from the MBA program is the interaction and experience sharing among peers. Therefore, we look for high-quality candidates from diverse backgrounds who can provide a broad spectrum of valuable experience to the class with selfless contribution.

2. **Career Alignment**. The MBA is a significant investment in terms of time, money, and other opportunity costs. Our goal is to help students achieve all of their post-MBA goals. The admissions team carefully considers how the applicant's goals and aspirations align with the program's strengths.

3. **Leadership Potential**. We are looking for outstanding candidates with leadership potential who have the capacity to make lasting contributions to the region or industry in which they are working. Our students are dynamic and talented individuals with a high level of integrity. The admissions team looks for examples that demonstrate leadership in the applicant's professional life.

Applicants significantly improve their chances of admission by demonstrating the three aforementioned qualities.

What are career opportunities for international students attending your program?

The continuous economic development of Asia, especially China, has driven many multinational corporations to the east. Corporations are looking to expand in the mainland market; hence, there is a strong demand for talent with a good understanding of Chinese culture and business practices. International students attending our program will augment their technical skills with an in-depth understanding and knowledge of Asian culture and business practices. Most of our students have successfully managed the career transition to Asia. Some of our international graduates return to their home countries for career opportunities as the Asia expert for their organization because they remain closely connected to the Asian market.

Last year, 95 percent of our graduates accepted a job offer within three months after graduation. Eighty-eight percent of graduates stayed in Asia, with Hong Kong (51 percent) as the most popular location. Seventy-six percent of them switched their job functions and 71 percent their industries after the MBA. Nearly half of them increased their base salaries by 75 percent or more.

Describe funding and scholarship opportunities at your school.

HKUST offers various scholarships and awards, ranging from 10 percent to 50 percent of tuition, to full-time MBA students, including:

- Merit scholarships—offered based on candidates' work and international exposure, academic performance, references, and interview performance
- Need-based grants—offered to admitted candidates with genuine financial needs
- Scholarships for non-Asians with Asia exposure or language proficiency in an Asian language
- Scholarships for Asians with international exposure
- Scholarships for underrepresented or minority groups
- Scholarships for candidates with extensive global experience
- Scholarships for women with impact
- Jebsen Scholarship for permanent residents of Mainland China and Hong Kong

Kuwaiti candidates may be eligible to apply for the MBA scholarship administered by the Kuwait Investment Authority. Spanish candidates may also be eligible to apply for the scholarship sponsored by LaCaixa Foundation and Casa Asia that covers the full tuition fee, flight tickets, and monthly allowances at HK$15,000, as well as other financial assistance.

Current Student Application Insights

BUKKY OLOWUDE, Yale School of Management

Why did you choose Yale SOM?

I chose Yale SOM for two reasons. (1) My cousin, whom I greatly admire and respect, graduated from Yale. I remember the impact that SOM had on her and the personal stories she used to share about her experience. (2) I wanted to attend a business school where I could make and leave an impact. Yale SOM, one of the youngest business schools (established 1976) in its peer set, has a strong student-driven culture. This means that you can create events or experiences that you feel will add to the student experience. The administration and faculty are incredibly supportive of student ideas and give them ample opportunity to test out their leadership skills.

How has having a new dean (Edward Snyder) impacted the school?

Personally, as an international student, I think his focus on making Yale SOM one of the most global business schools has been a big impact. He launched a new master's program, the Master of Advanced Management, a one-year program for top students from Global Network for Advanced Management (GNAM) schools who want to deepen their understanding of the most complex management issues facing leaders worldwide. So not only am I taking classes with students who already have an MBA from schools like INSEAD and IE in Spain, but I am also able to build my network at those schools when I take a Global Network Week intensive course. For instance, I recently returned from Beijing, where I attended Renmin University of China for a week to learn more about doing business in China, attended a Yale alumni event, and visited as well as met with company representatives from Tencent, Baidu, etc. In the spring, I may be going to Koç University Graduate School of Business in Istanbul to further my knowledge on developing an effective local to global strategy. Then, I will likely head to São Paulo to attend Fundação Getulio Vargas—Escola de Administração de Empresas de São Paulo (FGV-EAESP) to learn firsthand about Brazil's preparations for the World Cup in 2014 and the Olympics in 2016.

What types of students do very well at Yale?

Yale SOM naturally attracts intellectually capable students who are passionate about learning and elevating their skills. I think the additional layer that makes the students here special is that they have an entrepreneurial drive (i.e., a self-starter mentality). They are invested in our community, enjoy volunteering for social causes, and may want to work for either a for-profit or a nonprofit as long as the organization aligns well with their long-term goals. Women also do really well at SOM. There is a high number of my female classmates who display strong leadership as club leaders, members of student government, admissions interviewers, representatives on the Community and Inclusion Council, etc. Yale women, both single-handedly through their personal aspirations and collectively, are helping to break down the stereotypes of women in business! Yale really does train the entire student body to be leaders for business and society.

What admissions advice do you have for applicants applying to Yale?

If you want to meet a diverse range of students who have a social conscience and want to make the world a better place, either through for-profit or nonprofit careers, Yale SOM is for you. If you have an entrepreneurial drive and want to have an impact on your community, Yale SOM is for you. If you want to form a close bond with the majority of your classmates, Yale SOM is for you! We have one of the smallest classes, and you definitely get to know the majority of your classmates very well.

DENNIS TSENG, Yale School of Management

Why did you choose Yale SOM?

Most people mention the integrated curriculum, which is built around looking at problems holistically from multiple perspectives and not siloing business away from society and government or siloing separate business functions within an organization. Or they mention the access to Yale University overall, with SOM being truly integrated with the overall university, having 14 percent of students pursuing joint degrees, and 77 percent of the student body taking electives outside of SOM at the schools of law, medicine, forestry, drama, architecture, divinity, etc., as well as Yale College. Those are both good reasons to choose Yale, but for me, Yale became a no-brainer when I visited for Welcome Weekend. Every student, faculty member, alumnus, and staff member made me feel like I was coming home, like I'd been away for a while but now I was back, and they were glad to see me. The idea of "SOM Nice" wasn't just a myth; it was clearly engrained into the DNA of the school. Since I've been here, this has only been reinforced for me, and it's become very important that this culture of collaboration and encouragement continue to flourish at Yale.

How has having a new dean impacted the school?

I'm a big fan of Dean Snyder. Part of this has been based on the extreme transparency he has demonstrated. He has spent a good amount of time in front of the student body explaining his overall strategy for the future of SOM. The most impressive outcome of this has been the amount of ownership the student body has taken in executing on this strategy. Ted's insistence on strengthening student services and in enlisting students in advancing this goal, as well as his expansion of SOM's global reach through increased global learning experiences, have both been very noticeable from a student standpoint. One concern I've heard from alumni and current students is that these changes might affect the core essence of SOM—as an ethical business school training leaders for all sectors and all manners of organizations. I think this concern is justified, but also one that Ted is very cognizant of. For what it's worth, everything I've heard from all levels of the administration has been that the core DNA of the school will not shift, even as the school becomes better at what it does.

What types of students do very well at Yale?

SOM is full of top performers from a very diverse group of industries, and we're very proud of our diversity in backgrounds and in interests. I'd say that a common factor for students is that we're all generally excited by and supremely interested in the backgrounds of our classmates. This is an extension of the collaborative nature of SOM and creates the multiplier effect that is often felt as students continue to build on each others' strengths. Students who are single-minded in their focus to the extent that they aren't able to empathize with other viewpoints may find themselves struggling in this kind of environment.

What admissions advice do you have for applicants applying to Yale?

I can't provide specific advice since I am an admissions interviewer, but I will say that SOM believes in selecting the best students possible, first and foremost. After that, we really believe that it's up to those students to decide whether we are the right place to help them become the leaders that they see themselves becoming, and we do everything in our power to help them come to that decision. If, through the course of your research, you are convinced that SOM is the right place for you, that is great! Tell us that.

Alumni Application Insights

FERNANDO D'ALESSIO, Stern

Pre-MBA career path:
Investment banker (JPMorgan & HSBC).

Post-MBA career path:
Investment banker (U.S.-focused, advising family businesses and PE shops).

How many years of work experience did you have prior to the MBA?
Seven years.

What was your greatest concern applying to business school, and how did you address it?
I had heard from friends who had attended business school that it is a race to get a job and that a good part of the experience is about recruiting. I was concerned about whether I had too much experience. I always felt the more years of experience, the more you can get out of the program, but when visiting schools, I noticed I was on the older side. I realized that timing is a big deal, and if I could do it all over again, I would have applied three years earlier.

Why did you select your MBA program?

I applied to a few schools, and my focus was on programs that were strong in general management and finance. I also wanted a program that had a good environment for student activities. Location was also important to me since I wanted to stay close to or remain in New York City. Most importantly, given my seven years' experience, I wanted to make the most out of graduate education by taking the majority of my second-year classes with part-time students, and NYU Stern is known to have one of the top part-time MBA programs in the country.

What was the most interesting part of your MBA program?

At Stern, you have the choice to exempt out of classes, and since my undergraduate degree was in economics, I was able to exempt out of two required economics courses and take a proficiency exam to exempt out of statistics. I appreciated the fact that you could specialize in up to three majors, and I pursued a finance, management, and entrepreneurship major. But most importantly for me, I wanted a firm foundation in finance and entrepreneurship as well as interaction with experienced professionals, and I got a solid training in this area at Stern.

How did you find the academic part of your program?

It was challenging. There were different teaching methodologies used, and some professors used the case-based method and others relied on lectures or a combination. I liked having both, since some courses were suited for cases while others were better for the lectures. I appreciated the diversity of teaching approaches at Stern.

How did you find the social part of your program?

The social life at Stern was very active. But I kept a low profile since I was married and didn't party as hard as some of my classmates. Being in New York City is definitely a great advantage.

What was your job search like?

I adopted a focused approach from the very beginning. I had done mergers and acquisitions for seven years, so I wanted to complement my experience with new skills. I wanted a firm with a strong restructuring background or financial sponsor exposure, and I joined a firm that offered both after business school. In addition, I kept my options open and applied to a couple of consulting positions as well.

How did the MBA prepare you for your career?

Stern has a great program that helps career switchers. Once you are admitted to Stern, you have a lot of support. For example, there are programs that prepare students for a new career by providing them access to professionals from the industry. The school offers various workshops and one-on-one preparation to help students prepare for cases and mock interviews. I was especially impressed with how collaborative students were with each other, and it was common for second-year students to help first-year students.

What advice do you have for applicants to maximize their applications?

Know why you want the MBA. It is important to be well prepared. Before you apply, you should visit the schools and talk to students and alumni to make sure it is a fit. You should also study hard to make sure you nail the GMAT and get a solid score so you can check that box and move on to more challenging aspects of the application. If the GMAT is weak, you have already taken yourself out of the game before it starts.

RECY DUNN, Stanford

Pre-MBA career path:

I was an SEO intern at Merrill and worked at energy companies Texaco (Chevron) and Amoco (BP) as an analyst in sales and trading (energy); a year into it, I had an epiphany that I didn't want to be a trader. While interviewing for new opportunities, I had a layover in New York City, and in conversation with some friends, I joked about how it would be great to work at SEO (a nonprofit). I called, and they said, Come in to interview. A few weeks later, they offered me a job. I quit my trading job, sold my car on a Friday, flew to New York Saturday, and began work Monday morning. It was a huge pay cut but I enjoyed the work: it brought joy and meaning to my life.

Post-MBA career path:

I did an internship at Wells Fargo after my first year in business school and realized I hated the big-company experience. I accepted the fact that my passion was education. How do you make money doing what you love? I joined Platform Learning, a for-profit company with an education mission. Then I spent two years completing the Broad Residency at Urban Education with a placement in D.C. public schools. I currently work in a general management role as an advisor to the deputy superintendent in Prince George's County, Maryland.

How many years of work experience did you have prior to the MBA?

Five years.

What was your greatest concern applying to business school?

How to tell my story in a way that would help me gain admission. I felt I didn't have functional knowledge in a particular business area, plus I worried about my undergrad transcript. Since I didn't have the typical banker, consultant, or general management corporate exposure, I knew I had to focus on pitching my story effectively.

Why did you select your MBA program?

I chose Stanford GSB because of its reputation as an excellent general management program. I was also drawn to its program offerings and the truly collaborative environment where classmates committed to working together.

What was the most interesting part of your MBA program?

The education was top notch. I was amazed at how much access we had to faculty, the flexibility to work with them on new and interesting research. I also appreciated the exposure to the business executives who came to speak at the school. I found Stanford to be flexible, allowing me to pursue a joint degree program with a master's in education.

What surprised you the most about your program?

I was impressed with the number of opportunities and clubs on campus; there was something for everybody. Being a part of rugby club, marketing club, and the Black Business Student Association, I enjoyed the diversity of options that was available. My takeaway was realizing that management is more than accounting and finance; I learned the importance of organizational behavior and the role of interpersonal dynamics and softer skills when leading with impact.

What was your job search like?

The director of Stanford Career Services was an alumnus, which says a lot about the school's investment in its students' careers. My job search was more nontraditional since I was looking for an education position, so I had to do a little more ground work. But Career Services gave me access to tons of alumni and training to prepare me for interviews. They even had consultants come in to help students who didn't know exactly what they wanted to do career-wise.

What advice do you have for applicants?

Apply early and don't be afraid to let the board know who you are. So many people just try to simply explain their résumé. Be willing to let your guard down and definitely be introspective. Focus on essays and paint a picture for the admissions committee so they get a sense of where you were, what you were doing, what you were feeling. And finally, have a clear vision of what you want to do in the future.

FRED CHIMA, Columbia

Pre-MBA career path:

Worked at PricewaterhouseCoopers in the Assurance and Business Advisory Group, starting as associate and later promoted to manager.

Post-MBA career path:

Spent my summer after my first year in business school in banking at Citigroup (London). After graduating, I joined Credit Suisse First Boston in New York City in the Investment Banking Group.

How many years of work experience did you have prior to the MBA?

Four and a half years.

What was your greatest concern applying to business school?

Experience wasn't a concern since I felt I had enough. I was concerned about financing the MBA. I felt it was a big investment. I also wondered whether the MBA would get me from point A to point B. After careful research, I felt comfortable with the investment. Speaking to alumni who had gone to Columbia and made the jump to finance reassured me that my goal was realistic and feasible.

Why did you select your MBA program?

I wanted a program that was recognized internationally, since I was an international student. I also wanted a program with an excellent reputation in finance and technical depth. Furthermore, geographic location was important to me: I wasn't interested in being outside of the Northeast. For these reasons, Columbia was a good fit.

What was the most interesting part of your MBA program?

Coming into the program, I underestimated the depth of diversity of my class. I mean diversity in terms of experience/background, not just ethnicity. My class was incredibly diverse: former entertainers, a rancher, bankers, etc. And everyone has the same goal. You make friends with classmates from all over the world. The program puts you through quite a bit of change.

How did you find the academic part of your program?

Coming from a solid accounting background as a CPA, I felt that the first year wasn't as challenging. I could have exempted more classes but I wanted to take all the classes to make sure I wasn't missing out on anything. My second year was awesome. I got to pick the classes I was interested in. I like finance, but my passion really is the intersection of politics and business, so I took three to four classes from the School of International and Public Affairs (SIPA).

How did you find the social part of your program?

It was at first challenging (international students go through this I believe). MBA programs attract certain personalities (mostly socially aggressive and type A personalities) and if you aren't like that, it may be hard initially. Over time, however, everyone adapts. Business schools push you to adapt. Internationals may need a bit of adapting initially. After a semester, you'll find your stride.

What was your job search like?

I found it very distracting. I knew I wanted a career change. I was initially confused about how I would make my career transition from accounting to finance. I attended all the presentations in banking, which, by the way, was a big mistake (you lose focus); I didn't know if I wanted to be in New York or pursue an international role. As a career changer, I needed to pound the pavement, especially in a tough economy where many analysts were returning to old firms/industry, making it more competitive. I got my internship from interviewing through the Career Services Office. For my full-time role, it was through a connection I made while in business school.

How did the MBA prepare you for your career?

From a people/soft skills perspective, it was invaluable. Banking has two legs: how good are you technically and how good are you in getting along with people. The softer stuff is what I learned a lot about, the intangibles, how a team works, managing up and down, and becoming comfortable in unfamiliar environments. Technically, I felt it was a brush-up of my skills instead of giving me new skills. I may have survived without an MBA my first year in an associate role, but would I have survived beyond the first year? Not necessarily. As you move into a more senior role, your responsibility goes beyond basic accounting and finance skills and focuses more on looking at business in a holistic way. This is a skill set I got from Columbia! The cases and projects tend to look at things from an overall perspective. You think back to cases you did, the challenges the protagonists faced, and the solutions they came up with. Another benefit of the MBA is that it builds one's confidence. You have classmates with strong opinions. Even if you are quiet, you learn how to defend your ideas, and in banking, if you encounter people who are type A, you can hold your own. The MBA gives you credibility in your profession.

What advice do you have for applicants to maximize their applications?

First of all, think about what you want to get out of the program. It will help you focus on the schools to apply to. I don't believe you should apply to ten schools. Once you identify the programs, dig in and talk to the alumni and admissions people. It doesn't guarantee admission, but invest in them knowing you. Don't worry about financing the program. Get over the concerns about money. International students receive loans, so you should view the MBA as an investment.

For career changers, you should talk to as many people as possible in the career of interest. They will give you a lot of perspectives that will help you understand how to go about making the career switch. Even if you are an international student, don't be shy. You should assert yourself. Just because you are from another culture doesn't mean you can't speak up. Be introspective and assess what you bring to the table. I had a CPA and experience from a top accounting firm. I also knew what I wanted to do—mergers and acquisitions (M&A). I met with associates and found out what they did in the M&A groups at their firms. By learning exactly what skills were needed and specifics of the role, I was able to effectively market myself by capitalizing on my experience and my understanding of the career I planned to follow after business school. It paid off.

KHARY CUFFE AND SELENA CUFFE, Harvard

Pre-MBA career path:
Khary: analyst in Asset Backed Securities Group (Prudential); investment associate (Seedco)
Selena: business development (United Airlines)

Post-MBA career path:
Khary: baby care brand management (Procter & Gamble); wine importation (Heritage Link Brands)
Selena: food and beverage brand management (Procter & Gamble); Council on International Educational Exchange (CIEE); wine importation (Heritage Link Brands)

How many years of work experience did you have prior to the MBA?
Khary & Selena: Four years.

Did you meet at business school?

Khary: I met my wife as a prospective student during one of my visits to Harvard.

What was your greatest concern applying to business school?

Khary: Picking the right school and getting admitted.

Selena: Cost was a concern for me. I wondered whether it was a worthwhile investment financially. I also was concerned about how I would fund my education. Finally, I also wondered about the GMAT before taking it, but it turned out not to be an issue.

Why did you select your MBA program?

Khary: As a minority, I wanted a program that had good diversity and a strong brand reputation. Harvard had both. I was also attracted to the learning model at Harvard and found the entire academic experience engaging.

Selena: When I visited HBS, it immediately felt like a fit. During the class discussion, I found myself wanting to join in.

What was the most interesting part of your MBA program?

Khary: For me, it was the people I met, the variety of interests, and the opportunity to do a joint degree.

Selena: The Treks exposed me to places I may not otherwise have explored in my life. For example, meeting members of parliament in different countries and engaging in dialogue with them about the future of their country and how business fit into their vision was interesting. During a subsequent trip to South Africa, I learned that despite South Africa's $3 billion wine industry, blacks owned less than 2 percent. And there were no distribution channels for their wines to the United States. Subsequently I began to explore how to bring their wine to the States. As a result, in 2007, we launched Heritage Link Brands in the U.S. market to do just that!

What surprised you the most about your MBA program?

Khary: The caliber of classmates is remarkable. You can't help but wonder whether you can compete at that level. I certainly consider myself a confident person, but surrounded by rock stars, it has you stepping up your game!

Selena: I was surprised by how easygoing and approachable the professors were. Interacting with Harvard professors felt like sitting down with a friend over coffee. This is the case even after business school. The relationship with your professors is long lasting.

How did you find the academic part of your program?

Khary: I found it to be great. While it was challenging, I felt it was immediately applicable. I have been able to apply a lot of lessons I learned in business school to our company, Heritage Link Brands.

Selena: I found it to be challenging but not too stressful. I enjoyed it. It pushed my limits, but I never felt I was out of my element.

How did you find the social part of your program?

Khary: It was great. There were always a ton of activities to do. Student groups were very active and engaged.

Selena: It was very robust. There were more things to do than you could do in a day, week, or semester! It was complete fun, and there is something for everyone, regardless of your interests.

How did the MBA prepare you for your career?

Khary: From a technical standpoint, I didn't feel the MBA was as relevant. From a professional network standpoint as well as developing soft skills, it was absolutely helpful.

Selena: Business school gave me courage to become an entrepreneur. Two classes, The Entrepreneurial Manager and Entrepreneurial Marketing, for instance, provided the frameworks for how to build a business from start to finish.

What advice do you have for applicants to maximize their applications?

Khary: Visit the school, not during prospective students' day but when there isn't a special event going on, so you can get the "real" sense of the school. Once you decide you will apply, get help. Use a consultant or organization like Managing Leaders for Tomorrow (MLT). Talk to students from the school. And finally, with your app, be yourself.

Selena: I am a firm believer in getting students who are at the school to look over your application. They have insight into the culture of the program. Having said that, use judgment. I wouldn't share the application with everybody either.

CHRIS RYAN, Fuqua

Pre-MBA career path:
High-school teacher

Post-MBA career path:
Consultant, education company executive, independent film producer

How many years of work experience did you have prior to the MBA?
Six years.

What was your greatest concern applying to business school and how did you address it?
I was concerned more about getting in and less about what I would do afterward, as I thought I had that figured out. With regard to getting into school, I was worried that my nontraditional career path to that point would hamper my chances.

Why did you select your MBA program?
I had known about and liked Duke as a university for a long time (I almost went there for undergrad). So when I started looking at business schools, Fuqua was definitely on my list. Around that time, I met another teacher who was a year ahead of me in the process. He went to Fuqua and was very pleased with the program. When I went for the campus interview, I was struck by the atmosphere of the place—it felt both serious and welcoming, both focused and warm. At that point, I had a strong sense that Fuqua was the place for me.

What was the most interesting part of your MBA program?
My classmates, hands down. They brought an amazing diversity of experiences and backgrounds to the school. At graduation, I remember feeling that there was still so much more to learn about my classmates—but the two years were up.

What surprised you the most about your program?

What surprised me the most was how important extracurricular activities would be for me and for the bulk of students. During school, I devoted a great deal of time to video production, of all things! For many years, Fuqua has had a club called "Fuquavision" that puts together *Saturday Night Live*–style videos and shows them regularly to the entire school on Friday nights. As you can imagine, putting together a nearly hour-long program of videos every six weeks is very difficult and time-consuming (especially while trying to meet the other obligations of school), but it was also very enjoyable. Even more important, it gave me a chance to develop my skills and interests in filmmaking. Since then, I have been an executive producer on a film featured at the Sundance Film Festival, and I continue to write and develop projects. This aspect of business school was ironic for me, since I had even considered going to film school instead of business school.

How did you find the academic part of your program?

Both practical and interesting. I really enjoyed learning all sorts of mate- rial I had never studied before, both for its own sake and for its real-world utility, which was generally obvious. I found most of the professors not only excellent thinkers but also inspiring teachers. True, there were a few who were less than scintillating in the classroom (I imagine that's true at every school), but I was very happy to see that the administration took student concerns very seriously. As our class's representative to the Curriculum Committee, I was pleased to be part of the school's efforts to make the curriculum and teaching even better.

How did you find the social part of your program?

Outstanding. The dean when I was there, Rex Adams, used to put it this way: "No jerks and no weenies." Don't get me wrong—I probably qualify as a weenie, or at least a geek or a nerd. That said, what Rex was getting at was the collaborative culture, the "team Fuqua" ethos that really does pervade the school. I'm sure every major business school is fun and has its share of happy hours, etc. But one thing I loved about Fuqua that I think is unique, or at least rare, is that the single biggest social convener is a year-long charity effort on behalf of North Carolina Special Olympics—and not just raising money for them but interacting with the athletes and building bridges to and within the surrounding community. That's pretty cool.

What was your job search like?

I came in focused on management consulting as an initial career step into business. As a consultant friend had put it to me, a few years as a consultant can act as a kind of "residency" after business school (as if after medical school). There were many other aspects of the consulting path that appealed to me as well. With the immense help of Fuqua's Career Services Office and many second-years (including my teacher friend), I got summer offers from McKinsey, BCG, and Bain, and spent the summer with McKinsey. At the end of the summer, McKinsey made me a full-time offer, which I accepted.

How did the MBA prepare you for your career?

It helped me in several ways:

1. Developing leadership. As a high school teacher, I was used to directing the activities of students. However, I had only limited opportunities to exercise leadership among my peers. Fuqua gave me a chance to do just that.
2. Developing discipline among chaos. Since business school is so intense and "multifarious," so to speak, it is a great lab in which to figure out how to prioritize a multitude of commitments of differing types.
3. Developing specific knowledge/skills. As a consultant, a film producer, and an executive at a small, growing company, I have frequently drawn on specific ideas and techniques I learned or exercised in business school, from Excel modeling to negotiating contracts.

What advice do you have for applicants to maximize their applications?

Tough one! I think it's very important to figure out WHY you want to go to business school. It's not like, say, dental school: for one thing, you don't need a license to practice business, and also every business-school class contains a variety of folks with different dreams and goals for their careers. So you must go into the application process with a strong sense of what you want to go and do.

RACHEL ZLOTOFF, Kellogg

Pre-MBA career path:
I was a coordinator at Nickelodeon Consumer Product Department for three years (first in the apparel/home furnishing division and later in the packaged goods department). I was promoted to a manager position and had the responsibility of managing one person.

Post-MBA career path:
I did an internship at a consumer goods company in New York after my first year. I then concentrated on the Big Three consumer product companies and fortunately landed a job with one of them, Kraft.

How many years of work experience did you have prior to the MBA?
Two and a half years.

What was your greatest concern when applying to business school?
As an early-career applicant, I worried that I might not be admitted due to limited work experience. Therefore, I applied to more schools than most (seven programs) to increase my odds of being admitted. But despite that, I set a realistic expectation for myself: if I didn't get admitted, I had plans to reapply the following year. My application strategy was to show that my career experience was substantive despite working only a few years. It worked since I was admitted to five of the seven schools, including my first choice, Kellogg.

Why did you select the MBA programs you applied to?
I selected my programs based on their reputation as top schools, plus I focused on programs that had a collaborative environment. The culture of the program was a huge deciding factor for me.

What was the most interesting part of your MBA program?

I was most impressed by the opportunities offered at my program and the people that I met. They were the most interesting people I have had the fortune to work with. Their backgrounds, intelligence, and incredible achievements were all inspiring. I was constantly challenged each day.

What surprised you the most about your program?

My greatest surprise was how truly collaborative my classmates were. For example, not having a banking or accounting background, finance and accounting were not easy subjects for me. Classmates from these industries would sit with me and dedicate time to teach me these subjects outside of classes, and they wouldn't leave till I got it. Their dedication was unprecedented. Even the professors were accessible and easily approachable. They felt like friends, and many of them came to our TG happy hour events.

How did you find the social part of your program?

I found the overall Kellogg community to be very close, and there is more than enough opportunity to connect with your classmates. The real challenge is learning how to balance all the social activities with the academic demands.

How was your job search at Kellogg?

Kellogg attracted top marketing companies, and I had a lot of options when it came to recruiting. I interviewed with different marketing companies and focused my search geographically on Chicago and New York City. I chose Kraft for its marketing quality and general management scope plus its exceptional, best-in-class training. I was looking for a position that would give me solid training and enable me to build skills that are transferable outside of marketing. I also found the Career Management Center to be excellent. The career counselors were accessible and highly supportive. So was the Kellogg Career Network, which gave students access to hundreds of companies. Everyone I knew graduated with a job, most with multiple offers. Kellogg career opportunities were vast. If you wanted a job in nonprofit, banking, or consulting, you were able to find companies from these different sectors/industries recruiting.

How did you find the academic part of your MBA and how did the MBA prepare you for your career?

One of the main reasons I wanted an MBA was to build up my analytical abilities, especially in terms of using data to drive strategic decision. Today, in my new job, I am working on several strategic projects and am able to draw directly from my business education to come up with new ideas. I also have reached out to my former professors to discuss business issues. Even my marketing binders have been great reference points.

What advice do you have for applicants to maximize their applications?

Because networking is so important, make sure the MBA program is a good fit for you. Talk to as many people as possible to learn about their experiences; do not simply use school rankings to select an MBA program.

Pre-MBA Summer Program Insights

IVAN KERBEL, CEO, Practice LLC—The Practice MBA
Summer Forum; Wharton MBA

You were the former career director at Yale SOM and a Wharton alum. What did you observe during your time in the career office that led you to start Practice MBA?
Whether at an intimate program like Yale's (where the student body numbered less than 200 during my time there) or at a larger-scale program like Wharton's (where each class hovers around roughly 850 students), there are universal, shared aspects of the business school experience.

The most salient common feature is a lack of time to take advantage of all of the unique resources and opportunities available to business school students, coupled with a considerable set of fixed academic, extracurricular, and job-search-related demands that are part of every student's schedule.

All MBAs work extraordinarily hard once in business school, but not all of them start school with the same level of exposure to and facility with MBA-level skills, concepts, and social expectations. In particular, international students traveling to business school from abroad, as well as nontraditional MBAs (those from less intensely commercial backgrounds such as military service, teaching, sports, nonprofit work, and government roles), have a bigger set of hurdles to overcome in terms of hitting the performance benchmarks across each dimension of business school life, and especially with respect to competitiveness in the context of MBA recruiting.

In my experience, international students and nontraditional MBAs often have to put in a superhuman effort to compete on an equal footing with classmates who have attended undergraduate business programs and/or who have experienced rigorous professional development and on-the-job skills training in industries such as finance and management consulting.

I founded Practice LLC and The Practice MBA Summer Forum—a three-week, intensive summer program designed specifically for rising MBAs—to expand the amount of time that a newly admitted student has to develop both hard and soft skills to smooth out the transition process, reduce the risk of "false starts," and improve his or her ability to compete, contribute, and achieve great personal impact while enrolled in business school.

Describe the Practice MBA summer program.

The Practice MBA Summer Forum is an in-person, intensive course of study—up to 200 students from across the world can participate each summer by traveling to the United States before the start of their respective school years. The program includes social outings, such as baseball games and special dinner outings, as well as interaction with MBA alumni at leading organizations who will also participate in the delivery of specialized content as guest speakers.

The three foundational components of the Summer Forum curriculum are:

- Week 1: **Culture & Language Transition** (for international students)
- Week 2: **MBA Career Strategy Seminar** (all students)
- Week 3: **People Performance Lab** (all students)

Students participating in the program can choose to attend one or all weeks of the program, depending on their interests and needs.

Culture & Language Transition includes a daily writing/speaking exercise, full language immersion for all participants, and a comprehensive introduction to host-country culture and social standards in the academic, extracurricular, and professional settings. Based on the profiles of the students who register each year, our program will prepare rising MBAs for successful experiences not only in the United States, but also in the UK, France, and Spain, and will include specialized content to account for differences in country-of-origin culture for MBAs arriving to business school from Asia, Latin America, Africa, Eastern Europe, and the Middle East.

The **MBA Career Strategy Seminar** allows students to gain deep insight on the MBA recruiting process and to develop a successful strategy for both the internship and full-time job search. We hold group workshops and individual coaching that help students synthesize career self-assessment instruments (such as Myers-Briggs and Career Leader), align their abilities and interests with specific industries, functions, and organizations that recruit MBAs, build job-searching and interviewing skills, and understand the current market forces that affect the recruiting landscape for opportunities they are likely to pursue.

People Performance Lab is intended to maximize the effectiveness of students' efforts in all spheres of business school life by building both hard and soft skills, from mastering software and research tools critical to the MBA classroom and work environment (e.g., financial modeling via Excel) to absorbing personal and interpersonal effectiveness soft skills (from better organization and time management to improved communication, presentation, and influencing skills).

Students who attend Summer Forum have a unique opportunity to network with classmates enrolled in an exclusive set of peer MBA programs and to benefit from the accumulated know-how of program faculty who've worked extensively with elite MBAs and who are themselves MBA alumni and industry veterans. In 2014, we are developing two weeks of additional programming prior to the start and at the end of Summer Forum in partnership with the National Outdoor Leadership School (NOLS). We will be conducting Wilderness Trip Leader Training courses in Washington's Central Cascades Range that offer students an additional opportunity to network with fellow MBAs, find time to relax and recharge both physically and spiritually, learn valuable multiday outdoor expedition skills, and enjoy the unique, pristine beauty of the mountains, forests, lakes, and glacier fields that are abundant in this part of the Pacific Northwest.

Who is this program designed for?

The program welcomes rising MBAs who have been admitted to leading business schools in the United States and Western Europe. We feel that international students, as well as rising MBAs who are from nontraditional pre-MBA backgrounds, can benefit the most from our program and services.

When does the program start?

Summer Forum is held over a three-week period in July, roughly a month before most students arrive on campus. Deadlines for student registration usually fall in February and April.

Any final words of advice to applicants who are beginning the application process?

For most of us who've attended business school, the experience represents a period in our lives when we are surrounded by the most capable, intelligent, fun, and interesting set of peers we could ever hope for. It also means that in order to pursue our individual dreams and goals—the things that propelled us into business school to begin with—we must find some way to stand out and differentiate ourselves, even in the midst of such extraordinary company. The one remaining, relatively free period of time during which a student can broaden and deepen his or her knowledge and capabilities in order to handle the complexity and rigor of business school is the span of a few months prior to the start of school (when opportunity costs, performance demands, and overall stakes are lowest).

Our firm is the first to comprehensively address the personal, academic, and professional growth needs of newly admitted MBAs so that they can maximize their use of time and achieve the goals they've set for themselves once enrolled. We are firm believers that the best way to do this is to bring high-achieving MBAs together in an immersive, in-person learning environment led by veteran MBA coaches. We encourage students to explore a range of pre-MBA activities and options and to formulate a prematriculation strategy that helps them achieve the highest possible return on their larger investment in graduate school.

Ivan Kerbel is CEO of Practice LLC and The Practice MBA Summer Forum, an annual, intensive pre-MBA training program for newly admitted MBAs. He can be reached at ivan.kerbel@practicemba.com.

GMAT Perspective

BRIAN GALVIN, Vice President of Academics, Veritas Prep

What is Veritas Prep's unique approach to GMAT preparation?

The GMAT is a self-professed test of "higher-order thinking," and so we attack it in that way. While content is important, the GMAT is a reasoning-based test, so we emphasize "what you do" over "what you know." The GMAT is all about problem solving and making use of what you know, and so we train people to recognize clues in problems and have a set of tools to use to unravel them. For example, most students will have a handful of exponent rules memorized (when do you add the exponents, when do you multiply them, what do you do when the exponent is negative, etc.), but we find that knowing those rules isn't enough on most tough problems—you also have to know how to use them. So we focus on what we call the "Three Guiding Principles for Exponents," which are 1) find common bases (which usually means prime factor them); 2) multiply (which usually means factor addition/subtraction into multiplication and division); and 3) find patterns (since exponents are essentially "repetitive multiplication," they lend themselves really well to pattern thinking). And so with this, students can see ways to take abstract-looking problems and make them concrete by knowing how to get them in a position where they can then use that knowledge.

We also take reasoning one level higher with what we call "Think Like the Testmaker"—a look at the GMAT's playbook for how it creates a reward system, punishing those who don't quite think critically with trap answers and rewarding those truly astute thinkers with correct answers. For example, in sentence correction problems, the GMAT loves to "hide the right answer" behind a unique (but correct) grammatical structure that many will eliminate immediately. If you know, however, that the test loves to put what we call a "false decision point" toward the first few words of each answer choice, you can avoid making that obscure decision and patiently wait for a more concrete decision point. Knowing the GMAT's toolkit to misdirect…can be instrumental in avoiding traps and being alert to what truly matters.

There have been some changes in the GMAT test. What advice do you have for applicants on how to prepare?

The new section of the GMAT—the integrated reasoning section—is aptly named. It integrates some quantitative skills with some verbal skills (particularly critical-reasoning ideology), so the best advice for students preparing is to embrace the overlap. Doing integrated reasoning problems will help you improve on many quantitative and verbal topics and vice versa. So much of your integrated-reasoning preparation is fairly natural: keep studying GMAT quantitative and verbal, and pay attention to how those themes (critical thinking, quick analysis of numbers, etc.) pop up in your work life and business-related reading. In fact, business school faculty, in advocating for a GMAT section like integrated reasoning, proposed just such an undertaking so that prospective students would have to develop critical-thinking skills when it comes to "authentic" real-world data (charts, graphs, tables, etc.).

What is the best time to begin preparing for the GMAT?

Before you need to! If business school is potentially in your future plans, it's helpful to prepare for and take the GMAT when you have the time and ability to focus, and often that comes well in advance (months, if not years) of your application deadlines. For example, my favorite class to teach is our January/February class—the "New Year's Resolution crowd" as I like to call it. Why? They come in so eager to learn and without time-sensitive stress, and so they're much more relaxed and able to focus on learning and improving; their questions are much more about concepts and strategies and less motivated by pressure and stress ("What happens if I click D on the last question but don't have a chance to hit 'confirm'?" or "If my test is on Tuesday and my applications are due Wednesday, how much time should I spend on my GMAT vs. my essays?").

Some people respond really well to that sense of urgency, but for the most part, if students can prepare for and take their GMAT independent of their applications, they have more time and attention to devote to maximizing their score. And if they can plan their two to three months of study for a time of year or period of life when they have time to invest, they get a lot more out of it than when they're trying to cram it in around a busy work schedule, social schedule, or particularly, application schedule.

Add to that the calm and confidence that comes from having test day be "a test day" and not "the test day"—if you know that the worst case scenario is you retake the test four to six weeks later, it's a lot easier than going in with the thought "if I don't score well today, I can't apply this year"—and it's very helpful to prepare for and take the GMAT well in advance of your intended application dates.

How can someone with an initially low GMAT strategically raise his or her score?

We have three steps that every student goes through. There's what we call the "Skillbuilder" phase of our course, which is the review and conceptual understanding of the content that the GMAT tests—triangle rules, algebra skills, verb tenses, etc. If your algebra skills have atrophied to the point where you struggle to solve for variables in linear equations, doing a handful of cleverly written data sufficiency problems isn't the most effective use of your time and resources. Find drill problems on that subject and work to make that weakness a strength.

Once the basic skills and concepts are shored up, the next phase is what we call "Skills Meet Strategy." In that zone, we focus on recognizing which skills tend to be important in your toolkit in which types of problems or setups. The GMAT isn't a content-based test, at least not once you get to above-average level problems; the test is based on making common skills look like entirely unique problems. This phase is arguably the trickiest for students—they've mastered the content but hard problems don't look familiar, and so it's important to have a handful of goals for each type of problem setup.

Finally there's the dimension we call "Think Like the Testmaker." The authors of GMAT questions are quite adept at creating trap answers that are incredibly tempting to those who aren't thinking critically, and by the same token creating a reward system for those who do think critically. For example, in word problems, it's really easy to solve for the wrong variable, a mistake that often traps those who are relieved enough to have gotten an answer for their algebra that they lack the presence of mind to go back to double-check the question. The GMAT is a standardized test, which means that it's designed to elicit a standardized set of mistakes; learning the common ways in which the test traps some and rewards others can go a very long way.

What tools or books do you recommend for applicants who want to do a self-study?

Of course, we're pretty big fans of the Veritas Prep series—our books, our practice tests (which are scored and administered using item response theory, the same system as the official test), and our Veritas Prep on Demand video lessons. Obviously, we're a little biased, but what we like most about them is that they've been created over years—our instructors who wrote and filmed those lessons did so after many years and thousands of hours of experience learning the GMAT and its tendencies and strategies. There's a progression in becoming an expert on a test like this—it goes from learning the content, to learning how to make that content pop for students, and to learning how the authors of the test really create questions and what they're rewarding and punishing. And over that progression, you learn that many of the things you once thought were helpful or important may have only been correlated with success; they weren't really the cause. So with that in mind, we'd highly recommend using official resources (the Official Guide for GMAT Review, the GMAT Prep software, etc.) and study resources that have gone through a few progressions.

In a lot of ways, it's just as important to stay away from "bad" study material as it is to find what's good—a lot of material is guilty of writing questions specifically to test strategies that may not really hit what the GMAT tests, or of writing strategies that "feel good" but don't necessarily produce results. The GMAT is a pretty sophisticated test, and I'll readily admit to being guilty of a few of those mistakes even after I'd been teaching for a few years. If you're going to self-study, make sure that the resources you're using really understand the test, and for that, there's nothing better than the resources offered directly by the GMAT itself.

MBA Resources

I HAVE COMPILED A COLLECTION of resources to help answer additional questions you may have about the business school application.

COMMUNITY LEADERSHIP

Here are some great websites to link up with socially responsible organizations and explore ways to contribute your leadership in your community:

VolunteerMatch (www.volunteermatch.org)
BoardNetUSA (www.boardnetusa.org)
Smart Volunteer (www.smartvolunteer.org)
Idealist.org (www.idealist.org)
Change.org (www.change.org)

WOMEN AND MINORITIES

The Forté Foundation (www.fortefoundation.org) is an organization that promotes women in business. It provides a variety of resources to women considering a business career and education. Female applicants to business school who are members of the organization receive mentorship support, career advice, and access to female business leaders, and they attend admissions events where they can meet board members and receive scholarships to fund their MBA.

The National Association of Women MBAs (www.mbawomen .org) is dedicated to empowering women MBAs and helping them to take on leadership positions in corporate America and to enhance the diversity of the nation's workforce.

The National Society of Hispanic MBAs (www.nshmba.org) fosters Hispanic leadership through graduate management education and professional development. NSHMBA works to prepare Hispanics for leadership positions throughout the United States so that they can provide the cultural awareness and sensitivity vital in the management of the nation's diverse workforce.

The National Black MBA Association (www.nbmbaa.org) is dedicated to developing partnerships that result in the creation of intellectual and economic wealth in the black community. In partnership with more than 400 of the country's top business organizations, the association has inroads into a wide range of industries as well as the public and private sectors.

GENERAL MBA SITES

Poets & Quants (www.poetsandquants.com) is an online community that provides business school insights from deans, admissions boards, and other admissions experts. It provides in-depth analysis of MBA programs and how they are differentiated from other programs. Applicants are also able to get information about upcoming MBA admissions events and breaking news from business schools around the world.

MBA.com (www.mba.com) is a great website that every applicant to business school ought to visit. It includes information about assessing the value of the MBA to deciding which schools are the best fit for you. It also provides information about the GMAT, including the registration process, sample GMAT exams, and business school resource information.

Businessweek (www.businessweek.com) provides an online community for applicants applying to business school. Applicants are able to read interview transcripts from admissions board members at leading MBA programs as well as to participate in virtual chats where they can ask questions directly to the board members. Another major draw for applicants is that they can interact with each other through forums and discussion boards. Current MBA students also write about their MBA experiences.

MBA Podcaster (www.mbapodcaster.com) has expanded the way information is communicated to prospective MBA candidates. Instead of the traditional online chats, MBA Podcaster uses audio and video services to bring the most current admissions information to business school applicants. MBA Podcaster includes interviews and discussions with authorities in the MBA arena, including business school deans, admissions directors, admissions consultants, corporate recruiters, current students, and alumni. Topics include everything from a behind-the-scenes view of the admissions process to post-MBA job opportunities and current market trends. Each in-depth show discusses a particular topic of interest to an MBA applicant and interviews relevant experts to help make the application process more efficient and successful. The moderator/host leads the discussion and draws conclusions to help the listening audience plan effectively for their pursuit of an MBA. The company was founded in January 2006 by Leila Pirnia, an entertainment executive and graduate from Massachusetts Institute of Technology. MBA Podcaster is dedicated to providing listeners with accurate and unbiased information.

MBA Zone (www.mbazone.com) was founded by Brenda Mizgorski, a Wharton MBA, nearly ten years ago. This site was one of the first online communities for MBA applicants with information covering the application process, life as an MBA student, and life after business school.

Vault (www.vault.com) was started by MBAs who saw a market opportunity that wasn't being filled and jumped on it. They have successfully built an online community and an extensive collection of information, books, and other products covering a variety of careers and universities. This site is helpful for applicants who want to learn more about different careers and what a typical day is like in that industry. Vault also offers a database of available jobs for its members.

The MBA Tour (www.thembatour.com) is a high-quality independent information source regarding MBA admissions. Its events emphasize personal interaction between prospective MBA students, business school admissions representatives, alumni, and other like-minded education enthusiasts. Established in 1993, it has built a strong reputation based on representing top business schools from North America, Europe, Asia, and South America.

QS World MBA (www.topmba.com) is an online MBA platform where students can learn about business schools from around the world. Applicants can access the latest articles and reports on business education and the latest trends at business schools on this site. Additionally, QS promotes MBA tours across the globe, giving applicants an opportunity to connect with admissions board members.

INTERNATIONAL STUDENTS

InternationalStudent.com (www.internationalstudent.com) covers information on getting visas, securing financing for an education as an international student, and other related international topics.

EducationUSA (www.educationusa.com) is a global network of more than 450 advising centers supported by the Bureau of Educational and Cultural Affairs at the U.S. Department of State.

SCHOLARSHIPS AND FELLOWSHIPS

The Consortium Fellowship (www.cgsm.org) provides financial funding to minority candidates from MBA programs that are members of the Consortium organization.

The Robert Toigo Foundation Fellowship (www.toigofoundation .org) provides financial funding, mentorship, and support to minority MBA candidates interested in a career in the financial services industry.

LOAN RESOURCES

SoFi Loans (www.sofi.com)
GradLoans.com (www.gradloans.com)
Gate (www.gateloan.com)
FastWeb (www.fastweb.com)

GMAT PREP PROGRAMS

Following is a list of the different GMAT prep companies. You should research each of them to determine the ideal program to help you prepare for this important exam.

Veritas Prep (www.veritasprep.com)
Knewton (www.knewton.com)
ManhattanGMAT (www.manhattangmat.com)
The Princeton Review (www.princetonreview.com)
Kaplan (www.kaplan.com)

Bell Curves (www.bellcurves.com)
Manhattan Review (www.manhattanreview.com)

In addition, many GMAT forums provide students with access to admissions experts through online chats, blogs, and other resources to discuss and learn about the GMAT, test strategies, and admissions tips. They include:

BeatTheGMAT (www.beatthegmat.com)
GMAT Club (www.gmatclub.com)
The GMAT Pill (www.gmatpill.com)
Magoosh (www.magoosh.com)

INDEX

ABOUT THE AUTHOR

C HIOMA ISIADINSO IS THE founder and CEO of EXPARTUS (www
.expartus.com), a global admissions consulting and personal branding company that prepares applicants to gain admission to elite schools.
Chioma has more than sixteen years of admissions experience and is
a former admissions board member at Harvard Business School and
former director of admissions at Carnegie Mellon University School of
Public Policy and Management.

Chioma started EXPARTUS based on her vision of the power of personal
branding to help individuals differentiate themselves in competitive pools.
Her consulting practice has served applicants from more than fifty coun-
tries, including Nigeria, Colombia, Sweden, Switzerland, the UK, Turkey,
South Korea, Indonesia, India, Ghana, Australia, Kenya, Portugal, China,
Germany, and various other countries and cities within the United States.

Chioma is a sought-after international speaker on the subject of
admissions, personal branding, and leadership development. She
has been interviewed by *Financial Times*, the *New York Times*, and on
CNBC's *Power Lunch*. She writes an education column, Education
Without Borders, for *This Day* newspaper.

Chioma earned her Master of Education degree from the University
of Pittsburgh and graduated from Hobart and William Smith College
with honors in Psychology. She has designed and conducted numerous
personal development workshops in Nigeria, the UK, and the United
States to help applicants gain admission to elite universities.